Karate Masters

VOLUME 3

Karate Masters
VOLUME 3

JOSE M. FRAGUAS

P.O. Box 491788, Los Angeles, CA 90049

Disclaimer

Please note that the author and publisher of this book are NOT RESPONSIBLE in any manner whatsoever for any injury that may result from practicing the techniques and/or following the instructions given within. Since the physical activities described herein may be too strenuous in nature for some readers to engage in safely, it is essential that a physician be consulted prior to training.

Copyright © 2006 by Empire Books.

All rights reserved. No part of this publication may be reproduced or utilized in any form or by any means, electronic or mechanical, including photocopying, recording, or by any information storage and retrieval system, without prior written permission from Empire Books.

EMPIRE BOOKS
P.O. Box 491788
Los Angeles, CA 90049

First edition

05 04 03 02 01 00 99 98 97 1 3 5 7 9 10 8 6 4 2

Printed in the United States of America

Library of Congress: 2006012533
ISBN-10: 1-933901-04-7
ISBN-13: 978-1-933901-04-6

Library of Congress Cataloging-in-Publication Data

Fraguas, Jose M.
  Karate masters / by Jose M. Fraguas. -- 1st ed.
    p. cm.
  Includes index.
  ISBN 1-933901-04-7 (pbk. : alk. paper)
 1. Karate. 2. Martial artists--Interviews. 3. Large type books. I. Title.
  GV1114.3.F715 2006
  796.815'3--dc22
                             2006012533

*"In order to make the action exist unequivocally,
a hypothetical enemy outside the muscles is necessary,
and for the hypothetical enemy to make certain of its existence
it must deal a blow to the realm of the senses fierce enough
to silence the querulous complaints of self-awareness."*

—**Yukio Mishima**
Japanese Writer

Dedication

To my instructors, who gave me the keys to understanding and generously shared their knowledge for my personal growth and development.

Acknowledgments

I gratefully acknowledge the help of a wide range of people who assisted me with great will and generosity, some of whom, for reasons of privacy, have asked not to be publicly identified.

Special thanks go to designer Patrick Gross; France's Thierry Plée, long-time friend and president of *Sedirep* and *Budo Editions*; Norma Harvey of England; Billy Bly, founder and editor of *American Samurai*; Germany's publisher Schlatt (director of *Schlatt-Books*); John Cheetham, editor of *Shotokan Karate* magazine; wado-ryu stylist and writer Salvador Herraiz from Spain, who delved deep into his collection of photos and interviews to find additional material that could be included in this book; Christopher Hodgin of Anchorage, Alaska; Don Warrener, director of Rising Sun Productions; legendary karate-ka, writer and friend Terry O'Neill from England; Steven Heyl, director of *Doshin Martial Arts*, who kindly supplied additional information to complete some interviews; Okinawa karate great and master calligrapher Tetsuhiro Hokama; Harold E. Sharp, a true legend in the world of martial arts and who kindly supplied great photos from his personal archives; Isaac Florentine, film director and passionate karate-ka; Arthur Tansley of Tokyo, Japan ... your amazing talent as photographer is only surpassed by your kindness as a human being; Kylie Jackson from Australia, and finally to my wife, Julie, whose discernment is always tempered with kindness.

A word of appreciation is also due to my dear friend Masahiro Ide, President of *JK Fan* and *Champ* videos, for his generosity and cooperation in this project; I also want to thank Okuma-san from the JKA Honbu Dojo in Tokyo for his assistance, kindness and supply of great photographic material for some of the chapters; and I must acknowledge the help and support from the publishers of *Gekkan Karate-do* magazine [Fukushodo, Ltd., Japan]. Without their support, kindness and commitment to preserve the art of karate-do, this book would not exist.

I would foremost like to give my most heartfelt gratitude to all the masters appearing in this book. Not only did they generously give me an enormous amount of personal time for the long interviews, but they also provided me with great pictures to illustrate the work.

You all have my enduring thanks.

—Jose M. Fraguas

About the Author

Born and raised in Madrid, Spain, Jose "Chema" Fraguas began his martial arts studies with judo, in grade school, at age 9. From there he moved to taekwondo and then to kenpo karate, earning black belts in both styles. During this same period, he also studied shito-ryu karate under Japanese Masters Masahiro Okada and Yashunari Ishimi, eventually receiving a fifth-degree black belt. He began his career as a writer at age 16 as a regular contributor to martial arts magazines in Great Britain, France, Spain, Italy, Germany, Portugal, Holland and Australia. Having black belts in three different styles allowed him to better reflect the physical side of the martial arts in his writing: "Feeling before writing," Fraguas says.

In 1980, he moved to Los Angeles, California, where his open-minded mentality helped him to develop a realistic approach to the martial arts. Seeking to supplement his previous training, he researched other disciplines such as jiu-jitsu, escrima and muay Thai.

In 1986, Fraguas founded his own publishing company in Europe, authoring dozens of books and distributing his magazines to 35 countries in three different languages. His reputation and credibility as a martial artist and publisher became well known to the top masters around the world. Considering himself a martial artist first and a writer and publisher second, Fraguas feels fortunate to have had the opportunity to interview many legendary martial artists. He recognizes that much of the information given in the interviews helped him to discover new dimensions in the martial arts. "I was constantly absorbing knowledge from the great masters," he recalls. "I only trained with a few of them, but intellectually and spiritually all of them have made very important contributions to my growth as a complete martial artist."

However, there were some drawbacks to his position as a publisher, Fraguas acknowledges, that directly affected his personal martial arts development. "Of course, some people taught me because of my position as a publisher and not because who I was as a person. Even though I recognize that, I'm still grateful for the knowledge they shared with me."

Steeped in tradition yet looking to the future, Fraguas understands and appreciates martial arts history and philosophy and feels this rich heritage is a necessary steppingstone to personal growth and spiritual evolution. His desire to promote both ancient philosophy and modern thinking provided the motivation for writing this book. "If the motivation is just money, a book cannot be of good quality," Fraguas says. "If the book is written to just make people happy, it cannot be deep. I want to write books so I can learn as well as teach. Karate-do, like human life itself, is filled with experiences that seem quite ordinary at the time and assume a fabled stature only with the passage of the years. I hope this work will be appreciated by future practitioners of the art of the *empty-hand*."

Originally from Madrid, Spain, he is currently living in Los Angeles, California. He can be contacted at: mastersseries@yahoo.com. O

Introduction

Some of my best days were spent interviewing and meeting the masters in this book. There is little I enjoy more than reading a great interview while time slows and sometimes even seems to stop. Having the opportunity to meet and interview the most prestigious martial artists of the past four decades is something that every martial artist doesn't have the chance to do. Hopefully, in some small way, this will help make up for that.

Meeting the masters and having long conversations with them allowed me to do more than simply scratch the surface of the technical aspects of their respective styles; it also allowed me to understand the human beings behind the teachers. Some of the dialogues and interviews began by simply commenting about the superficial techniques of fighting, and ended up turning into a spiritual conversation about the philosophical aspects of the martial arts. Although these masters are all very different, they share a common thread of traditional values such as discipline, respect, positive attitude, dedication and etiquette.

For more than 25 years I've interviewed these martial arts masters, one-on-one, face-to-face, with no place to run if I asked a stupid question. Many times it was a real challenge to not just talk to them, but to make the questions interesting enough to bring out their deepest knowledge. I tried to absorb as much knowledge as I could, ranging from their training methods, to their fighting methods, to their philosophies about life itself. Their different cultural backgrounds never prevented them from analyzing, researching or modifying anything they considered important. They always kept their minds open to improving their arts and themselves. From a formal philosophical point of view, many of them followed classical philosophies and religions—but they all tempered that with vast amounts of common sense.

They devoted themselves to their arts, often in solitude, to the exclusion of other "normal" pursuits. They worked themselves into extraordinary physical condition. They ignored distractions and diversions and concentrated on their mental and physical training. They got as good as they could possibly get at performing and teaching their chosen art while the rest of us watched them, leading our "balanced lives," and wondering how good we might have gotten at something had we devoted ourselves to it as ferociously as these masters embraced their arts. In that respect, they bear our dreams.

If you read carefully between the lines, you'll see that none of these men were trying to become a fighting machine, or create the most devastating martial arts system known to man. They focused, rather, on how to use martial arts to become a better person. There are many principles that once discovered open a wide spectrum of possibilities, not only to martial arts, but to a better existence as individuals.

The interviews often lasted as long as three or four hours. I would begin at their school and finish the conversation at a restaurant or coffee shop. Much of this information had never been published before and some had to be trimmed either at the master's request or edited to avoid misunderstandings. It is not the questions that make an interview. An interview is either good or bad depending on the answers. Considering the masters in this book, I had an easy job. My goal was to make them comfortable talking about life and training—especially those who trained under the founders of original systems. In modern times, there are not many who have had the privilege of living and learning under these legendary founders.

"The masters are gone," many like to say. But as long as we keep their teachings in our heart, they will live forever. To understand martial arts properly, it is necessary to take into account their philosophical methods as well as their physical techniques. There is a deep distinction between a fighting system and a martial arts. Unfortunately, the roots of the martial arts have been de-emphasized, neglected or totally abandoned today. Martial arts are not a sport. Someone who chooses to devote himself to a sport such as basketball, tennis, soccer or football—which is based on youth, strength, and speed—chooses to die twice. When you can no longer do that sport, due to the lack of their required attributes, waking up in the morning without the activity that has been the center of your life for 25 years is troubling and unsettling. In contrast, the martial arts can and should be practiced for life—they never leave you.

A true martial artist is like a musician, painter, writer or actor—their art is an expression of themselves. The need to discover who they are becomes the reason for an endless search for the perfect technique, great melody, inspiring poetry, amazing painting or Academy Award performance. It is this motivation to reach that impossible dream that allows a simple individual to become an exceptional artist and master of his craft.

Many of the greatest teachers share a commonly misunderstood teaching methodology. They know the words they could use to teach their students have little or no meaning. They know that to try "self-discovery" in quantitative or empirical terms is a useless task. A great deal of knowledge and wisdom comes from oral traditions, which martial arts, like every other cultural expression, has. These oral traditions have always been reserved for a certain kind of student and considered "secrets," given only to a special few who have the minds and attitudes to fully grasp them.

Alexandra David-Neel wrote: "It is not on the master that the secret depends but on the hearer. Truth learned from others is of no value, the only truth which is effective and of value is self-discovered ... the teacher can only guide to the point of discovery." In the end, "the only secret is that there is no secret." As Kato Tokuro, arguably the finest potter of the last century, a great art scholar, and the teacher of Pablo Picasso said: "The sole cause of secrets in craftsmanship is the student's inability to learn."

To find out what karate-do means to you, what it does for you, and what it holds for you, is a deeply personal process. Each path is different and we all have to find a personal rhythm that fit us individually, according to what surround us.

As human beings, we are always tempted to follow linear logic towards ultimate self-improvement—but the truth is that there are no absolute truths. You have to find your own way in life whether it be in martial arts, business or cherry picking. Whatever path you pursue, you have to distill the personal truths that are right for you, according to your own nature. The quest for perfection is very imperfect, and not in tune with human nature or experience. To have any hope of attaining even a single perfection, you have to concentrate on a single pursuit and direct all your energy towards it. In this sense, perfection comes from appreciating endeavors for their own sake—not to impress anyone—but for your own inner satisfaction and sense of accomplishment.

It is important to have a feeling of responsibility; and putting yourself into an art as genuinely as you can, without any sense that you are going to get something back in return, reverberates throughout time and space. We need to honor those who came before us, as well as nurture those who will come after, so the art can grow and expand—you've got to send the elevator back down.

Martial arts are a large part of my life and I draw inspiration from them. I really don't know the "how" or the "why" of their effect on me, but I feel their influence in even my most mundane activities. All human beings have sources or principles that keep them grounded, and martial arts are mine. That is when the term "way of life" becomes real. In bushido, the self-discipline required to pursue mastery is more important than mastery itself—the struggle is more important than the reward. A common thread throughout the lives of all the masters is their constant struggle towards self-mastery. They realized that life is an ongoing process, and once you achieve all your goals you are as good as dead. But this process is not all driven by action. Often the greatest action is inaction, and the hardest voice to hear is the sound of your own thoughts. You need to sit alone and collect yourself, free from technology and distraction, and just think. This is perhaps the only way to achieve mental and spiritual clarity.

I don't believe that books are meant to be read fast. I've always thought that writing is timeless and that reading is not a detraction. So take your time. Approach this book with the Zen "beginner's mind" and "empty cup" mentality and soak up the words of these great teachers. They will help you to not only grow as a martial artist but as a human being as well. O

Contents

1 Tetsuhiko Asai
Master of the Unexpected

17 Tino Ceberano
The Hard Way

41 Teruo Chinen
A Peaceful Man

57 Malcolm Dorfman
A Legacy of Passion

79 Hideharu Igaki
The Budo Spirit

87 Yasuhiro Konishi
Over a Giant's Shoulders

101 Shojiro Koyama
The Perfect Balance

139 Akio Minakami
A Warrior's Journey

155 **Anthony Mirakian**	**201** **Seinosuke Mitsuya**	**213** **Kunio Miyake**
The Legendary Pioneer	The Distant Dream	The Power of Will
227 **Tom Muzila**	**249** **Hironori Ohtsuka II**	**265** **Edmond Otis**
Conquering Fear	A Heart of Peace	The Art and the Way
279 **Ryusho Sakagami**	**289** **Shigeru Sawabe**	**303** **Tatsuo Suzuki**
The Gentle Master	A Legacy of Excellence	The Pure Essence
315 **Katsutaka Tanaka**	**327** **Mikio Yahara**	**337** **Gogen Yamaguchi**
The True Way of Budo	The Unconquerable Spirit	Simply "The Cat"

Tetsuhiko Asai

Master of the Unexpected

A MAN WHO PRACTICES WHAT HE PREACHES, TETSUHIKO ASAI SENSEI IS ONE OF THE MOST SOUGHT-AFTER KARATE INSTRUCTORS IN THE WORLD AND ONE OF THE FIRST KARATE-KA TO EVER COMPLETE THE LEGENDARY JAPANESE KARATE ASSOCIATION INSTRUCTOR'S COURSE. IN SEARCH OF A FUNCTIONAL APPROACH THAT WOULD BE PRACTICAL AND RELEVANT IN THEORY AS WELL AS IN AN ACTUAL SELF-DEFENSE SITUATION, HE HAS COMPLETED AN IN-DEPTH STUDY OF ALL THE MAJOR STYLES. HIS GREAT PERSONALITY MAKES HIM A TRUE MASTER OF THE ART IN EVERY SENSE. HE TELLS HIS STUDENTS TO LISTEN AND RECOGNIZE THE TRUTH CONCERNING KARATE. "ASK YOURSELF [THE FOLLOWING QUESTION]: 'IF IT CAME DOWN TO A SITUATION DEMANDING FIGHTING ABILITY IN THE NAME OF HONOR OR LIFE, WOULD I HAVE IT ... HERE AND NOW?'" ALTHOUGH HE IS AN EXCEPTIONAL MASTER OF THE PHYSICAL ASPECTS OF KARATE, HE IS A STRONG PROPONENT OF THE IDEA THAT THE GREATEST VALUE OF TRAINING IS THE REFINEMENT OF CHARACTER THAT IT PRODUCES. "A SOUND BODY MAKES A SOUND MIND." ASAI SENSEI IS ONE OF THE LEADING VOICES IN THE WORLD OF JAPANESE KARATE AND WORKS QUIETLY IN AN EFFORT TO SHARE HIS KNOWLEDGE AND EXPERIENCE WITH A THE YOUNGER GENERATION OF PRACTITIONERS AROUND THE WORLD.

Q: Tell us a little bit about yourself.
A: I was born in Shikoku in 1935. I studied judo and kendo before getting involved in karate at Takushoku University. This is where Grandmaster Funakoshi, Nakayama Sensei and Okazaki Sensei were in charge of the training. I entered the JKA instructor's course. After I graduated, I was sent to Hawaii and Taiwan to teach the art. It was in Taiwan where I had the opportunity to meet several Chinese kung-fu masters with whom I shared training and knowledge. Some people approached me to learn and others challenged me, so I had to fight. I still keep in touch with some of my friends from my time in China.

Q: Your father played an important influence in your life. What can you say about him?
A: He was a very strong man and many people consider him an eccentric.

Karate Masters

"If your muscles are not relaxed, they simply can't be fast [and you can't] produce power. It is necessary to know how to relax the muscles and use the natural energy of your body. Karate is good for health, so students need to find out how to do it right."

He was very strict with me, and he had an ironclad code of ethics. He always said that once you begin something you can't stop. You must finish it. I respect my father very highly and this sense of commitment has been the guiding principle of my life.

Q: Sensei, in your classes you always stress the importance of relaxation. Would you elaborate on that?

A: This is a mistake that many practitioners make, regardless if they are Japanese, European or American. The problem is everywhere ... West and East. Students come to class with the excitement of [participating in] hard training. Due to their passion and youth, they are too tense in [virtually] every action they make. In order to practice karate properly, you need to learn how to relax the muscles and use them properly to generate speed. If your muscles are not relaxed, they simply can't be fast [and you can't] produce power. It is necessary to know how to relax the muscles and use the natural energy of your body. Karate is good for health, so students need to find out how to do it right. Unfortunately, many instructors around the world never learnt the right way and always practiced with tension and hard movements. This is one of the reasons why people think karate is a hard style while the truth is that it is not. It is important to look at the art from a softer point of view. For instance, men should try to emulate the way women do karate. Women are not built like men, so they use more technique and more subtle ways of doing the movements instead of relying on muscle and strength. If a man tries to use this approach, he will discover that the techniques will flow more naturally. Then he can add the natural power he has in his body to accentuate the action.

Q: What is the key factor in becoming a good karate-ka?

A: There are many factors, and all of them must work together to bring the best out of the practitioner. Hard training is important. You have to put your mind into it. Strive to find a good instructor; learn the right technique, timing, kime and the proper use of the body; and use your natural energy. If you do these things, everything else will fall into place.

You should strive to control every part of your body at will. This is a true sign of mastery, and it goes beyond any style. It doesn't matter if you practice shotokan, shito-ryu, goju-ryu, et cetera. If you control your body at will, you'll be one of a few people who can do that. If you take a *tsuki*, as an example, you'll see that anatomically there are no great differences between a shito-ryu exponent and a shotokan practitioner. The important thing is to perform the technique with a certain spirit in a certain atmosphere. This is one of the main principles we were trying to develop at the old JKA. We wanted to use the human body in the most efficient way for the martial arts. Once you follow this rule, you'll see an infinite amount of possibilities, although the human body is limited. In fact, the only limit in martial arts training is the limit of the human body.

"The important thing is to perform the technique with a certain spirit in a certain atmosphere. This is one of the main principles we were trying to develop at the old JKA. We wanted to use the human body in the most efficient way for the martial arts."

Q: What are the main aspects of your teaching?
A: My teaching is for health, and that's the reason why I emphasize relaxation all the time. Making the muscles tense is not good for your body and can cause many injuries during training. I want the students to learn and understand how to use the body properly and how to produce the right kime without using useless movements or unnecessary tension. Proper kime involves going through the target and not stopping your technique short. Of course, having control over your techniques is very important. But, in order to be effective, you need to be able to generate devastating power in your punches and kicks without holding back any energy. To do this, you must use the principle of snapping your body. Try

Karate Masters

"The martial arts have been around for a long time, and the ancestors based their styles on natural movement and relaxation. Today, people don't want to use the old traditional methods to use both physical and inner strength because it is easier to lift weights."

to use it like a whip. This is a difficult concept to master, but it is extremely important and should be practiced from the very beginning.

Karate has five different aspects that should be developed. First, there is the martial side of it or the combative and self-preservation of the individual. Second, the health benefits derived from its practice. Third, is the physical activity, which is always good. Fourth, the sportive element that brings people together. Last but not least is the development of character and spirit. My approach to teaching includes all of these elements because I consider them all necessary. Nowadays, we don't need karate like we did after the war; it is a completely different approach. Karate needs to be useful for modern society. I want to return to the roots and to the original essence and reason of karate ... a time in which there are no limitations. Karate is not only for young people.

Q: Do you think modern training methods like weightlifting are responsible for this?
A: Maybe a little. The martial arts have been around for a long time, and the ancestors based their styles on natural movement and relaxation. Today, people don't want to use the old traditional methods to use both physical and inner strength because it is easier to lift weights. There is no reason why the old and new methods can't work together, but it is important to understand how both work and the direction you want to take in your training. Weightlifting creates muscle mass and a rapid increase in strength, but this kind of training works against the relaxation necessary for karate-ka to generate internal power, which is more important than muscle power.

Q: Weight training causes tense muscles?
A: No. Tense muscles come from the incorrect use of the body during training. You can do two training session with weights everyday and still be relaxed, and you can punch 1,000 *gyaku-tsuki* and be tense for a

week! It is a matter of knowing how to use your body properly when executing a karate technique. You need to understand how your body works and how to correctly use the training methods.

Q: So, you don't use weights in your training?
A: No, I don't. I focus more on speed than [developing] strength with weights.

Q: What should a student look for if he is interested in karate for self-defense?
A: First, you must study the vital points and attack those. Forget about your powerful reverse punch to the stomach. Self-defense is a whole different situation. Attack the eyes, the throat, the groin, the knee and all the vital areas where you can infringe a lot of pain with simple natural weapons. If you train with this concept in mind, you'll always have real karate in your hands. You will also have an effective karate, and this will bring self-confidence to you. It is not about muscle; it is about knowing what tool to use and what targets to hit. The art of karate is practiced barehanded and its essence is to render an opponent unable to fight by using a single technique. If you want to put a nail all the way into a piece of wood, you don't use a screwdriver. You use a hammer. Learn what weapons are more appropriate to hit certain parts of the human body, especially when you have to protect yourself against a much bigger aggressor. In that case, you want to hit the targets that really hurt him. Attacks to vital points require speed and accuracy. Otherwise, all you get is an aggressive opponent!

"Forget about your powerful reverse punch to the stomach. Self-defense is a whole different situation. Attack the eyes, the throat, the groin, the knee and all the vital areas where you can infringe a lot of pain with simple natural weapons."

Karate Masters

Q: How is your personal training?
A: I train everyday for more than two hours. I have a routine of exercises that I practice daily. These are a very important part of my training. They keep my body flexible and limber. Flexibility is an open door for relaxation, and I make this principle my main objective. It is important to try to keep all joints loose and supple. I have tried everything, and I am constantly learning and absorbing. I am not an expert in every style I practice, but I have picked up the ones I could do well and that suited my personal style. Also, I recommend [that you should] use your imagination when training and think about karate. Look at the things and the live creatures around you. Study them and try to absorb the knowledge they have. You may think that this is crazy, but you would be amazed at the amount of important knowledge surrounding us.

Q: How would you describe yourself?
A: I'm not sure. I try to be honest and stick to my principles. I'm very demanding on myself, and that allows me to judge myself first. I have to live with myself—not with my critics—so I try to be at peace. I don't really spend time talking about others. Life is very short, and I have a lot of things I want to do and accomplish. I'm a martial artist, not a politician. I always welcome anyone who wants to train with me, regardless of his association with other karate groups. I like to do karate and not waste time talking and arguing. I have nothing to hide. From the technical point of view, I am a researcher. I may study a technique for 10 years because there is a period of study, of trial, for any new technique before I can really accept it as useful. Then I must make sure it is teachable. If I am the only one who can do it, then there is no point [in pursuing it]. My goal is to become a total martial artist and do research just for myself.

Q: Sensei, when you were part of the old unified JKA, your way of physically expressing karate was substantially different from the rest of the top instructors. Why?
A: As I said before, I can't talk about others. My karate has always been the product of my personal training and experiences. And I had many experiences in other martial arts systems that some of my old peers in the JKA never had. Japanese karate has been very closed-minded for many years. [Contrary to what they believe], the karate way is not the only way. There are many other good ways and approaches that can be beneficial to all karate-ka, if they know and learn how to use them to complement their karate. Shotokan sometimes is too straight-lined. It was like a horse

Asai

"My karate has always been the product of my personal training and experiences. And I had many experiences in other martial arts systems that some of my old peers in the JKA never had. Japanese karate has been very closed-minded for many years."

with blinkers on. You have to study hard, see what is missing and then try to compensate for this. Before I started getting older, I always thought that shotokan should have a soft side because it is natural to the body. For many years, the JKA tried to create hard and strong people. And that's good, but it is not the only way to do it. I have always looked at Chinese chuan-fa [kung-fu], kendo, aikido, judo and any other art that could make my karate more versatile and adaptable. I tried to develop a shotokan that would be practiced by people of all ages ... not only young and strong people.

Q: You are using two words—versatility and adaptability—that fit into the Chinese way of combat.
A: Well, that's the way I have always thought. Some may think this is new, but I have always believed in this and practiced my karate based on these premises. That's probably the reason why my karate has always had a

Karate Masters

"True karate is capable of adapting to the situation and changing accordingly. That is the essence of life. Change is simply the product of education. The more you learn, the more you realize other things."

very different flavor when compared to other JKA head instructors. Adaptability and versatility are concepts not only found in the Chinese arts. True karate is capable of adapting to the situation and changing accordingly. That is the essence of life. Change is simply the product of education. The more you learn, the more you realize other things. Therefore, it is natural for you to change and adapt to that knowledge. Some people may say that my karate is always changing. Although that is not completely correct, it is not incorrect either. In my approach to karate, I have been strongly influenced by the Chinese styles I have studied. The Chinese seem to be more natural and casual when doing things, and that affects the way they train and conceive the martial arts. In karate, we have the same movements and principles, but you have to look closely to discover them.

Q: Based on your comments, what is missing in the hard approach to shotokan that the JKA used for so long?
A: A soft side and—instead of using force—the use of more circular and evasive defensive actions using body angling and techniques to re-direct an opponent's energy. You block softer but you hit as hard as always.

Q: Do your training methods still reflect those that Nakayama Sensei developed?
A: The basics and essential aspects of karate are the same. I haven't changed any of those. Because I have studied other methods and systems, it is logical to think that I included my own point of view and flavor to the art. The late Grandmaster Funakoshi established the roots, Nakayama Sensei developed the foundation and now it is up to us to expand the art in different ways to meet the current needs of students and society. Many people may think that my style of teaching is very strange, but this is only because I emphasize aspects that we usually don't see in regular karate. I am now researching ways of training for life. I'm trying to develop techniques and training methods that we can use until we die. It's an unlimited world, and we must try to expand. It is like a telescope. Don't look down the wrong end at a little circle; look through the wide end so you can see more.

"The late Grandmaster Funakoshi established the roots, Nakayama Sensei developed the foundation and now it is up to us to expand the art in different ways to meet the current needs of students and society."

Q: Do you still believe in thousands and thousands of repetitions of the same technique as a good training method?
A: It depends on your age and your goal. However, the answer is yes. I do believe in this kind of training because it builds a strong spirit and deter-

Karate Masters

"Competition has changed a lot throughout the years. In the old days, it was more of a one-punch, one-kill [mentality]. We really were aware of any possibility and making a single mistake meant defeat. That is the true spirit of budo, and this spirit can be maintained in modern competition."

mination to keep going no matter what. People need this kind of training, but they [also] need to learn how to relax and take care of their bodies. Otherwise, they will have problems and injures later on. Don't forget to stretch and massage the muscles. Remember what we said about tension. Relaxing and contracting the muscles improperly can cause many injures.

Q: Are you against the sport aspect of karate?
A: Not at all, but karate is a martial art—not a sport. The sport aspect of karate has allowed the art to spread greatly. In itself, that is not particularly bad, but it sure brings consequences if you do not watch out. I was one of the first competitors in karate history, but karate for me has always been a martial art. The problem arises because the competitions standardize the way instructors teach and students practice. Basically a "competition style" has been created, and all of the fighters look the same. The participants lose their own identity because the sport approach has been taken to the extreme.

Competition has changed a lot throughout the years. In the old days, it was more of a one-punch, one-kill [mentality]. We really were aware of any possibility and making a single mistake meant defeat. That is the true spirit of budo, and this spirit can be maintained in modern competition. That's why I like the idea of shobu-ippon. It represents what true budo is. The system for shobu-ippon set the fighter's mind in a different direction, than, for instance, the six-wazari format. The training methods changed according to this. Today, competitors simply jump and throw techniques without real kime or meaning behind them. If they are losing by three wazari, they think, "It's alright. I can still catch up!" Competition karate is only a very small part of karate. I have great students who are tournament champions, but this doesn't prevent them from training real budo karate. In sport or competition karate, you can always find shortcuts to win. In traditional karate, there are no shortcuts of any kind. Shiai-kumite is not even a *complete* form of kumite.

Q: What do you mean by a complete form of kumite?
A: I mean that you can only use certain techniques allowed in sport competition. I truly enjoy dojo kumite because you can use anything you want ... headbutts, elbows, knees, throws and even locks. In short, all the real tools of true karate. Karate is a complete package; you simply need to understand how to bring it to life and make it work for yourself.

Q: Are there some other important differences when fighting under the mentality of shobu-ippon?
A: I wouldn't say that it is because this one-blow, one-kill concept, but when I was competing the use of *ma-ai* [distance] was different. We tried to bring the opponent into our distance so we could strike with a decisive blow. The distance was longer than in modern competition. Now, it seems the proper distance doesn't matter anymore. The competitors know that—even if they are hit—they won't die from it [the strike]! The real dimensions of danger and menace have disappeared.

"We have to be able to look at what is happening without any kind of preconception or prejudices. There is traditional *karate,* modern *karate and* contact *karate. These are the facts, and they are here to stay. We must be able to accept these different trends, try to find unity and assimilate them."*

Q: What should be done to improve the current situation of the art?
A: That's a very difficult question. We have to be able to look at what is happening without any kind of preconception or prejudices. There is *traditional* karate, *modern* karate and *contact* karate. These are the facts, and they are here to stay. We must be able to accept these different trends, try to find unity and assimilate them, but there are some limitations to this because there are things that cannot be called karate.

Karate Masters

"It is important that the public has a clear idea of what is and is not the art of karate. I can be honest with myself and everybody else, but the love of my life is karate."

Q: Such as ...
A: Such as everything that is excessively sport biased because that doesn't deserve to be called karate. It is important that the public has a clear idea of what is and is not the art of karate.

Q: You don't make your living teaching karate. Does this situation make things easier for you?
A: Yes it does, because I can teach whomever I want, and I don't rely on memberships to put food on my plate. I can be honest with myself and everybody else, but the love of my life is karate.

Q: What is your opinion of the split that occurred in the JKA after the passing of Masatoshi Nakayama?
A: It was sad, but it wasn't the first time that there were problems inside the JKA. [When he was alive,] everybody stuck together out of respect for him. When he died, it was open range.

Q: Let's talk about kata. Has the format of kata changed throughout the years?
A: Yes, and I think it is natural. All of the head instructors of the old JKA trained and practiced the same kata. However, when one [of them] left Japan and lived for 30 years in another country, it was logical that some changes (his feelings and teaching methods) were going to occur. This is natural, and there is nothing wrong with that. The essence of the form is still there and nothing has changed, but the personal flavor the instructor put into it [changed] because of his evolution as a martial artist.

Q: How important is the bunkai of kata in karate and does it have any real value of self-defense in modern society?
A: Kata represents the history of the art. All the tradition in these forms [has been] passed down from masters to students throughout the generations. The kata were structured and formatted by the old masters to preserve realistic knowledge of self-defense. It is very important to study the form and to understand what you are doing and why are you doing it. It's occasionally difficult to completely decipher the bunkai and realistic applications of kata movements because they are not so obvious at first. The variations in the use and study of the forms bring new perspectives and ideas to the kata, and this is always good for the art. The main idea is to use the kata as a training method and the bunkai as the actual application in combat. It is very important to link the actual form with the application against an opponent. This is practiced in yakusoku kumite, and it brings the movements from kata alive in a combat situation. It is here in which you use your own ideas and imagination to create and develop [concepts] while maintaining the original flavor of the specific kata. You can also use different kata to develop different attributes and qualities. Not all kata are designed for the same thing.

Q: Explain this concept.
A: For example, let's say that a student needs to develop hip rotation. Well, there are specific kata that put a strong emphasis on this principle. Another student may need to develop bodyweight shifting. He uses other kata to improve this particular aspect of his karate. Different kata help to

Karate Masters

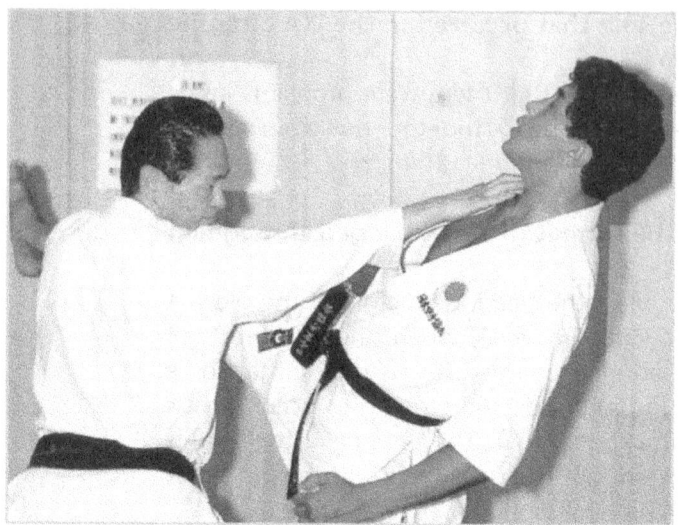

"I know about 140 different forms, and each and every one of them teaches me something different, but I am Japanese and my karate is Japanese. A shotokan practitioner shouldn't be fixated on only training the standard kata of the style."

develop different attributes. Not all kata were created for the same purpose. You need to know what your weak points are and choose the kata that will help you to improve those. That's when kata becomes a training method for specific purposes.

Q: You have studied several Chinese styles of chuan-fa [kung-fu]. What are the differences you see between Chinese and Japanese forms?
A: Well, as we talked about previously, the Chinese always stress the relaxation aspect of it. The stances are very fluid, and the transition between positions is always done in a very natural way. Karate should be the same ... because it is natural. Natural is always the answer to the question. I know about 140 different forms, and each and every one of them teaches me something different, but I am Japanese and my karate is Japanese. A shotokan practitioner shouldn't be fixated on only training the standard kata of the style.

Q: Therefore, is it better to keep your stances high in karate because that is more natural than making them low?
A: In the beginning and for training purposes, the student must work techniques from low stances. This builds muscle and strengthens the practitioner's hips. Everyone needs this kind of training in the beginning. Don't forget that strong leg muscles will prevent knee injuries later on. After years of training and experience, when the student knows how to use the hips properly, it is OK to use higher stances. Students can use deep stances for specific techniques and higher stances for something else. It doesn't really matter as long as the student knows what he is

doing. But this is pretty much up to the individual. There is not a set rule that everybody must follow.

Q: You have created the Japan Karate Shotokai. Why?
A: I simply wanted to express karate in my own way. Karate has taught me to overcome my fears and myself and to get along with and work with others. I am an engineer of the art ... not a politician. I want to train and teach people ... not argue about things. I don't have time for that. I want to create collaboration and support among the students. This organization is a martial arts organization, not a group for politics. Division in the world of karate is not good, but it is a fact. The reason for this is very simple; ego. Everybody wants to be the boss, but nobody wants to be the Indian.

"Make karate training part of your life and set realistic goals that you can achieve. Set a goal and work hard to accomplish it. Define where you are going. Study new ways and develop new ideas that can improve what you are doing."

Q: What advice would you give to karate practitioners?
A: To truly understand what budo means, I would tell them to put their hearts into it and never stop training. Budo is Japanese culture, and sometimes it is hard for non-Japanese to understand. That's why it is important that students first understand their own culture and then absorb what budo can offer.

Make karate training part of your life and set realistic goals that you can achieve. Set a goal and work hard to accomplish it. Define where you are going. Study new ways and develop new ideas that can improve what you are doing. Be creative. Time is essential because it allows us to look at the same thing differently. Karate—like a human being—needs time to grow. There is no end to expanding. Consider yourself always a student and never think that you are already there. Never give up. O

Tino Ceberano

The Hard Way

EVERY MAN, AS HE GROWS OLDER, SEEKS SOME REAL OR SYMBOLIC ACHIEVEMENT WITH WHICH TO CAP HIS CAREER. AFTER RECEIVING HIS 3RD DAN FROM THE LEGENDARY GOGEN "THE CAT" YAMAGUCHI, A YOUNG TINO CEBERANO LEFT HIS NATIVE COUNTRY OF HAWAII TO START LIFE IN MELBOURNE WITH THE PURPOSE OF ESTABLISHING THE STYLE OF GOJU-RYU KARATE IN AUSTRALIA. FROM SMALL BEGINNINGS, THIS STYLE OF KARATE HAS GROWN AND MULTIPLIED, BECOMING THE MOST WIDELY PRACTICED OF KARATE STYLES IN AUSTRALIA.

SENSEI CEBERANO HAS TRAVELED BACK AND FORTH TO JAPAN ON MANY OCCASIONS FOR HIS OWN [REASONS] AND FOR HIS STUDENTS' SENIOR GRADINGS. AND, WITH HIS INVOLVEMENT IN THE INTERNATIONAL KARATE SCENE OVER MANY YEARS AS THE CHIEF REFEREE OF WUKO, AS WELL AS HOLDING THE TITLE OF VICE PRESIDENT OF THE SAME ORGANIZATION, HE HAS CONTRIBUTED TO ESTABLISHING THE ART IN DIFFERENT COUNTRIES AROUND THE GLOBE.

AFTER THE DEATH OF GRANDMASTER GOGEN YAMAGUCHI, THE SENIOR OFFICIALS OF THE GOJU-KAI GRANTED CEBERANO SENSEI HIS INDEPENDENCE AS A PROPAGATOR OF THE GOJU-RYU SCHOOL. THIS DECISION ALLOWED HIM THE PRIVILEGE OF FORMING HIS OWN ORGANIZATION. THE INTERNATIONAL GOJU KARATE-DO (I.G.K) WAS FORMED AND RECOGNIZED BY THE OKINAWAN GOJU RYU RENMEI.

IN FEBRUARY 1992, HIS STANDING AND TECHNICAL EXCELLENCE RESULTED IN AN INVITATION TO BE TESTED FOR HIS 7TH-DEGREE (NANADAN-KYOSHI) GRADING. CEBERANO SENSEI BECAME THE FIRST WESTERNER TO BE GRADED FOR THIS LEVEL UNDER THE AUSPICES OF THE OKINAWAN BUDO INTERNATIONAL.

IN THIS SENSEI'S OPINION, THE ART OF KARATE-DO ADDS UP TO A BASIC ATTITUDE—AN ATTITUDE THAT PLACES THE HIGHEST IMPORTANCE ON SELF-KNOWLEDGE, TRANQUILITY AND RESPECT. "KARATE IS A UNIVERSAL ART. IT BELONGS TO HUMANITY, NOT JUST TO THE JAPANESE AND OKINAWANS," HE SAYS SMILING.

Q: How long have you been practicing the martial arts?
A: Since 1951. I started on the island of Kauai, Hawaii. Prior to that, as early as 1949 on the sugar plantation camp where we lived on the island of Kauai, I received an introduction to Filipino arnis from our fathers,

Karate Masters

"As a young boy of ethnic background [Filipino/Spanish] growing up in a multi-cultural society in the islands of Hawaii, the martial arts were evident and saturated well into our lifestyles."

uncles and the elders of the village. This got the youngsters started in an ethnic cultural inheritance that was part of the norm for many of the local boys who grew up in the villages.

Q: In how many martial arts have you trained?
A: I have been involved in arnis, judo, jiu-jitsu, kenpo, karate, kobudo and tai chi.

Q: Who were your first teachers?
A: My father and granduncle were our senior teachers of arnis while we were on the island of Kauai. My uncle's name was Apo Sedong Cabacungan, and he was from Hanapepe. My next instructor, Dr. Rex Glacier, happened to be from the Kalaheo Judo Dojo, and he was associated with the Hawaii Judo Association under Professor Sakabe, who happened to be with the Hongwangji Mission in Honolulu. Next came my first instructor in kenpo … Sensei Fred Imperial. He was under the lineage of the Lone Pine Tree System of Kenpo Hawaii. My next mentor and the most influential instructor leading me into the martial arts proper was Master Masaichi Oshiro of Honolulu, Hawaii. He was the first instructor/pioneer of goju-kai karate under Grandmaster Gogen "The Cat" Yamaguchi. My instruction in kobudo came from many [instructors] in Japan and Okinawa. There was Inoue Mokatsu Hanshi of the Shinken Taira Kaiso lineage Rukyu Kobujitsu Hozon Shinko Kai, Teruo Hayashi Hanshi of the Hayashi Ha Shito-ryu and many others, including the masters of the Okinawa Goju-ryu Federation.

Q: Would you tell us some interesting stories of your early days in the martial arts?
A: As a young boy of ethnic background [Filipino/Spanish] growing up in a multi-cultural society in the islands of Hawaii, the martial arts were evident and saturated well into our lifestyles. As we put it amongst our col-

leagues or even peers of renown, recalling those days of the 1950s and mid-1960s, we had something special that we all inherited. The mixtures of these passed-on technologies bore special traits, influencing our very nature of compatible fighting skills for what we were then and became as we ventured out into the world beyond our imagination. Mention that [you were] a local boy from Hawaii, and [people knew that] you would were a happy-go-lucky individual who would not back down from any beef [provocation]. We would go "Duke City" (have a go) as a matter of survival or [to] really kick butt. Our service careers often noted that the local boys from Hawaii were the guys who had a bit of something. From that time on, there was a generation of pioneering of those who left Hawaii and went to the states. There was Prof. Richard Kim, Master Ed Parker, Prof. Wally Jay, Master Gordon Doversola, Master Ted Tabura, Master Bill Ryusaki, Master Ben Largusa, Master Ted Lucay Lucay and many more. While [many others] made significant contributions, there are just too many to list. But, having said that, I do have to add one more. This is a pioneer from way down south. Down under, in fact. I am talking about Australia. This [contribution] occurred during the transition. The transition of the martial arts becoming a household word. I can say that it has been an interesting period of time, and it will be even more promising in the future. I am a part of this transitional phase much, just as I was part of the pioneering state from those years during the early 1960s. The person I am talking about, of course, is me.

"The transition of the martial arts becoming a household word. I can say that it has been an interesting period of time, and it will be even more promising in the future."

I will mention some of the old stories from my Hawaii days because these will linger on forever and will be well remembered by those who have experienced what are sure to become legacies.

My first kumite [experience] was at our dojo in the Liliha branch of the goju-kai. My instructor and sempai was Antone Navas. He was a sen-

Karate Masters

"Our study in the martial arts is in fact motivational. [In so doing, we must] sustain endurance and develop tolerance and perseverance. Most importantly, we must make spiritual gains that come from the fighting spirit. This is zanshin *or internal fortitude."*

ior student of instructor Masa Oshiro. Navas was a gentle giant. A man in his rightful place amongst the best, he was also a riding companion of the famous Sons of Hawaii, a motorcycle gang known throughout Hawaii at the time. Having come from another style prior to this, I thought that he was going to teach me kumite and take me through the paces, which was the case in the matches before he called on me. In my entire life, I had never encountered anyone with his enormous strength. We started our usual sparring mode, only I was like a little dog trying to hit and run, mainly to avoid this man's strength and skill, as he was as fast as they come. He got hold of me, and I was bounced from one side of the dojo to the other. I lost all momentum, balance and got so disoriented that I felt like a rag doll. He then picked me up, and to my amazement, told me how I should evade and use various tactics to succeed. He then took me aside and said, "Remember this. To fall seven times, is to rise eight. Life begins now." Those words have sunk in well. To this very day, I reflect on [them] in my teaching. Our study in the martial arts is in fact motivational. [In so doing, we must] sustain endurance and develop tolerance and perseverance. Most importantly, we must make spiritual gains that come from the fighting spirit. This is *zanshin* or internal fortitude. Call it what you may, but it is our power source that we call on instinctively at the best of times. In those years of progress, those beautiful words from my sensei/senpai of the Hawaii Goju-Kai Dojo carried me. They carried me through my days here and throughout the world of which I have served as a student and propagator in this art.

Q: When you started teaching, how did the Westerners respond to traditional Japanese training?
A: Very interesting indeed! I was one of a kind when I arrived in Australia at the time I did. The first time it was in 1962. The second trip was in

1963. I eventually returned to marry an Australian girl whom I had befriended on two occasions while I was on tour as a Marine. Let it be known that karate in those parts was hardly known. As a Marine who had the privilege of doing what I knew best, I had the opportunity to show many people something they will never forget ... goju *sanchin* and *tensho* kata, as well as *seienchin*. In August of 1963, I returned to Melbourne, which is in the state of Victoria, to marry my Australian fiancé. I considered residing there even though I was still a reserve Marine on partial duty.

At one point, I was invited to the Dandenong Judo Club. This is where two well-known exponents of judo were trainees. One was Peter Armstrong, a stuntman in the film industry, and Mr. Malcom Brown was studying to become an accountant. Later, Brown taught tae kwon do and became a sponsor to a very well known instructor in the art. When a person in Australia claims to be the first goju-ryu propagator in the country, we should call a spade a spade.

"As a Marine who had the privilege of doing what I knew best, I had the opportunity to show many people something they will never forget ... goju sanchin *and* tensho *kata, as well as* seienchin.*"*

Now, let me get back to the Westerner's response to the traditional training question. I guess I can sum it up by saying that the students were receptive to the traditional teaching. Or at least the traditional method prevailed. I can also honestly say—for what it is worth—that I would describe [that the whole matter] was a challenge. Our [stereotypical] character trait of an "Aussie" is that he is very liberated, an individual with a lot of freedom who puts on a personalized display and may at times be very skeptical unless proven otherwise. The last statement says it all, as my experience proved only too well what it meant to be a foreign pioneer in this strange country who was tested time and time again. As we say here, "It was my way or the highway." Yes, I am proud to say that tradition prevailed and was accepted. I could go on and on in describing how hard it was to get people to adjust. Instead, let me say that the best of part of this undertaking had been [exposing] the mystery of this hardly known art of the Orient. The only information available was traditional; therefore, it was literally accepted, provided I proved the worthiness of it.

Karate Masters

"I would like to acknowledge the many masters of whom I hold in reverence ... their capability, their presentation of their skills in describing the word art as in the martial art."

The presentation then was ritualistic. It gained momentum when the guest masters of Oriental origin arrived and many more have since arrived. However, there aren't any more or any fewer martial artists here who still adhere to the traditional philosophical state. The motivational attributes that contribute to its select presentation are still here. And most importantly, there is a linkage to why the art remains significant to modern science and a formidable combative technology.

Q: Were you so natural at karate that the movements came easily to you?
A: I couldn't very well consider myself a natural except that I was able to do everything that was asked of me. If natural means that I was able to do things perfectly, then I am fooling myself. I had some memorable lessons, and sometimes it takes a lot of repetition. But I was an eager student and a "sponge" for learning. I've proven myself to others, and it has been a great experience then, now and will still be for years to come.

Q: How has your personal karate changed and developed over the years?
A: In answering this question, I would like to acknowledge the many masters of whom I hold in reverence ... their capability, their presentation of their skills in describing the word art as in the martial art, and most importantly, their propagation level in presenting a development format that science presents as the mechanics of training. I believe that my personal karate has changed dramatically because of the many influences I've had from my own father, including in the early years of boxing training. I also became involved in physical education as a teacher. Later, I became a national coach in sport karate, and I had to study the biomechanics of movements in the martial arts. While doing this, I can account for the progression in scientific movements that relate to what had been missing

in my karate of earlier years. Other integrated study of various disciplines in the arts also influenced my standard of creativity and the likes of precision to realistic techniques as well.

In essence, I believe that my training has purpose now, and with that level, there is a maturing consequence that is better, more concise and better understood. A new weapon of this time appears more realistically sound than taking an ancient outdated weapon of yesteryear to fight in this era of today.

Q: What are the most important points of your teaching philosophy?
A: Let me start with my own philosophy as written when I first exposed it to literal recording a long time ago, "It's not the style but the man." The importance of this statement allows freedom for all exploratory measure, as in personal study and the continued interest in the why, how and what for. I choose to go by the following words as my own in the area of teaching: "A teacher with the tools of his trade fires the imagination of his students." We live in a society of advanced technologies. We refer to the availability of many other "ology" and what proves to be the development factor of the individual's quest for the answers that are within grasp of these facility. Do not stop at your expansion. Pursue the thoughts of your roots and origin and seek your truth but be mindful to reality. It is often too much to concede to other ulterior motives for this is the beginning of the end.

"I choose to go by the following words as my own in the area of teaching: 'A teacher with the tools of his trade fires the imagination of his students.'"

Q: With all the technical changes during the last 30 years, do you think there is still pure shotokan, shito-ryu, goju-ryu, et cetera?
A: Considerations of purity are measured on what indoctrination has implied ... believe what I say and not what I do. This is a way of saying that we know so much, but we must continue to pursue knowledge and progress with the times. To answer your question, let me refer to the goju-ryu system, because that is what I am familiar with, especially now

Karate Masters

"Pursue the thoughts of your roots and origin and seek your truth but be mindful to reality. It is often too much to concede to other ulterior motives for this is the beginning of the end."

that I have gained insight [into topics], some of which not even many of my senior goju-ryu peers are up to par with on educational development. We modern thinking practitioners have discovered the study of martial arts as a science. It is noted [or comprised] of skill-related subjects that make real the inner functions acceptable or questionable. I would like to mention that the Japanese did not really know—in-depth—what the Okinawans had been concealing for many years from the fold of their sovereignty rulers. And now this plays a major role in the recovery and exposure of advanced technology that we all can appreciate. And that is the linkage of the Chinese styles and their influence on what we find rather valuable at this point in time. So we are advancing, and in doing so, rather that undermining the status quo of our origins in the styles, we are contributing to the enhancement of the technology.

Q: Are different ryu important?
A: In regards to choosing a training center, each practitioner can make that choice. However, to the experienced senior practitioner, he should understand that Okinawa, which is where karate jitsu originated, is but a small island with three specific locations from which the following styles originated: shuri, tomari and naha. It is very important for a practitioner's studies to include the relations and the techniques, which means he must be open to a wider and broader interest in his continued study.

Q: What is your opinion of full-contact karate and kickboxing?
A: Kickboxing is a justifiable practice because it promotes the art of the Thailand, which is muay Thai. In the full-contact karate circuit, knowing that it may be controversial, to say the least, the sport must create what the boxing circuit has done, and that is make safety a priority for amateurs and professionals and [establish] rules that [ensure that] future practitioners can enjoy the sport. This eliminates the untold [number of] promotions to world championships. This [action] may even launch these sports into the Olympics.

"In the full-contact karate circuit, knowing that it may be controversial, to say the least, the sport must create what the boxing circuit has done, and that is make safety a priority for amateurs and professionals and [establish] rules that [ensure that] future practitioners can enjoy the sport."

Q: In regards to the art of karate, how would you describe the life and dedication of Yamaguchi Sensei?
A: Without question, he was a master in his own rights, an innovator before his time, the figure responsible for creating a respected worldwide organization and the man who brought forward a truly subjective study of karate that many followers to this very day understand only partially. In his lifetime, he was a towering strength of the goju-ryu foundation ... without question. I've had the privilege of living under his roof, training with him personally and getting placed in a position of relative importance. I have since gone independently on to pursue further study with the Okinawan masters. These are significant masters who contributed to my continued interest in the arts and have contributed greatly to my level of expertise.

"We are experiencing a transitional point in which sport, if it continues to take over, may bring disadvantages to those who portray or promote this [aspect of karate]. The clarity in practice makes real [or confirms] that Bugei is making distinct gains over the budo and perhaps a new transition to the karate-jitsu will place karate into a better position of propagation in the Western sector."

Q: Do you think that Western karate is at the same level with Japanese karate?
A: Yes, at this point in time. However, I'm sure there may be a Japanese master who would say that Westerners lack this or that. It is interesting to note that the martial arts are a worldwide study and the interest in the professionalism and science of the arts are growing. It's just like the wheel that turns in whichever way it advances. This is the nature of progress.

Q: If you were to compare the fundamental differences between Japanese karate-ka and Western karate-ka, can you see any fundamental differences?
A: On a whole, I have not been updated on the development of Japanese karate-ka. Therefore, I will have to base my answer on those to which I am exposed. My opinion is that modern study makes it possible for an individual to make inevitable progress and development in whatever he wants and needs to excel. This stands strongly with today's practitioners ... whether they are Westerners or Asians.

Q: Karate is nowadays often referred to as a sport. Do you agree with this definition or do you think it is only budo?
A: I would like to comment on what is naturally the effectiveness of karate's growth. We are experiencing a transitional point in which sport, if it continues to take over, may bring disadvantages to those who portray or promote this [aspect of karate]. The clarity in practice makes real [or confirms] that Bugei is making distinct gains over the budo and perhaps a

new transition to the karate-jitsu will place karate into a better position of propagation in the Western sector. My comment on this stems from personal observation and experience from international exposure.

Q: Do you feel that you still have further to go in your studies of karate and budo?
A: Most certainly. This study will go with me to the grave. It is my life, my ambition and my legacy will forever be: "It's not the style, but the man."

Q: At the present time, how do you see karate, in general, and goju-ryu around the world?
A: I do not wish to speculate and then retrieve my statements, but here goes. Karate is a tool, as in other disciplines, that most practitioners see as a motivational activity with a purpose. It will continue—and with proper delivery of its correct technology and with correct teaching—for a long time. The goju-ryu technology will become an influential subject to steer an interested person to [undertake an in-depth] study in culture, skills and compatible techniques. They will also discover a formidable combative technology.

"Karate is a tool, as in other disciplines, that most practitioners see as a motivational activity with a purpose. It will continue—and with proper delivery of its correct technology and with correct teaching—for a long time."

Q: Does kobudo help empty-hand karate?
A: Yes, definitely. It enhances many skills, including balance and evasion, directional power and specific hitting techniques. I recommend this totally.

Q: What's your opinion of makiwara training?
A: I have done this for many years, but I have not reached [a level of] satisfaction from its benefits. With my knowledge of both the biological effects of using this and better ways to enhance my power, I have

Karate Masters

"Sport and tradition do have their place, but I use them in a different way. I balance them against all of the components in our practice. We must not put aside what has been our study, but we must continue to make the study interesting and creative for all to follow."

reverted back to corrective training and proper use of other implements in developing my personal skills.

Q: To progress in the arts, how should a sensei schedule his personal training?
A: Many years ago I had the privilege of training with my other revered teacher and master of kobujitsu ... Inoue Motokatsu Hanshi. He was an astute and very knowledgeable practitioner of many arts. He would practice daily, beginning as early as 5:30 a.m. He worked on various skills and even traveled from one country to another. In his system, he used a miniature calendar on which he scheduled the techniques that he was going to study that day. While traveling, he'd merely turn to his calendar and refer to the item he was going to be working on. Then he would visualize his entire practice. What a remarkable man he was and how he trained us will remain in our hearts for the rest of our time.

Q: Self-defense, sport or tradition. When teaching the art of karate, what is the most important element?
A: The martial arts, as in many other facets, remain integrated largely because of their origin and imbedded items of rudiments and progressive development. In the daily teaching of the martial arts, I see a composite of all [of these items], which can be made presentable by a lesson plan that includes all of them. Of course, there may be variables and interesting progressions of why various items are taught.
Sport and tradition do have their place, but I use them in a different way. I balance them against all of the components in our practice. You see, they all are part and partial of the art. We must not put aside what has

been our study, but we must continue to make the study interesting and creative for all to follow.

Q: Sensei, do you have any general advice you would care to pass on to the karate-ka?
A: Take your training and progression seriously. And don't overlook the time factor. We seem to think that we will never get old and that our bodies will always be strong, willing and able. For those who belong to the school that promotes the study of this art for life, pursue this like a daily meal. Sustenance will contribute to the welfare and continuation of the body ... similar to your desire to learn more. It never ends. And the mind, the body and the spirit will coexist to bring satisfaction in this practice, if you so choose.

Q: Some people think that it is necessary to go to Japan to train. Do you agree?
A: Definitely not. We have many qualified instructors in the world who can provide quality training. Of course, it should be noted that such a pilgrimage to Japan could be a novelty, as well as visiting Okinawa. By all means, you should do so if you so desire. Obviously, there are cost and logistics to consider, but the trip may "center" you and you may experience innovative training methods. [These benefits have been obvious from others throughout] these past years.

"The manner in which we were taught was accepted as if it were the standard rule. If you did not follow those methods or conform to that way of training, you were told that you would never learn."

Q: Since you began training, what do you consider to be the major changes in the art of karate?
A: Attitudes and receptiveness to traditional teachings. The manner in which we were taught was accepted as if it were the standard rule. If you did not follow those methods or conform to that way of training, you were told that you would never learn. It is, of course, very enduring to teach that way. The repetition and many hours of physical exercises were

Karate Masters

"In my early years, I was fortunate to have my father teaching me what values were all about. I appreciated what I got, made something of it and considered myself lucky for what came my way. In essence, start what you finish or go until it no longer serves you."

strenuous and there were dangerous implications [to the training] that hurt many students. However, the respect and courtesy were exceptional. If you suffered an injury, you'd take it as a mark of honor ... rather than [an incident in which] someone was trying to injure you purposely. We have rules bound by litigation today that make our responsibility in the dojo very restrictive. For most, it is a form of training that caters only to its client rather than teaching the art for what it is and how it will be beneficial to its practitioners.

Q: With whom would you like to have trained with that you have not?
A: In the art of karate, I would nominate Taira Sensei, the weapons master of Okinawa, and, of course, our founder and creator of the goju-ryu, Master Chojun Miyagi.

Q: What would you say to someone who is interested in learning karate-do?
A: What do you wish to gain from learning karate-do and how did you decide that it is karate-do that you desire to learn? The reasoning behind these questions is to be certain that we gain a student and not a person of ill repute or someone with ulterior motives who would waste our [the instructor's] time. So it's good to know before hand know exactly where we stand.

Q: What keeps you motivated after all of these years?
A: Someone just asked me this question recently, and I answered it by

telling him that I have a desire to better myself through physical conditioning. But there is more to it than meets the eye. Yes, the beginning was a challenge because there was a lot to tolerate, and it's important to focus on every detail. This literally can make or break someone. In my early years, I was fortunate to have my father teaching me what values were all about. I appreciated what I got, made something of it and considered myself lucky for what came my way. In essence, start what you finish or go until it no longer serves you. Attributes to motivate exist … like a burning cell that activates every muscle in your body. I feel great and see the light of the next day descending upon me as my

"If one removes the bunkai from kata, it becomes a superficial practice in which meaningless maneuvers simply become a dance and nothing more. The 'guts' of kata lie in its bunkai or what can be practiced as kyogi-kumite."

desire to carry on. I do *kokyu* breathing to refurbish my energy and life, and this [is motivational]. [Simply] living is motivational, especially when you are happy and positive.

Q: Is it necessary to engage in free fighting to achieve good self-defense skills for a real situation?
A: It would be every now and again, but this is not really a measure of [true] defense. So, the best way to improve your skills and understanding of the mind in responsive action is to spar. Not only will you derive these [aforementioned] benefits, but you will also eventually understand the instinctive relays of energy and cardio threshold. All of these are a specialty of my innovative workout. I will release this when we next meet.

Q: What is your opinion about mixing karate styles? Does the practice of one nullify the effectiveness of the other? Or, on the contrary, can it be beneficial to a student?
A: It is most beneficial. Barriers of style have now been lifted and most certainly bring advantageous results that all students will enjoy and appreciate. Put aside the stigma of "my style" or "my way," as it is every-

Karate Masters

"To search is to find. Upon doing so, answers will be granted by virtue of ones understanding or duplication."

one's way, and it will open the door to accept the art in its expanded science ... ready to explore.

Q: Modern karate is moving away from the bunkai in kata practice. How important do you think bunkai is in the understanding of "kata" and karate-do in general?
A: If one removes the bunkai from kata, it becomes a superficial practice in which meaningless maneuvers simply become a dance and nothing more. The "guts" of kata lie in its bunkai or what can be practiced as *kyogi-kumite*.

Q: What is the philosophical basis for your karate training?
A: The words that began in biblical times and for those who were seeking the truth certainly precede the common anecdotes of martial arts philosophy. To search is to find. Upon doing so, answers will be granted by virtue of ones understanding or duplication.

Q: Do you have a particularly memorable karate experience that has remained as an inspiration for your training?
A: Yes, I have a most memorable moment that will never be repeated in all my life. This incident enabled me to share moments of energy exchange with my Grandmaster, Gogen Yamaguchi. The year was 1972, and the location was the Adelaide Hills in South Australia. We were at a vintage resort property where we were scheduled to shoot a local television feature of this great master. We were in a cherry orchard in the rear of this beautiful resort. There was mist, and it was a bit eerie. We were in our gi, prepared for a kumite match and the setting was similar to Old Japan. It was the grandmaster and the lowly student. The grandmaster, with his shoulder-length hair, not only looked awesome, but his form was excellent and he was fierce. When the order for hajime was given, it felt like I shouldn't be there, let alone have to face up to our Kancho, Hanshi Gogen Yamaguchi. It ended as it started … I was taken for being star struck. Even if I moved to execute, I was checked and there was an answer to everything I delivered. It was the greatest experience that anyone could have encountered. It felt like I was a magnet. I was stopped before even getting started. It will be my story to tell my grandchildren when they too reach a period in time for their lessons. This will be my inspiration to the day I pass on, for what it was and what took place on that morning in South Australia.

Q: After all these years of training and experience, explain the meaning of the practice of karate-do.
A: What karate-do means to me may differ for others. In answering this, I will explicitly refer to my experiences that have influenced my growth in this homogeneous society that can be measured for progress and development. Let me expound on the features of this path—the empty-hand way—that have had a grip on my life and [provided] continued satisfaction and given direction to my ever-growing quest to the attributes by which I follow. It is a unique study, for it encompasses the concern of the elements in life that impose on a serious practitioner the inner depth of mental exploration, the physical energy one puts to test on progressive development, and the soul seeking attributes that lead to the character development and further influence of what evidently becomes a chosen way.

In summary, what I have gained from this study and involvement stays with me as chronological development that I come to recognize as the same thing my dear Sensei Inoue Motokatsu mentioned during one of his lectures to us and that is this journey takes you undisturbed as long as you are on track. Our lives reach a point of cognition to realism or what is known as *heiho* awareness. In essence, the applications are universal.

Q: How can a practitioner increase his understanding of the spiritual aspect of karate?
A: First, he must have tremendous desire. Personally, I would rather explain what and how this became a venture for me and explain what transpired as I became a spiritual being rather than have someone else explain that based on observances of me. What started as a physical motive for practicing [the martial arts], I [soon] recognized a very unique feeling. I started to feel uplifted and [experience] a power surge of energy during many training sessions. A relaxed state or a state of contentment followed. It was a feeling of having an awareness of everything around me and thinking that I can go on and on with this feeling of control with my senses, my body and mental awareness. Yes, this reality struck me even greater when training in special sessions with masters and other sensei who directed me to search for the inner strength of what comes as spiritual enhancement. I was prepared for change and this became inherent to my studies of religion and other beliefs.

I believe that this is the key to one's search and discovery … being desirous of change. We must consider our belief in the mind, the body and the spirit. When these points or elements of noted existence surface, grasp every opportunity to expand your study, for there lies in it a worthwhile experience that will never set you back and keep you on track with the "Do" of martial arts.

Q: How much training should a "senior" karate-ka be doing to improve at his art?
A: There are several definitions to the term "senior karate-ka." I refer to seniors in terms of ranking in age, maturity and time spent training. Let me advise everyone right now that biological age need not be a deterrent to anyone's involvement in the art. Improvement is not always of the physical nature, but certainly there can be a mastery of skills on a different level, such as theory, correctness of application and philosophical aspirations that bring motivational attributes. It seems like this is the case for many seniors who are no longer able to execute the techniques as easily as they once did in their youthful past. Maturity is the key and hence the practice must be a balanced circuit regime to suit the practitioner's schedule, physical condition and motivational incentive. And, of course, it all highly depends on the individuals desire to maintain the practice.

"A successful karate-ka must be able to engage, exchange, and enjoy his art and, most importantly, contribute or convey to his fellow man the understanding—coded by our practice of respect, courtesy and awareness to others—when called upon."

Q: Is there anything lacking in the way karate is taught today, especially when you compare it with those who were being taught in your early days?
A: In today's teaching, much of the instruction borders on the physical attributes. Unfortunately, the time factor of these workouts limits the intensive motivational and inspirational attributes [that also belong in the sessions]. There's also too much emphasis on sport. Students should realize that the sport element is only a segment of properly learning the martial arts. The sport aspect seems to be the motive most of the time and the attitude [encouraged] is to win at all costs just for the sake of winning. Precedence seems to be on the ego, and it seems like this is the case at most dojo. That is where their priorities are. Understanding the traditional values in practice also lacks details. Ritual exercise means nothing without the understanding and practice of courtesy and respect to the sensei and fellow students, including oneself. Infliction of pain or receiving pain is something that must be suppressed. There are certainly ways it can be cor-

Karate Masters

"Yes, I support supplementary training, as I too adhere to physical training with a difference. Your body needs to be nurtured, and you should choose to follow your desires. This is the modern era of physical fitness, and the technology available certainly surpasses that of yesteryear."

rected and administered with agreeable purpose and positive results. If these changes are met, then things will be better than they were yesterday.

Q: What are the most important qualities of a successful karate-ka?
A: A successful karate-ka must be able to engage, exchange, and enjoy his art and, most importantly, contribute or convey to his fellow man the understanding—coded by our practice of respect, courtesy and awareness to others—when called upon. Once we become involved with the martial arts, we become missionaries to the cause. The cause merely puts us there amongst those who came before us. It engages us as we share this art and for our future existence of surviving the elements that we sometimes take for granted. Let us work together on this, as we do have to sustain this very important study.

Q: If a student wants to partake in supplementary training such as weight training or stretching, what do you suggest?
A: Modern training provides many different modes and circuits of exercise and personal systems that suit every possible development. Yes, I support supplementary training, as I too adhere to physical training with a difference. Your body needs to be nurtured, and you should choose to follow your desires. This is the modern era of physical fitness, and the technology available certainly surpasses that of yesteryear. Your mastery of the arts must be sorted out as you wish. Past criticisms only led to envy and suppressed motives. Later, you discover the loss of understanding of what it was, what it is and what will be.

Q: What are the most important attributes of a student?
A: To be totally happy and satisfied with his training, to be able to perform and be content with his knowledge and progression of study, and to be able to walk away from any danger when provoked. In a state of higher attributes, a student must also grow in other areas of his life, including health, protection, vocation and motivation.

Q: Why do a lot of students stop training after two or three years?
A: For obvious reasons. First, they lack the foresight to reach the levels to which they once strived. In other cases, they are an undefined subject because they are essentially just a puppet in training ... rather than absorbing and relating to the studied technology. In other cases, they become bored because they do not improve. As I mentioned earlier, the mind, body and soul must all be on track. Otherwise, a student's career is going to be shortened.

Q: There is very little written about you in magazines. Unlike some martial artists, you obviously do not thrive on publicity. Why?
A: I have had write-ups in all of the Australian magazines, the European magazines and several American publications. Among other things, there has been a word or two mentioning my participation in some of the tournaments in the 1980s and the 1990s. I am honored indeed for your interest in this interview and this may launch my existence in a manner that I will be most proud. My role has been known amongst many from the many years of worldwide service in karate-do. I take pride in my work and contribution to our martial arts. It is not a lack of desire to [have stories] published about me. Instead, it's been circumstances. While I was in Australia, I was a leader, propagator and a senior practitioner who created

for those who wished to learn. I have had my day in competitions, my role as a top worldwide adjudicator and an executive for many years that put me well into the driver's seat, headed in the right direction. Perhaps now that I am in my maturing years and still active in teaching and propagating this opportunity will launch new, creative innovations that will be a subject for exponents worldwide. As I reiterate, my role out there has been that of a player. I did not exist to be highlighted or grandstanded but to be innovative and productive. I have produced world champions from Australia, worked with movie celebrities, provided security for prominent people and worked with heads of State from many countries. Still, I remain humbled by the fact that I've been there done that and am still going enjoying everything that has been given me. So, again I am indeed grateful for this opportunity, not only for myself but also for my colleagues, because this is a start for us all.

Q: Have there been times when you felt fear in your karate training?
A: Yes, I suppose we [all] may—from time to time—encounter such experiences, particularly when on duty and having to engage in the inevitable. [Let me now] reflect on what my instructor once said to me, "To fall seven times, is to rise eight. Life begins now." Choice words.

Q: What are your thoughts on the future of karate-do and what's your opinion about karate entering the Olympics?
A: I am happy to answer that with convictions of pro and con that will reveal the many reasons that provoked conditions of today's karate-do, as well as respond to the many conditions that play a role in the sport's participation into the Olympics. First, the future of karate-do lies basically in its propagation and creative interest to combative technology, as it was an art. Our directions changed over the times and created ulterior motives that caused the climatic conditions of politics in sport-oriented training. If we are to follow the "Do" of karate, then it should be concerned with defense first—not attack. The competition mode totally destroys the ideals of the karate way. Second, in the event of karate-do being admitted to the Olympics, I dare say that our competitions would be a drawing card for the spectators. This is proving itself as a low-scaled version of karate in its origin.

Now, I want to comment about something from the earlier years of WUKO's development commission. This pertains to the kumite rules for *shiai*. At the time, there were only three foreign members of the elite Referee's Council that had been privy to these meetings. That was Sensei

Frank Nowak and Jerry Thompson, as well as myself. Our chairman was Sensei Teruo Hayashi of the FAJKO. The subject was the inclusion of *sanbon shobu*, a replacement for *ippon-shobu*. All technicalities aside, we were involved deeply in the concepts of other shiai. These other items would have been more conclusive and definitely would have brought credit to karate-do in its implementation should they had been introduced and applied as rules. However, that was not the case, so the game continued with progressive changes [implemented] to highlight the current style of competition rule to suit all participants. One major but very sad and controversial system [that had developed] had been the start of political conflict from all groups and all styles. This eventually led to fragmentations too wide and broad. Thus, the objective of unity died. The biggest thing that it [the fragmentation] created is egoism. Ideals and the code of a karate-ka [were not important]. Instead, winning at all costs and at all risks became important. I regretfully expose a long kept feeling of remorse and disappointment because of the disservice that it [this whole process] had done to many. My role is, as I said, to teach. Hopefully this lesson will not go unmanned for its corrective nature and still may be reinstated to bring again a resurgence of the karate-do that we knew of the past. For the future, I can think of another alternative to the Olympics, but I will reserve that for a well-planned program that is now on the drawing board.

"Karate-do evolved not only from our humble masters from Okinawa but also for many years outside of Japan. It continues to grow with so much interest that motivational experts recognize it as a formidable practice both for the body and the mind."

Q: Is there anything else you would like to add for the readers?
A: They should understand that there is a beginning to all of this. Karate-do evolved not only from our humble masters from Okinawa but also for many years outside of Japan. Today, it has developed into a major household word, and it's important in regards to physical education and cultural attributes. Furthermore, it continues to grow with so much interest that motivational experts recognize it as a formidable practice both for the body and the mind. O

Teruo Chinen

A Peaceful Man

He is one of the world's leading instructors of Okinawan goju-ryu karate and one of a mere handful of karate-ka who is still living and training today who can authentically claim to have trained under the legendary founder of goju-ryu ... Grandmaster Choyun Miyagi.

Proud of his early links to the "source," Chinen Sensei recalls the training in the old days. "The dojo was dirt-floored, and the school was a L-shaped backyard. There was not any glamour about it."

Only a lifetime dedication could have produced such awesome skill and power that is Chinen Sensei. Very few around the world can match his dynamic and powerful techniques and actions. A retired schoolteacher, he is not a believer in too much mysticism or any other form of "ism." He believes—as a Buddhist—in the capabilities of the mind to enhance an individual's potential but not from a cryptic or inexplicable perspective. For him, the connection between physical technique and thought is of the outmost importance. His knowledge and understanding of Chinese culture and philosophy surprise many. For him, however, it is a simple way to understand the roots of karate. As a master of karate-do, Chinen Sensei has been around long enough to have seen most things, and that's probably the reason why he is a man who really is at peace with himself.

Q: What would you tell us about your family involvement in the martial arts?
A: My family has a long tradition of martial arts. I was born in Kobe City, Japan, in 1914. My father was a Navy career man in Okinawa. In 1945, we moved there, and this is where I met Miyagi Sensei years later. My father was a shorin-ryu practitioner. My grandfather was a shorin-ryu instructor, and my uncle was an expert in the bo. In fact, he had kata named after him, such as Chinen-no-kou. I was the first member of my family who took the goju-ryu style of karate. My family accepted it well, but my brother gave me a hard time for a while because he thought I should have stuck to the family tradition of shorin-ryu.

Karate Masters

"I didn't know who he was, but I remember Miyagi Sensei was a stern and quiet man. His movements were very soft but extremely powerful, limber and flexible. The combination of such power and flexibility was incredible."

Q: Sensei, what is your relationship with Chinen Masami Sensei of yamanni-ryu?
A: Yamanni-Chinen-ryu has always carried two arts. One is the weapons system and the other is shorin-ryu karate as I mentioned in the beginning. Masami Chinen was my granduncle. He lived in Shuri, Okinawa, and worked at the Shuri City Hall, as did my brother. I used to call him granduncle Shobi. My father adopted the Japanese ways and did not use the *Masa* name for his children. Later on, my brothers and I all received Japanese names, and they are as follows: Akira, Hirokazu, Teruo and Toshio. No more Chinese names and no more Masa line!

Q: How did you come to live near Miyagi Sensei and how do you remember him?
A: My mother's younger brother was a police officer in the Naha district, and his chief happened to be Chojun Miyagi, who was providing instruction at the police academy. He had several houses, and one of these was three blocks away from Miyagi's. My uncle, being a single man, didn't need the spacious house and gave it to my mother for us to live there. We were a large family (six brothers and sisters), and there was no father. As far as the training concerns, I was just a kid, much too junior to receive serious attentions from Miyagi Sensei. Of course, I didn't know who he was, but I remember Miyagi Sensei was a stern and quiet man. His movements were very soft but extremely powerful, limber and flexible. The combination of such power and flexibility was incredible. His hand strength was incredible and his movements very precise. Only those actions required to do the job were executed. There were no unnecessary movements whatsoever. His reputation was that of a humble man and a kind individual. Of course, at that time there were challenges, but Miyagi Sensei never did this out of a bravado attitude.

He came from a very wealthy family. Because he didn't have to worry about money, he put all his time and energy into karate. He could simply afford to do that. His group of students was comprised of different levels of skill, and he treated them according to their specific skill and understanding. He personalized the instruction for each student. This is the main reason why you see students of Miyagi Sensei doing the same things but slightly differently. He personalized the instruction and gave each student what he really needed at that period of time. Another factor was the stage of his life that Miyagi Sensei was at that time. It is not that anyone is doing it wrong, but they learned it differently at different times.

I have heard really silly stories about Miyagi Sensei, such as the one that he could leave his footprints on the dojo ceiling because of his ability to do a back flip so high that he kicked the ceiling. To begin with, the dojo was outside. It didn't have a ceiling! Miyagi Sensei was way too intelligent to risk damaging his body that way. He was very powerful man, but he was only human.

"I have heard really silly stories about Miyagi Sensei, such as the one that he could leave his footprints on the dojo ceiling because of his ability to do a back flip so high that he kicked the ceiling. To begin with, the dojo was outside. It didn't have a ceiling!"

Q: Who introduced you to him?
A: My uncle took me to his dojo one evening. He told Miyagi Sensei that my family was practitioners of shorin-ryu and asked him to accept me. He said yes and that was it. No paperwork! My first class involved standing basics and front kicks, deep knee bends, stand-up [techniques] and kicks. That kind of stuff.

Q: How was the training afterwards?
A: It was a quiet. There was no yelling or loud kiai. In fact, the kiai we practiced was very internal. The reason for this is the dojo was located in the middle of a residential area, so yelling was not really appropriate! He was a police officer. Therefore, the last things he wanted were screams and yells coming out of his place.

Karate Masters

"Kata and supplementary training were the basics of the training. The supplementary training included the makiwara, chiisi (stone lever weight), nigiri game (gripping jars) and many other [traditional items]."

Q: How did he direct the classes at that time?
A: Well, he was not in a good health, so he sat down a lot and directed the classes. He observed and gave instruction. We did a lot of kata. Kata and supplementary training were the basics of the training. The supplementary training included the makiwara, *chiisi* (stone lever weight), *nigiri game* (gripping jars) and many other [traditional items]. There were not a lot of students and the assistants always took good care of every disciple. Miyazato Sensei was one of them.

Q: Did Miyagi Sensei choose the assistants personally?
A: It was not that kind of structure. There weren't "assistants" as we understand today. They were "seniors" taking care of the "junior" students. Miyagi Sensei would say, "Go help this student." And they did.

Q: How do you remember the death of Miyagi Sensei?
A: From a historical point of view, I was too young to really understand what was happening. I remember that police agents were all around Miyagi's house. I realized that he was a very important individual, and I believe everybody knew the end was near because he had been sick for a long time.

Q: When did you start your training under Eiichi Miyazato Sensei?
A: Miyazato Sensei was Master Miyagi's senior student. When Miyagi Sensei died, Miyazato Sensei received all the training equipment and established his own dojo to continue the teachings of Master Miyagi. Of course, I went with him. I remember we had to move the equipment from one place to another, and I took the makiwara and the chiisi. It was a nice walk. It was only two miles or so! At that time we didn't care about rank of promotion of any kind. We simply cared about karate. We didn't need a belt to know who was good and who wasn't. Belt ranking came later, and it originated from the art of judo. They were using only three belts: white, brown and black. Additional colored belts came afterwards

as instructors experimented with introducing incentives for regular training.

Q: How was it at Miyazato's dojo?
A: It was a typical Okinawan building. It had a household Shinto shrine with the statue of Busaganashi. The dojo had an open door ... Japanese style. It was beautiful, and I really liked it.

Q: From where did the word Jundokan come?
A: It was Miyazato Sensei who gave birth to Jundokan. There is an old Chinese poem called *Jundo Seisho*. Translated, this means, "Do the right way." Miyazato Sensei took a quotation from it.

Q: When did you receive your rank from Miyazato Sensei?
A: It was around 1958 when I was going to Tokyo to teach. Master Miyazato presented me with a black belt. There was no rank designated or certificate presented. In 1974, when I was dispatched to South Africa to teach, Miyazato Sensei gave me a certificate proclaiming the rank of *rokudan*—6th Dan.

"In Okinawa, the training is more individualized and personalized. Of course, the teacher corrects your mistakes, but the class structure follows the Chinese example in which students work on their own."

Q: How different are the Okinawan and Japanese teaching methods?
A: They are very different. In Okinawa, the training is more individualized and personalized. Of course, the teacher corrects your mistakes, but the class structure follows the Chinese example in which students work on their own. At a certain moment in time, the whole group can go through drills or kata at once, but most of the training is individually done. In Japan, the training follows a more militaristic approach. This training structure is very good for young and talented students because you can truly create great karate-ka ... if they survive this kind of structure. Everybody does the same techniques over and over again. Many schools in Japan use this approach, and the technical level [of students] becomes really good. Everybody is cut by the same mold so the individual doesn't receive personal attention as in the Okinawan approach. As I said, it is

Karate Masters

"You must adapt the art to the country where you live and teach. Kata must stay the same, but the concept of the form must change in relation to the culture of the country where the instructor is teaching."

good for young people who are physically strong and who have a decisive mind.

The Okinawan counterpart is more subtle, more tailor-made for the individual student. The teacher treats each student, taking into consideration the ability, age, and physical make-up and peculiarities of each individual. People are quite different—different body structures, philosophies, customs, and ways of expressing themselves—so it is natural that their karate will develop differently. The Japanese approach is more like, "Let's go to train very hard for two hours." When the time is up, they just get on with it and do it. Okinawans follow the Chinese way more. They have a 24-hours martial arts mind. When they feel like training, they just do it. They don't care about the time. The Chinese are more relaxed about it; therefore, I think it is more natural. From my point of view, the art has more possibilities of blossoming this way. If you don't understand how Chinese people think, you may never understand the philosophy behind your karate. The Chinese are very dramatic and exaggerated ... maybe because the country is so big geographically. Chinese history is 10 times longer than Japan's. The Chinese mind goes with the Tangtse and Hwan Rivers ... slowly but surely. Even conversations between Chinese people are a little mystic; they never reveal their entire mind.

Q: Is your Jundokan International organization separate from the Jundokan in Okinawa?

A: Yes, it is separate. The reason that it is separate is that you must adapt the art to the country where you live and teach. Kata, for example, must stay the same, but the concept of the form must change in relation to the culture of the country where the instructor is teaching. Some may think I am saying something stupid, but that is exactly what the old Okinawan masters did when they learnt kung fu and shifu from the Chinese masters who brought the art to Okinawa. These Okinawan practitioners (who later became masters of karate) took the teachings and adapted it, giving it an Okinawan flavor and creating the birth of Okinawan karate.

Q: Do you advocate training in other disciplines?
A: I do. I have grades in kendo, judo and Okinawa weaponry, too. I think that the study of other martial arts forms may assist the students to gain a better understanding of their main art.

Q: You acknowledge that goju-ryu has a strong influence from Chinese arts. This is very unusual for an Okinawa teacher.
A: Well, I don't know if it is unusual or not, but I always give credit where credit is due. For the astute observer, the relationship between goju-ryu and some Chinese styles of kung fu—especially pa kua—is quite obvious. You can see those influences in the circularity and the footwork. We can also see similarities in *kakie* and *tui shou* [pushing hands] from tai chi chuan or the chi sao of wing chun.

"I think that the study of other martial arts forms may assist the students to gain a better understanding of their main art."

Master Kanryo Higaonna, Miyagi's teacher, traveled extensively to China's Fukien Province and trained strenuously for more than 15 years under the legendary Ryu Ryuko. Higaonna Sensei returned to Naha, Okinawa with a great number of kata and knowledge that he passed onto Miyagi Chojun. Miyagi Sensei refined these techniques and kata. In 1931, he named the system goju-ryu. The name (hard and gentle style) reportedly came from an amalgam of some of the Eight Precepts of Chinese kenpo found in the ancient Bubishi manuscripts. There is a particular verse that translates as: "Everything in the universe is controlled by the opposing principles of yin and yang and the way of inhaling and exhaling embraces hardness and softness." Everything is breathing ... hard and soft.

Q: When did you come to the United States?
A: I came to the United States in 1969. Between 1958 and 1969, I was in Tokyo at the Yoyogi dojo, helping Mr. Higaonna Morio teach *gaijin* at his

Karate Masters

"To be honest, it was harder to work with the instructors than with the students. I believe it was a mix of ego and the difficulty of changing what they were doing for so long. I totally understood the situation and gave them as much private instruction as I could."

school. My first intention was to go to Brazil to teach because there had been an outpouring of demand for goju-ryu teachers in Europe, South Africa and South America. However, because the situation was unstable at the time, I ended up in the U.S. I was ready to go to Brazil because Miyazato Sensei called me and told me his wife's brother had company in Sao Paulo, and he was thinking about sponsoring me so I could open a dojo to teach goju-ryu. Then, the country had a *coup d'etat,* and the political situation was inappropriate, so I did not go at that time. I decided to accept the offer to visit the U.S.

I only wanted to stay in the United States for a short period of time, maybe three months or so. However, when I came to Spokane, I saw the low technical level of karate there, and I decided to stay longer. I knew it wasn't anybody's fault. I understood there had been many teachers before, many bridges, and the messages often got crossed. There was such a gap between the practitioners and me! I didn't want to make any instructor uncomfortable, so I offered to help correct what they were doing and establish some kind of foundation on which we could build. To be honest, it was harder to work with the instructors than with the students. I believe it was a mix of ego and the difficulty of changing what they were doing for so long. I totally understood the situation and gave them as much private instruction as I could. I knew it would take time to fix the problem, and I also knew that sometimes it is better to start from scratch instead of trying to rebuild the whole thing. Because things were still chaotic in Brazil, I figured I might as well stay in the U.S.

Q: When did you form Jundokan International?
A: I believe it was around 1980 when Higaonna Sensei formed his own organization, and I decided to stay with Jundo Seisho under Miyazato

Sensei. My idea was that Jundokan International would be a foreign office of Jundokan Okinawa. I wanted to support Miyazato Sensei, and that's why I chose the name of Jundokan International.

Q: What are the characteristics that set goju-ryu apart from other styles of karate?
A: As an art of budo, all styles and systems of karate-do lead to the same goal. So, in the spiritual goal ... there are no differences. Technically, goju-ryu uses the duality of hard and soft to deal with any technical approach. We use the circular movements in most of the actions because it is more natural and it dissolves the incoming energy from the aggressor more fluidly. The fighting distance is shorter than in other styles, and this simple fact effects the chambering position of the fist in *hikite*, the targets we hit in combat, et cetera. For instance, because the fighting distance is shorter, the fist usually is chambered higher than in other karate methods. Why? There is not enough room to punch. Furthermore, there are many fast and short circular techniques. Some of these techniques involve the snapping of the wrist to increase the power at the moment of impact. When the distance is short, speed is not that important but power is. The technique does not have to travel that far, so the practitioner needs to be able to generate a powerful blow. At this short distance, speed is not relevant. Instead, it's how powerful your strike is, especially if you hit each other simultaneously. The training methods used to develop power in short distances are circular. Because using your whole body produces maximum power, goju-ryu stylists need to shift their body in circular motions to get an added advantage.

"Technically, goju-ryu uses the duality of hard and soft to deal with any technical approach. We use the circular movements in most of the actions because it is more natural and it dissolves the incoming energy from the aggressor more fluidly."

Q: Is this the reason why goju-ryu stylists do some of the kata that other styles practice with slight changes in direction?
A: It is. In goju-ryu, everything is very subtle. Things are not so obvious like they are in other karate styles in which you can see through the tech-

Karate Masters

"People train for different reasons, and those [reasons] should be respected. I have changed my teaching methods in some ways, but the essence of the training is the same."

niques clearly. In goju-ryu, everything is in some kind of disguise. A technique may look easy, but it may actually be difficult to master. For instance, goju shares some kata with shito-ryu. However, in goju, the angles in some of the techniques are different. We also stress tension and proper breathing—at all times—in the techniques and kata.

Q: Like in sanchin and tensho?
A: Yes. Sanchin teaches the student how to properly use oxygen and send it to all the parts of the body. This kata also helps to judge the student's level when practicing other forms. I do believe that strong basics are the secrets to becoming a good karate-ka. Tensho is one of my favorite kata because it deals with breathing, and breathing is the key of life. If you are capable of focusing on one thing for an extended period, that [ability] can translate to something else. In the Western world, students don't like to spend too much time repeating the same technique. Thus, instructors should adapt and change their teaching approach. Sometimes this creates problems in the long run. People train for different reasons, and those [reasons] should be respected. I have changed my teaching methods in some ways, but the essence of the training is the same. I may change with times, but the quality of what they receive is the same. Chi or Ki comes through breathing. Breathing comes from the *tanden* and promotes the smooth flow of energy throughout the body. The amount of benefit you derive from this varies; it depends on the practitioners. All styles rooted in Chinese systems practice this, along with stimulating chi through movement ... and goju-ryu does this also.

Q: You mentioned tensho kata. Does it have roots in Chinese kung-fu?
A: Yes it does. Tensho represents the kata of white crane kung-fu. A woman created this style. In Okinawa, tensho kata is considered to be at the same

level as *pechurin* [suparimpei], but I always teach it to beginners so they can develop the proper breathing pattern and greater lung capacity.

Q: Sanchin kata is an important part of the goju style of karate. What can you tell us about it?
A: It is true that sanchin is one of the pillars of goju-ryu, and its importance and meaning go beyond the well-known translation of three battles. It also goes beyond the body-mind-spirit principle. This form is the basic training form for many Fujianese [Fukien] styles of chuan-fa [kung fu], primarily those with the animals, as the system's white crane. Sanchin seems to have originated some 300 years ago and is considered to be a white crane kata. This form was the basis for the breathing method, strength, stance and strategy in the Southern Shaolin temple. The training in sanchin takes place in three stages, which are training in the form, training the chi [Ki] and training the spirit [*shen*]. Training the form is learning the pattern of the kata and the moves along with their applications. The training of the Ki is the training of the principles behind the moves. This involves the study of how the principles are used to give the correct energy application and the flow of the energy throughout the sequence of the moves. This understanding can be then applied to other kata or forms. The training of the spirit is the final and most difficult phase of sanchin development. This means the ability to direct Ki and to use it as the will directs. It also involves achieving the correct state of mind required for combat. These arise only after a very long time of dedicated training. Finally, the idea of the number three goes beyond all these things we have talked about. In sanchin, the number three symbolizes a three-dimensional approach to the form, but this is extremely difficult to explain in written format without the proper physical explanations of the technique.

Q: What is your opinion of karate being a sport?
A: Karate is not a sport, but some aspects of karate can be used as a sport activity in competition. Budo is the most important thing I teach. Sport makes a student focus on speed and not the power behind the techniques. Everything evolves around who is the one scoring faster and not necessarily the one who is more powerful. Your opponent in a real confrontation will fall because of power—not strictly because of speed. It is not that speed is unimportant, but you want to make sure that you don't throw away power for useless speed. Karate was never designed for sport. Yes, you can use the front kick and the reverse punch to score a point, and that may be enough for tournaments. However, self-defense is a dif-

ferent thing altogether. You can't build a house with just one tool; you need a number of tools. And to protect ourselves, we need a variety of tools. Today, sport karate is very good and it [has reached a] high level all over the world, but there is a great danger [in that] because true karate spirit and attitude can't be maintained in sport karate training. This can be achieved only with the correct approach, and that is up to the instructor. Karate should be for everybody from children to older people. Everybody can derive benefits from proper karate training, regardless of their age. Perhaps when the students are young they can focus on competition. When they get older, they will need more than that. That's when the art and true karate-do comes along. You have to cultivate the art and the true karate when you are young. You can't think that it will be there when you are older if you haven't taken care of it before.

Q: Why haven't you been an advocate of the tales attributed to the old masters?
A: I'm trying to steer clear of that mysterious approach to karate training. You know those claims. "My punch is so deadly that I can't go to tournaments." Or, "Meditation brings the ultimate enlightenment." That type of stuff. I'm tired of hearing that sort of thing. Speed and power in karate come from correct training methods, strong conditioning and endless repetitions. I believe conditioning is one of the most important aspects of training, and I ask my students to do the same.

Q: What are your recommendations for makiwara training?
A: My first advice is that a student should only start under the supervision of a qualified instructor. Makiwara training is not a joke because it can ruin your hands if it is not done properly. I have always been attracted to it because of the view of those bloodstained, straw-padded posts in Miyagi's backyard dojo. Training with a makiwara is very important in the development of proper impact and kime in the techniques, but, as I said previously, it has to be properly taught. Otherwise, it can cause arthritic problems later in life. Remember, your hands are a wonderful piece of physical engineering, and you can cause irreversible damage to them. Treat your body with respect. Calluses are just a byproduct of the training. Training with a makiwara improves your timing, impact, and coupled with properly taught footwork, can greatly enhance your dexterity in striking on the move. To me, training with a makiwara represents the last hope in maintaining the essence of the original spirit of traditional karate. It's [makiwara training] the kind of karate that—unlike others—doesn't

promote hands and feet as soft as a baby's because there isn't an emphasis on sport competition. The feeling for self-protection has been lost, and makiwara training keeps this feeling.

Q: What do you mean by treating your body with respect?
A: We all want to live well and have a long and happy life. To do this, we must take care of our body and provide it with the utmost respect. During my 20s and 30s, I carried a wounded body. But as a teacher, I don't want my students to suffer the same injuries. I have done my best to develop good teaching skills that are physically harder but safer. We no longer practice some of those conditioning exercises that may not be so good.

Q: How important is bunkai in the understanding of karate?
A: Very important. Miyagi Sensei broke the different kata into a wide variety of applied physical situations that could be used in self-defense scenarios. He explained the bunkai by having an attacker perform an aggressive move and then—using the move from the kata. My way of teaching is geared towards continuing Miyagi's interpretation of the different kata in goju-ryu. What it is interesting is the fact that the true meaning of the techniques may not at first be evident. Sometimes the real bunkai may be very difficult to detect and has some kind of secret meaning behind it. Sometimes you find that the bunkai is applied in a different direction or using other principles to make it effective in combat. If you don't know how to unlock these principles and techniques, you may never find the real reason behind the technique. As I said previously, Chinese philosophy is very mystical, and in many ways, bunkai is also mystical. If kata movement goes to the right, you must think the answer is to the left. If one looks at the sky, then the enemy may be on the ground. Leave 10 percent of your karate a mystery and enjoy it. Use your imagination.

"During my 20s and 30s, I carried a wounded body. But as a teacher, I don't want my students to suffer the same injuries. I have done my best to develop good teaching skills that are physically harder but safer. We no longer practice some of those conditioning exercises that may not be so good."

Karate Masters

"Sometimes you find that the bunkai is applied in a different direction or using other principles to make it effective in combat. If you don't know how to unlock these principles and techniques, you may never find the real reason behind the technique."

Q: **How important is the concept of style in karate training?**
A: Nowadays, people talk about different styles and peculiarities of this or that particular method. When I started training, there were only three in the town of Naha. They were shorin, goju and uechi. When I moved to Tokyo in 1958, there were more than 10 different styles. They referred to them as styles, but they were very similar. I never thought that there were that many differences. It was mostly a way of calling the school after the sensei's name.

Q: **You are residing in the United States. What is your opinion about the level of martial arts in that country?**
A: I truly think that the technical level in the U.S. is very high. Sometimes, from the outside, people only see some "watered down version" of karate, but you should look at the top Japanese masters teaching there. There are great traditional instructors, and their students are very good. The U.S. is a melting pot because you have top instructors from Korea, Japan, China, Okinawa, et cetera. The intense competition has meant that the instructors of the various arts have really had to polish up their skills. And they have "borrowed" techniques and ideas from other styles and systems to make what they are practicing and teaching better. This has always been always a feature in martial arts history. Not even goju itself was a pure one-family style.

Q: **What is your opinion about kickboxing and other similar fighting events?**
A: I don't object to the full-contact karate or kickboxing scene, but for dojo training they should stick to one style and teacher. "Window shopping" is not good for martial arts. I believe that these kinds of events and

activities have their place, but they are not budo.

Q: Do you think it is a good idea to have one single federation that controls all karate styles?
A: My opinion is that karate is an individual or private thing. An organization overseeing distinct and separate martial arts, such as the Okinawan systems, would eventually hurt the quality of those methods. Culturally and traditionally, the Okinawan martial arts are too individual and distinct to be grouped together arbitrarily, so I don't think that approach is positive for karate or any other martial art style.

Q: It is obvious that your approach to training is more Chinese than Okinawan or Japanese. Why?
A: Basically, your body tells you when it wants you to move. In me, that response is through kata. The psychological response in me is due to my major field of study, which is the history of China. My need for training is spontaneous, and I will do so anytime and anywhere.

"The training of the Ki is the training of the principles behind the moves. This involves the study of how the principles are used to give the correct energy application and the flow of the energy throughout the sequence of the moves."

Q: What are your hopes for the future of the art?
A: I hope that the next generations will not only improve technically but also know how to share their knowledge. People must pass on the traditions and not lose them. In the old days in China and Okinawa, the teaching was done behind closed doors. Now, thanks to the media, karate-do is no longer a secret and it is within everybody's reach. It is up to us to preserve its value in the world. I feel strongly that the future of karate-do is still very positive, but hard practice is the key. O

Malcolm Dorfman

A Legacy of Passion

Malcolm Dorfman Sensei was born in Johannesburg on March 31, 1947. He was captain of the University of Witwatersrand judo team in 1966 and thereafter joined the university karate club. He made rapid progress and four years later was selected to the first national team to tour overseas. In 1978, after being chosen as the Springbok captain, he retired from the team. He went abroad many times to train with karate masters, including M. Nakayama Sensei and the instructors of the JKA headquarters in Tokyo.

Malcolm Dorfman Sensei was well known in the famous "Hornet's Nest," the elite instructor's class of the original Japan Karate Association. This was before the group fragmented. Since 1974, when he first trained there as a *san-dan*, he has been to Japan almost 20 times and trained in the "Hornet's Nest" for an extended period of time on each visit.

Although he recognizes the fact that fighting was the main focus of his early training, his goal changed along the way. "As I became more and more engrossed in karate, I discovered that the art possessed a stimulus that could not be gained in any other art of sport. I became sold on the art."

After the split occurred at the original JKA, Malcolm Dorfman Sensei opted to go with the Karate No Michi World Federation. At the international dan grading examinations, held the day prior to the 2000 Karate No Michi World Championships in Cardiff, Wales, he was awarded the rank of 8th dan by the Japanese Master Panel [International Shihankai] under Yahara Sensei. In addition, he was appointed as a director on the International Shihankai, making him the only non-Japanese member of this board.

Q: How long have you been practicing the martial arts?
A: My martial art introduction began approximately 45 years ago when I took judo between the ages of 12 and 14. However, I gave it up for soccer for three years, and then I resumed judo training again at the university when I turned 17. In 1966, I started my karate career at my university karate club, initially training in both judo and karate for one year. Eventually, I focused solely on karate.

Karate Masters

"Besides judo in my early days, there was a four-year period in the 1980s in which I trained in kendo, both in Japan and in South Africa."

Q: In how many styles have you trained?
A: Shotokan is the only karate style that I can truly say I trained in. I think many practitioners learn a kata here and there from other styles, and I was no different, but I certainly won't claim great proficiency in or knowledge of other styles. Besides judo in my early days, there was a four-year period in the 1980s in which I trained in kendo, both in Japan and in South Africa.

Q: Sensei, who were your first teachers?
A: As a beginner, my instructor was the late Vic McFarlane. No one outside the university will even know his name, but the encouragement he gave me in my first few months motivated me greatly. I then joined the dojo of Stan Schmidt Sensei in 1967, where, as my sensei and mentor, he was instrumental in putting me on the correct budo path. In 1973, a year after attaining *san-dan*, I decided that karate was to be not only my lifestyle but also my profession. Thus, I started my own dojo. For the next decade, I trained in the famous early morning S.A. JKA instructor's class (Early Birds) that Schmidt Sensei led. In addition to this, I went on a worldwide mission to train with many of the legendary Japanese shotokan masters. In particular, I trained with M. Tanaka Sensei, who became my mentor during this period. I also travelled regularly to Japan to train under Nakayama Sensei and in the JKA instructor's class at the Honbu Dojo.

Q: Tell us some interesting stories of your early days under the top JKA instructors.
A: I could write a book on this subject alone. There are so many stories, some amusing and some really serious. I will never forget the first time Tanaka Sensei invited me to train at his personal dojo on the outskirts of Tokyo. He had arranged for Imura Sensei, the future Shoto Cup kata champion, to meet me at the nearby station to prevent me from getting lost. I was looking for a car, but to my surprise, Imura Sensei arrived on a delivery bicycle, the type with a basket in front. "Get in," he said. I can imagine how ridiculous I must have looked sitting in this basket while riding through Tokyo.

On a more serious note, in 1986 I returned to Japan for my 6th dan examination and to train at the Honbu Dojo. At that time of the year, the instructors were concentrating on the forthcoming All-Japan Championship. As I was not a regular opponent, all the aspiring and wannabe champions wanted to practice on me. This went on every day for a week, resulting in numerous *shiai* bouts with the Honbu Dojo instructors who were entering the championship. At the end of the week, one of the instructors, Yokomichi-san, who was also a member of the Japan national team, walked up to me and said—in a very formal and severe manner—"Marukom-san, next time you and me shiai." I hadn't given the bouts during the week much thought, but I suddenly realized that I hadn't been beaten yet. This was about Japanese honor, and they were thinking, "How dare this *Gaijin* have the audacity to beat us in our own domain." Monday arrived, and so did Yokomichi-san, wearing a different gi. I noted that this was his tournament gi, complete with the Japanese flag on the left breast. Ueki Sensei judged this "practice" match. I thought I was in a war. Yokomichi came at me with such ferocity that I realized that I better reciprocate in the same manner or I wouldn't be standing at the end. It was so vicious that after [the referee yelled] "yame," the normally austere and serious instructors watching—including Tanaka Sensei, Yahara Sensei and Isaka Sensei—had huge grins on their faces. They loved it. The only problem was that I scored two points to his one, and my opponent never spoke to me for the remainder of my trip to Japan.

Q: How did the Westerners respond to traditional Japanese training when they visited the JKA Honbu Dojo?
A: From the time I started training there in the early 1970s, most Westerners felt it was abusive and stayed only a short time. Perhaps we South Africans were a bit crazy, because, although it was scary and really tough, we kept coming back year after year. I have great respect for the courage of my colleagues, especially Stan Schmidt, Norman Robinson, Ken Wittstock, Eddie Dorey and Rob Ferriere because they all endured those early days. Today, the training in Japan does not have the same harshness and intensity. That is detrimental for budo, but it is certainly more conducive for the regular Western karate-ka to train there.

Q: Were you a natural at karate? Did the movements come easily to you?
A: By the time I started karate, I had lost the natural flexibility of youth, so form definitely did not come easily to me. However, I found I had a greater natural affinity for such aspects of kumite as timing and distancing. Although my form did improve with hard work, it was at a far more grad-

Karate Masters

"I found I had a greater natural affinity for such aspects of kumite as timing and distancing. Although my form did improve with hard work, it was at a far more gradual pace than my kumite. Strangely enough, my first "big" title was in kata."

ual pace than my kumite. Strangely enough, my first "big" title was in kata.

Q: How has your personal karate developed over the years?
A: In virtually every way except for budo spirit, I think I am almost unrecognizable from my initial years. Technically, priorities, attitude, maturity. Everything is different. From a predominantly kumite-orientated karate-ka in my competition years in which my priority was to be able to fight better, be stronger and be tougher, I changed to a karate-ka who wanted to understand technique better, understand the scientific basis behind the technique, improve the method of delivering the technique and discover a better way of explaining this technique to the students. As a result, my personal shotokan developed into a very precise and technically orientated form of karate, far removed from the youthful version in which technical flaws were at times overlooked to ensure success at kumite.

Q: What are the most important points of your teaching philosophy?
A: Initially, the priority of my philosophy was teaching my students to win, whether it was against an opponent in the dojo, in a tournament or in the street. Of course, budo concepts such as courage, combined with correct protocol, was very much part of this philosophy. But I never emphasized the fact that karate is both hard and soft, whether it is physical or mental. Compassion did not form a major part of my teaching philosophy. However, years of teaching, marriage, bringing up my own children, injury and life experiences have tended to mellow me and have given me a better understanding of human nature. I started to realize that it [compassion] can be combined with a budo approach. Thus, over the years, I brought it more and more into my teaching philosophy. That is where I believe I am now, and I believe this current philosophy makes me a better teacher.

Q: With all the technical changes during the last 30 years, do you think there is still pure shotokan, shito-ryu, goju-ryu, et cetera?

A: I think the answer must be no. However, I won't answer for goju, shito or wado. As a shotokan practitioner, there are so many differences from the shotokan of Gichin Funakoshi Sensei compared to the JKA shotokan method of M.Nakayama Sensei and the SKI shotokan method of H. Kanazawa Sensei. As mentioned above, there are the continual improvements in technique and training methods, which in many cases create a different look. You only have to look at the old JKA black and white 8 millimeter movies and compare the kata of Nakayama Sensei, Kanazawa Sensei and other old masters with kata done by their students of today, and you will see that it looks like a different style with the same name.

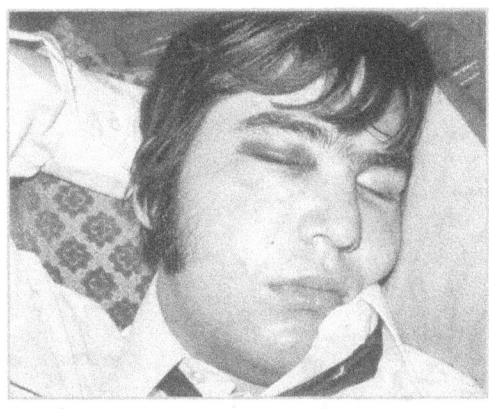

"Years of teaching, marriage, bringing up my own children, injury and life experiences have tended to mellow me and have given me a better understanding of human nature."

Q: Do you think different ryu are important? And what are the main differences between the different shotokan methods that have appeared after the old JKA split?

A: I think that they are important in the sense that every ryu has both a wealth of knowledge and tradition. If there were to be one merged ryu, it would be a great pity, because the unique essence of the individual ryu would be lost. Each ryu has so much to give to its adherents. I commenced in shotokan because it was the nearest available style. Had I commenced in goju-ryu, for example, provided I had a good mentor, I'm sure it would have been equally rewarding to me after a lifetime of study.

In regards to the different shotokan methods since the split, I'm not convinced major technical differences have resulted. Each one of the following "new" chief instructors—Asai Sensei, Yahara Sensei and Abe Sensei—took classes at the original JKA Honbu Dojo in Ebisu and learned and had the same basics from Nakayama Sensei. They do, of course, have their own individuality, which permeated and is reflected in their own students, both before and after the split. The fact that these instructors now head their own organizations changes very little, especially as many countries have seminars in which they invite Yahara Sensei, Abe Sensei and

Karate Masters

"To know you have the power, both mentally and physically—without having to implement it unnecessarily to the detriment of another human being—is an objective and art worthy of a lifelong study and practice."

Asai Sensei at different times. To categorize the essence of the three instructors, I'd say that Abe Sensei is *Mr. Correctness,* Yahara Sensei is *Mr. Dynamics* and Asai Sensei is *Mr. Innovations.* And, of course, they are all brilliant.

Q: What is your opinion of full-contact karate and kickboxing?
A: I'm not a fan. I appreciate the toughness of the two sports and the hard training that is necessary, but I fail to understand why people want to deliberately knock each other out. On the other hand, to know you have the power, both mentally and physically—without having to implement it unnecessarily to the detriment of another human being—is an objective and art worthy of a lifelong study and practice.

Q: How would you describe the life and dedication of the late Nakayama Sensei to the arts of budo and specifically to karate-do?
A: He was an amazing man and his passing was a huge loss to the karate world. To the layman, his techniques did not appear impressive, but on closer examination, a knowledgeable karate-ka would be amazed at his understanding of the dynamics of each and every technique. He had compassion for karate-ka with problems and an ability to solve these problems with sublime ease. He had uncanny insight into the character of those in his presence and once told me that he could judge a karate-ka's character by his kata performance. His extraordinary organizational skills became abundantly evident when he died, and no one had his ability to engender loyalty and unity. The JKA, until his death, was without doubt the greatest karate organization in the history of karate. He developed it and held it together with his quiet magnetism and great judgment.

Q: Do you think that karate in the West is on the same level with Japanese karate?

A: In some aspects, the answer is yes. In fact, in some instances I believe that the West is on an even higher level, especially in situations in which there is a conflict between traditional Japanese training methods and modern scientific exercise technology. However, if we define or categorize Japanese karate as a budo art, then the majority in the West have lost the way. I think Western practitioners were on the right track in the early years, but they deviated from this track in the mid 1980s.

Q: In terms of approach or physical capabilities, are there any fundamental differences between Japanese karate-ka and European or American karate-ka?

A: "East is east and west is west and never the twain shall meet." Japanese culture and Western culture are different.

"If we define or categorize Japanese karate as a budo art, then the majority in the West have lost the way. I think Western practitioners were on the right track in the early years, but they deviated from this track in the mid 1980s."

While there is some attempt to understand one another, we have all seen over the years that this [attempt] is often fraught with difficulty. This disparity holds true for karate ... both in approach and the physical differences that are blatant when comparing the average Japanese body structure to the average long-legged and tall Westerner from Northern Europe. Karate was created around the body structure of the typical Japanese. The result is that Westerners often struggle to emulate the form of the Japanese. However, the greater reach of the Westerner is often a huge advantage in kumite.

Q: Karate is nowadays often referred to as a sport. Would you agree with this definition or do you think it is only budo?

A: Every karate-ka has his own definition or idea as to whether it is a sport or budo and trains accordingly. Personally, I believe karate is a budo system with a sporting aspect for those budo karate-ka who feel the competitive urge. However, this must then be the traditional *shobu-ippon* system to be defined as budo with a sporting aspect. The WKF system is an example of sport karate.

Q: Do you still have further to go in your studies of budo?
A: Can anyone who prides himself on having an active mind ever stop learning? Budo karate is both an art and a science. Like any other art or science, there is an unlimited amount of knowledge out there.

Q: At the present time, how do you see karate in the rest of the world?
A: Unfortunately, with the possibility of Olympic participation dangled as a carrot, sport karate seems to be the way of the majority. But there are karate-ka like me who will continue the budo traditions and pass them on to our students in the hope that they will continue in the same vein and receive the same intellectual and physical benefits that this lifestyle offers.

Q: Does working with weapons enhance empty-hand karate?
A: Yes, but I must qualify this. Any supplementary training that helps coordination and skills must be of value. Understanding how weapons can be utilized will improve one's ability to defend against an attack with similar weapons. But to use the weapon itself effectively, one must be more than competent or it will be a liability. The saying that "a little knowledge is a dangerous thing" is certainly appropriate and applicable here.

Q: What's your opinion of makiwara training?
A: Like most things, makiwara training is good in moderation. First and foremost, it will develop good kime. Second, a conditioned hand will minimize the risk of injury to the hand on impact. However, overdoing makiwara training increases the chances of arthritis later in life and deforms the hands with no real tangible advantage over the conservative makiwara trainer.

Q: When teaching the art of karate, is self-defense, sport or tradition the most important element?
A: This is dependent on the type of student or group you are teaching. A group of women may need an emphasis on the self-defense aspect, while a group of teenagers may want an emphasis on the competition aspect. However, it would be remiss of any sensei—whether a group's main inter-

est is sport or self-defense—not to feature tradition as an important facet of the karate education. People join for various reasons, discover the tradition and true essence of karate-do, and find that their priorities change as they realize the value of the traditional side. I feel a budo dojo should emphasise tradition and self-defense over the sporting element but should not neglect sport training for those who are keen on competing.

Q: In training, what's the proper ratio between kata and kumite?
A: The proper, and I may add the natural training ratio of kata and kumite, not only changes with age, maturity and grade, but it is also dependent on an interest and flair for one or the other. If I use myself as an example between the ages of 20 to 30, as a *sho-dan* to *yon-dan*, my priority was

"Understanding how weapons can be utilized will improve one's ability to defend against an attack with similar weapons. But to use the weapon itself effectively, one must be more than competent or it will be a liability."

kumite, and the ratio was at least 7 to 3. I also trained my kata diligently, but it was more for grading examination or tournament purposes. As I got older, while still training and teaching kumite, my focus shifted towards training and teaching technique and kata. Now, every Friday in my dojo I hold a special kata class and every Tuesday my son Shane, the current KWF World and South African champion, holds a special kumite class. The reasoning is very straightforward. I am at the stage and age in which, after four decades of study, I have a deeper understanding and insight into technique, while he, at 29, is at his physical prime, focused on kumite and is better suited to demonstrate fighting techniques and strategy. He is no different than me when I was that age, and he will no doubt change his priorities and training ratio when he gets to the phase that I am at now. However, for young children, my viewpoint is very different. I believe that children should focus on technique, and as a result, the kata/kumite ratio should be 7 to 3. I remember a point Tanaka Sensei made, and I totally agree. I quote: "Children's karate should first be beautiful; they have time to be strong."

Karate Masters

"For those karate-ka who want to avail themselves of the wonderful attributes that karate has to offer must remember that it doesn't happen by magic or with natural ability alone."

Q: Do you have any general advice you would care to pass on to the karete-ka?

A: Karate training will improve anybody who trains correctly. For those karate-ka who want to avail themselves of the wonderful attributes that karate has to offer must remember that it doesn't happen by magic or with natural ability alone. Instead, it takes sheer, hard training, commitment, and the discipline to overcome obstacles and plateaus. Next, some want to give karate up because of a fallout with a sensei or another karate-ka. This is not a valid reason. There are many teachers and karate is a lifetime study. Give up karate if you don't like karate—not because you don't like another human being. Go elsewhere where you are comfortable.

Q: Some people think going to Japan to train is highly necessary; do you agree?

A: It is dependent on why one does karate. For the person who does karate as an interesting physical fitness regimen rather than an aerobic or keep-fit class, the answer would be no. For the competitive karate-ka who does karate as a sport, especially WKF multi-point competitions, he would probably be better off training in France. But the karate-ka who does karate as an art and science, as a way of life, a budo practitioner, I would say it is imperative to go to the source, the place of origin, in order to experience the attitude of budo in a Japanese dojo and see and feel the culture of Japan. There are still some older Japanese masters around who have a wealth of knowledge. For a genuine budo practitioner, it would be a great pity not to experience their deep understanding of karate-do. Furthermore, to train in a class of spirited Japanese karate-ka would be an unforgettable experience.

Q: What do you consider to be the major changes in the art of karate since you began training?
A: The most obvious change is the emphasis towards sport karate, but there is also a major change in the general softness in both attitude and the physical side of the majority of the current karate-ka when compared to the karate-ka of the 1960s, 1970s and 1980s. Technically, today's karate-ka are superior, but, in general, they lack the spirit of the samurai and the willingness to absorb physical pain to achieve the goal of being a budo karate-ka.

Q: If you could train with anyone, who would that be?
A: I trained under and with so many of the great Japanese JKA karate-ka that one more would not change much for me. I also experienced Nishiyama Sensei's teaching several times in his dojo on Olympic Boulevard in Los Angeles between 1975 and 1987. This was not his instructor's group. However, I would have loved to train with the group that were in his great JKA-USA (AAKF) instructor's class of the late 1960s and early 1970s. To train alongside karate-ka like Frank Smith, Ray Dalke, Tonny Tulleners, James Yabe and James Field would have been a great test and challenge, perhaps equal in many ways to training in the Hornet's Nest in Japan and in our own famous Early Birds class in South Africa. While my karate career took me East in the 1970s, and that was the basis of my development, I think I missed out on something great in the West.

"The most obvious change is the emphasis towards sport karate, but there is also a major change in the general softness in both attitude and the physical side of the majority of the current karate-ka when compared to the karate-ka of the 1960s, 1970s and 1980s."

Karate Masters

"With regular training, based predominantly on karate, I have maintained a fit and strong body, which has allowed me to engage in activities that most people my age cannot do or find difficult to do."

Q: What would you say to someone who is interested in learning karate-do?
A: First, I would find out briefly what his perception of karate is. In most cases, I have found that the perception differs from what they will find in a regular dojo. Second, I would briefly explain what he is most likely to find at a dojo, what to look for with regards to etiquette and class structure, and advise him to visit several dojo to assess which would suits him best.

Q: What keeps you motivated after all these years?
A: With regular training, based predominantly on karate, I have maintained a fit and strong body, which has allowed me to engage in activities that most people my age cannot do or find difficult to do. The need to continue an active lifestyle, which gives me such wonderful quality of life, keeps me motivated. Added to this, the study of this art is so mentally stimulating. I look forward to every day knowing that I am still able to explore this passion to which I have devoted nearly four decades of my life.

Q: To achieve good self-defense skills for a real situation, do you think it is necessary to engage in free fighting?
A: If the dojo kumite is hard and of a high standard, it must be beneficial to your self-defense skills, but it must also be supplemented with thought and practice of simulated street type situations. At the initial stages of my kumite interaction at the JKA instructor's class, the fights were so real that my defense, speed and reflexes improved at an amazing rate … simply due to necessity.

Q: What is your opinion about mixing karate styles? Does the practice of one nullify the effectiveness of the other? Or, on the contrary, can it be beneficial to a student?

A: Actually, a few years back I discussed this with Isaka Sensei. His point of view was that there was always still so much more to study in shotokan that he had no time left to study other styles. To a large degree, I think he is correct, but I differ in one way. I believe that if you have the time and inclination, no knowledge is wasted, and to extract what suits and complements your training methods from other sources certainly can enhance your repertoire and will not nullify your effectiveness. However, devoting too much time studying another style will detract from the study of your own style, making you a jack-of-all-trades and master of none.

"If the dojo kumite is hard and of a high standard, it must be beneficial to your self-defense skills, but it must also be supplemented with thought and practice of simulated street type situations."

Q: Modern karate is moving away from bunkai in kata practice. How important do you think bunkai is in the understanding of kata and karate-do in general?

A: To perform a kata with feeling and passion, one must be able to visualize an opponent or opponents. This is not possible without understanding the bunkai of that particular kata. There are also many effective self-defense techniques that one can discover by understanding the bunkai of the kata. However, much of the bunkai is very theoretical and debatable as to whether it will work in a practical situation. As a result, the average black belt holder will not gain much from the majority of bunkai applications in this regard. For the advanced black belt or top sensei who is truly studying karate-do as an art, this knowledge is of value.

Karate Masters

Q: What is the philosophical basis for your karate training?
A: This is not any different than my teaching philosophy, except that I went the extra mile in my gruelling personal routines. Initially, I only knew how to train, train, train. If I had trained that hard with my students, only a handful would have remained. Shane, my older son, is the only student who experienced a similar hard and harsh training regimen as I imposed on myself, and this was especially the case in his late teenage years. He commenced training at the stage in which my training was only about this hard karate. I [can now] see in him the results of that philosophy. Ten years later, in keeping with my teaching philosophy, my own training philosophy became more orientated towards technical perfection and my attitude became more moderate. My younger son, Saville, was a product of this stage of my life. He is very technical and kata orientated, and I see in him the transition and change in my own philosophical basis for training. At this phase of my life, all of my training encompasses long fluid movement to combat the natural stiffening and shortening of ligaments and tendons as the years go by. To avoid joint abuse, I also train softer, more relaxed and with less heavy repetition.

Q: Do you have a particularly memorable karate experience that has remained as an inspiration for your training?
A: In nearly four decades, there are many, but there is one in particular that made a difference to my kumite and my life, both inside and outside of the dojo. In my first period of training in the JKA instructor's class, Yahara Sensei and I were engaged in an interesting kumite bout. He had indicated to me that he wanted to do *yukuri* (slow and leisurely) kumite, so we interacted and exchanged a variety of techniques. Although at that stage I was a *san-dan*, I was rather inexperienced in the ways and attitudes of this very different and new class. I took the word yukuri literally and enjoyed this interesting exchange with this great fighter immensely. Suddenly, for no reason, Yahara Sensei exploded into action with a vicious *ippon-ken*, putting my nose somewhere around the corner, and there was blood everywhere. The next day, at a cocktail party to celebrate the very recent opening of this new JKA Honbu Dojo, Tanaka Sensei, whom I regarded as my mentor, saw my very obvious fat and puffy face and asked me what had happened. I described the incident and complained to him how unfair I thought it was. To my surprise, his response was very different from what I expected. He said, "I think maybe something is wrong your defense." I thought about what he said for days and realized he was right. From that day on, I adopted the philosophy to expect the unexpected and

this has helped throughout the rest of my karate career and in life in general. This is also a philosophy I expound to all my students.

Q: After all these years of training and experience, could you explain the meaning of the practice of karate-do?
A: Karate practice is about life and developing skills that serve one not just in the karate sphere but also in all walks of life. These skills extend beyond the obvious benefits of health and self-defense and encompass abilities such as improved focus and concentration and the discipline to endure life's obstacles. Furthermore, karate-do training enhances one's ability to both read an opponent—in the street or in business—and have the insight and knowledge to implement the correct strategy to overcome this adversary. The balance of hard and soft gives an understanding of human nature and creates a compassionate human being. Age limits physical prowess, but with the correct approach to karate training, the opposite applies with respect to wisdom.

"Karate practice is about life and developing skills that serve one not just in the karate sphere but also in all walks of life."

Q: How can a practitioner increase his understanding of the spiritual aspect of karate?
A: First, I am not one to sit under a waterfall and meditate. I am a physically active person, and my understanding of the spiritual side must relate to and go hand in hand with this active concept. I talk to my students about active meditation and use the example of a top marathon runner whose body is at the stage of exhaustion. At this stage of the race, there is something more than just courage and determination that makes the runner continue, drive on relentlessly and perhaps even win against all odds.

Karate Masters

"Age limits physical prowess, but with the correct approach to karate training, the opposite applies with respect to wisdom."

Something takes over in that person's mind, be it a state of void or a state of mental focus. There have been a few occasions in my long career in which I have experienced a similar state of mind, and this has created and further increased my understanding of the spiritual side. It is not something a sensei can teach. It is a latent potential in a human who has courage, determination and the desire to achieve, but it can only manifest in truly challenging and real circumstances. To have anything less than that is a simulation of the spiritual aspect and cannot truly improve any spiritual understanding.

Q: How much training should a senior karetka be doing to improve?
A: Every senior karate-ka is different and every "senior" should know what is good for his own improvement. So, I can only explain what works for me. My usual routine is to train extremely hard with my senior students on Monday and that entails kihon, kata and kumite. I train very hard again on Friday, but I focus on kata only. On Tuesday and Thursday I train lighter. The emphasis is on technique. On Wednesday, I train with my little kids in their class, and I do the simple techniques with them at their pace, concentrating on doing the most perfect movements possible. I do this as an example to them, because children of this age don't listen, but they will mimic what they see. I also do this because it helps me to eradicate bad technical habits that may have developed. On Tuesday, Thursday and Saturday, I do weight training for strength and muscle conditioning. I also ride a stationary bike for non-weight bearing cardiovascular training. [Anything] more than this will be counterproductive and increase my risk of injury. Through this weekly routine, I have maintained a good standard in some physical aspects and improved in other aspects that usually deteriorate with age. It is essential for a senior karate-ka to have a constructive, planned and monitored physical train-

ing program. As for the mind, hopefully wisdom will improve with age and influence the approach and practice of the art.

Q: Is there anything lacking in the way karate is taught today compared with those who were taught in your early days?
A: In my early days, there were fewer instructors and the majority were genuine. What they lacked in knowledge they made up with spirit and a desire to learn and practice genuine budo karate. The dojo had an ambience of reality and only the tough survived. Karate was a mystical superhuman art, the sensei was a respected figure in the community and the Japanese masters were semi-gods. The sensei taught his students with his heart, and the students took anything he dished out and believed in him. I use the male form, because female sensei were few and far between in the early days. Today, there is a "dojo" in virtually every school hall and in every suburb. In so many cases, the instructor is a disgruntled former student who failed, left and who promoted himself to a high dan. Potential adult students and parents of potential students are misled and confused to whom and where they should go. The standard of karate has been watered down. And many students are promoted quickly

"It is essential for a senior karate-ka to have a constructive, planned and monitored physical training program. As for the mind, hopefully wisdom will improve with age and influence the approach and practice of the art."

Karate Masters

"Nothing beats the quality of being hungry to succeed, be it in sport or in business or in any sphere, but it must be tempered with the correct attributes to complement and supplement this hunger."

because instructors are competing with other "sensei" who have very little else to offer to keep the student. Those students who land in a genuine dojo—many times only by coincidence—are lucky. Even then the mysticism has been removed by too much emphasis on competition karate and exacerbated by sport karate on TV. This gives rise to the image that this is what karate is [all] about. Even at this age, people who are ignorant of true karate training ask me if I am still competing. This is the perception of karate for so many people. In addition, I find that there are few students that I can really call karate-ka, as opposed to students who just do karate. As a result, even the genuine sensei cannot teach the average student the way and at the level karate should be taught ... the way it was taught in the early days.

Q: What are the most important qualities of a successful karete-ka?
A: Nothing beats the quality of being hungry to succeed, be it in sport or in business or in any sphere, but it must be tempered with the correct attributes to complement and supplement this hunger. Karate is no different and necessitates a cool head and calm mind to channel this hunger into a systematic development. Without these qualities, the karate-ka cannot reach the maximum level of his potential. Hunger for success, however, may create impatience. One must ensure that lack of patience does not result in an attempt to short circuit the system or the potential success will not reach fruition. One cannot deviate from the arduous path of karate-do.

Q: What advice would you give to students about supplementary training such as weight training, stretching and running?
A: Strength, flexibility and good cardio vascular conditioning are extremely important for any karate-ka, and for that matter, participants of all sports. Karate training has areas in which there are physical limitations, and this is where supplementary training comes in. However, this training must be scientifically based and well monitored. For older karate-ka, it [supplementary training] is especially advantageous as an age retarding process. For tournament karate-ka who are interested in bolstering performance, it is essential to supplement karate training with weights, running or cycling, and stretching routines. For the regular dojo member, it will enhance his general physical ability, making him a more effective karate-ka. Light weights for children are fine, provided no weight bearing exercises on the spine form part of the program, such as squats with a weight on the shoulders or shoulder press.

Q: What are the most important attributes of a student?
A: While it is always good to have a student with natural talent and the ability to win championships, these are not the most important attributes for a student to possess. More importantly, a student should possess loyalty, the will to train regularly and diligently, adherence to the protocol and ethos of karate-do, the will to help those lower in grade or less fortunate, as well as the will to put back into the dojo and into karate-do what they have

received. Furthermore, they should believe in karate as a lifelong study. Students with these attributes form the core of any dojo and organization.

Q: Why is it, in your opinion, that a lot of students start falling away after two to three years of training?
A: There are two major reasons. First, after the initial fast rate of improvement through the kyu grades, improvement slows down drastically and eventually plateaus are reached in which there is no tangible improvement. Karate now becomes more difficult. Without really hard work and dedication, improvement seems so far off. The majority of karate students are not your dyed in the wool budo practitioners, so easier pastimes are sought at this stage. Second, the monotony of repetition [becomes a factor]. Unless the sensei is innovative, a student will become bored. Link this to reason No. 1, and you have another resignation from your dojo. There are, of course, many other reasons. For instance, *jiyu-kumite* becomes part of the grading syllabus (post shodan), increasing the risk of physical punishment, an aspect that many karate-ka dislike. Unless there is success as a motivating factor, only your genuine budo practitioners are likely to push on.

Q: There is very little written about you in magazines, et cetera. You obviously do not thrive on the publicity like some martial artists. Why?
A: I believe I am a very practical person. The publicity I wanted and needed was in the city and surrounding areas where my dojo was situated. Locally, I have been fortunate to receive considerable publicity (both directly relating to me, as well as the achievements of my students) in the press and on television. This was primarily for marketing reasons, because ego does not pay the mortgage or my two sons' education, nor does it give me sufficient income to be a full-time karate professional with the time to devote to my study of karate-do. I never found the need to seek publicity out of my domain and perhaps that is the reason why that much has not been written about me outside of my own country. I also felt that without a practical reason, such as I mentioned above, pushing the publicity aspect did not conform to the ethos of karate-do.

Q: Have you felt fear in your karate training?
A: In the first few years of training in the JKA instructor's class in Japan, I felt fear often. I will never ever forget the feeling, day after day, as I placed my foot on the first rung of the steel spiral staircase that led to the door of the JKA Honbu dojo, wondering which instructor would smash me today.

Fortunately, the fear diminished year by year, as my ability improved and as they accepted me more and more, but the memory remains.

Q: What are your thoughts on the future of karate-do and what's your opinion of karate entering the Olympic Games?
A: Sadly, karate-do will become more and more a sport, but fortunately, I believe there will always be a traditional budo dojo somewhere for those who realize where the real karate lies. If karate becomes an Olympic sport, karate will receive far more media exposure, but it will not be karate-do.

Q: Is there anything else you would to add for the readers?
A: To achieve the most value from karate-do, it should form part of one's lifestyle. It should be a regular habit, not a seasonal pastime or recreation. An essential inner spirit can be fostered and developed with karate as a way of life, provided one is honest with oneself and not validate reasons and excuses for not training. The true karate *no michi* (road, path, way of the empty hand) is not for the fainthearted. O

"Sadly, karate-do will become more and more a sport, but fortunately, I believe there will always be a traditional budo dojo somewhere for those who realize where the real karate lies."

Hideharu Igaki

The Budo Spirit

A TRADITIONAL JAPANESE KARATE MASTER WHO CAME TO AMERICA TO SPREAD THE ART OF THE EMPTY HAND, SENSEI IGAKI HAS ADAPTED THE RIGOROUS METHODS OF TRADITIONAL EASTERN LEARNING INTO A WESTERN TEACHING SYSTEM THAT CHALLENGES HIS STUDENTS WITHOUT DRIVING THEM AWAY. DRIVEN BY A TRUE LOVE OF KARATE TRAINING AND THE BUDO LIFESTYLE, SENSEI IGAKI PASSES ALONG HIS ENTHUSIASM TO ALL THOSE HE MEETS. MORE THAN ANYTHING ELSE, HIS ADVICE FOR KARATE PRACTITIONERS EVERYWHERE IS SIMPLY TO "URGE KARATE-KA EVERYWHERE TO ALWAYS TRY TO IMPROVE THEIR SKILLS. THEY SHOULD NEVER BE SATISFIED."

THE COACH OF NUMEROUS U.S. CHAMPIONS, SENSEI IGAKI IS A MASTER INSTRUCTOR AND STRATEGIST WHO HAS STARTED TO MAKE INROADS ON THE INTERNATIONAL SCENE AS WELL. HE HAS GUIDED SEVERAL OF HIS AMERICAN STUDENTS TO ELITE FINISHES IN WORLD COMPETITION—RARIFIED ATMOSPHERE FORMERLY RESERVED FOR ELITE JAPANESE KARATE-KA. NOT LETTING HIS STUDENTS BE LIMITED BY CULTURAL DIFFERENCES, IGAKI IS SPREADING THE BUDO SPIRIT TO AN ENTIRELY NEW GENERATION OF WESTERN PRACTITIONERS, AND PROVING IN THE PROCESS THAT THE BUDO SPIRIT HAS UNIVERSAL APPEAL AND APPLICATION.

Q: Would you tell us some interesting stories of your early days in karate training?
A: I started in judo when I was around 7. I took it for three years or so. Judo is better suited for the larger competitor, so I switched to karate at the age of 10. It was very rare for a kid to start karate. Most kids took judo. I was pretty young when I started, so I can't really say that those first years were very serious. The Sugatasanshiro Judo TV show was popular at that time. There were no children in Nakahara Sensei's karate class. When I signed up for class, Nakahara Sensei thought I would quit. So he didn't charge me anything for the first month. When I trained I was placed close to the door, so if I decided to quit I could go home easy. The first month I only did *shiko-dachi* and *chudan-zuki*. That is all. After the second month, I was allowed to line-up with the other students who were all adults. Nakahara Sensei finally took my tuition fee. I had to practice with adults. Kumite was hard. I'm not talking about fighting the black belts, they have

Karate Masters

"For four years I did professional kickboxing. The reason is because I wanted to work on some different things. I also wanted to see if my karate would work, so to speak. Although the techniques are different, there are some common threads that you can use in order to make karate more real and contact oriented."

good control. When I was matched up against a white belt, though, I hated it. For them, it didn't matter if the opponent was a kid or not, they punched me and kicked me as hard as they could. Not only that, but often they would lose their balance and fall on me! It was an experience. But I learned even if the punch or kick wasn't done correctly, if it hit me it still hurt. My karate style was *tani-ha* shito-ryu. Mr. Takashi Nakahara was my first instructor. After I became a black belt, I began to train at Mr. Fujitani's dojo. Mr. Fujitani was a direct student of Kenwa Mabuni, the founder of shito-ryu. I also studied other systems, not in depth though. I have an instructor's rank in *tenshin koryu kenpo,* a style of jiu-jitsu. But I don't really have enough time to continue my training in that art.

Q: You did some kickboxing, didn't you?
A: Yes, for four years I did professional kickboxing. The reason was because I wanted to work on some different things. I also wanted to see if my karate would work, so to speak. Although the techniques are different, there are some common threads that you can use in order to make karate more real and contact oriented. It was a great experience but that is in my past. Now I am concentrating on my karate students and their training.

Q: When did you come to the United States?
A: I came to this country in 1979. Like many Japanese my age, the United States is a sort of dream country, so different from my homeland. I had the opportunity to come to the United States to teach karate. When I came to America, I taught my first class just like in Japan. There were about 75 students. It was just hard work. I gave no explanations and I

never praised anyone. Next day, everybody quit. Now I teach in a totally different manner. I explain more in class. I look for the positive improvement in my students. Whenever they do the technique correctly I tell them.

Q: Were you a natural at karate? Did the movements come easily to you?
A: No, I don't think so. I had to practice at home after every karate class. I have to thank my father for fixing the *tatami* at home so many times! Even now, I am correcting my technique. I must keep training. I want my skills to become better every day. I think I understand better now how techniques work, how the human body works. This has helped me to improve my skills and those of my students.

Q: Do you think that karate in the Western world has caught up with Japanese karate?
A: I don't know if you should think of it in terms of catching up. The karate is different as are the cultures. Some of the non-Japanese competitors I saw at the last World Championships were very skilled. You could tell that their karate was good. Yet, it was not quite the same as Japanese karate. Does it have to be the same? Karate has been practiced internationally for decades. Some of the best instructors left Japan to teach in various parts of the world. Those instructors taught students who, in turn, taught more students. It only stands to reason that some of those sensei could have produced students equal to the best in Japan. For most Japanese, karate is a martial art. They don't have the concept of a separate sport or of self-defense. But in America they tend to separate it into part sport, part self-defense, et cetera. The most obvious physical difference is size. The European and American karate-ka are usually bigger physically. Due to this physical fact, the movements become different. This influences how everyone tries to generate power and speed.

"When I came to America, I taught my first class just like in Japan. There were about 75 students. It was just hard work. I gave no explanations and I never praised anyone. Next day, everybody quit."

Karate Masters

"The good karate practitioner puts themselves in a dangerous situation in their mind when they practice. This kind of mental rehearsal helps to increase the intensity of the workout. It also helps them to prepare for the real situation. Too many karate practitioners rely merely on technique."

Q: Do you feel that you still have further to go in your studies?
A: Yes, I still have a lot to learn. There are so many things—techniques, conditioning, mental training, et cetera. I believe the instructor must compete with the students and stay one step ahead of them. I have to do this for my benefit and the benefit of my students and the National Team members. For me, every aspect of the art is important. Karate is one entity. It should not be separated into categories. I have never learned or taught a class in that manner. I try to teach a more complete karate.

Q: Do you think it is necessary to engage in free-fighting to achieve good fighting skills in the street?
A: I think so. Proper free-fighting teaches many things applicable to self-defense. For example, a very important aspect of skill development is the attitude one takes during training. The good karate practitioner puts themselves in a dangerous situation in their mind when they practice. This kind of mental rehearsal helps to increase the intensity of the workout. It also helps them to prepare for the real situation. Too many karate practitioners rely merely on technique. But a technique by itself doesn't work. We must know how techniques work, how to use them. Then we must make them work. In addition, we need to have the correct spirit—the courage. Do we have the guts to use it? We must have a strong fighting spirit in any combative situation.

Q: Do you have a particularly memorable karate experience which has remained with you as an inspiration for your training?

A: When I started karate, Nakahara Sensei didn't have his own dojo. He was teaching at a city gymnasium two times a week and outside at a park the other four days. One day a typhoon came. I went to the park anyway to see if Nakahara Sensei was there or not. I saw my teacher, Nakahara Sensei and my senior, Kankawa Senpai, there ready to practice. The three of us practiced under the roof of a park shed. I was very impressed with my teacher. This memory reminds me that even when somebody doesn't show up for class, I will still be there for my students and the team. Like any other successful person, a successful karate-ka must have the desire to achieve their goals no matter how difficult. They must want to win. Winning can mean many things—good health, self-confidence, fitness, kindness, not only taking a trophy back home. We should aim for winning, but winning in life—as a human being—not only as martial artist and karate-ka.

"Like any other successful person, a successful karate-ka must have the desire to achieve their goals no matter how difficult. Winning can mean many things—good health, self-confidence, fitness, kindness, not only taking a trophy back home."

Q: What is your approach to working with top athletes?

A: I want to help the athlete become as good as they can be using their talents. I do not want to create robots who do only what their coaches or instructors tell them to do. Each athlete is unique and must be treated accordingly. I try to help them become aware of their strengths and capitalize on them. Of course, there are some problems common to most of the athletes. These days we are working on a few things. First, the ability to close the distance to the opponent effectively. Too often, a fighter is

Karate Masters

"You need effective footwork and body mechanics. We talk about 'controlled off-balance' movements. Anytime a person moves, they are technically off balance. Once the fighter is not concerned so much with being hit, they can begin to see the scoring opportunities."

slow in closing the gap between himself and the opponent. You need to know how to do it deceptively so your opponent won't notice. Also, the athlete must be in the proper position once they get to the target. They must be able to score with a powerful technique. To do that, one must make use of their entire body, not just the hands and feet. The other factor is that they have to not leave themselves open for counterattacks as they close the distance.

Q: How can these sorts of things be corrected?
A: You need effective footwork and body mechanics. We talk about "controlled off-balance" movements. Anytime a person moves, they are technically off balance. It is just how well they can control that instant that makes the difference between a normal step and falling down. Of course, there are also differences between taking an ordinary step and trying to move quickly towards an opponent.

Q: You also talk about being comfortable in-close with your opponent?
A: Yes, most point fighters are uncomfortable when they are in tight with their opponent. Yet, often-times, this is an excellent opportunity to score with a good technique. We work mostly on defense at this range. Once the fighter is not concerned so much with being hit, they can begin to see the scoring opportunities.

Q: Some major changes have been made to the competition rules in order to make it more exciting for the spectators. What is your reaction?
A: I look upon the changes as an opportunity for the athlete to demonstrate even more of the total karate arsenal. The competitor will have to be able to deal with everything from jumping kicks to throws. I am already working on different training programs for several of our athletes. I think this will be a very interesting change but we still have to wait to see how this will finally affect the overall development of the karate as sport.

Q: Can you tell us about your future projects?
A: I have been working on a textbook of sorts for the kumite competitor. It goes into a lot more specific detail than most books I have seen on the subject. It should be available in the near future. I am also working on scripts for a series of videos that would be used in conjunction with the textbook. I hope these projects will help all karate-ka, regardless of rank and style in their journey.

Q: Do you have any general advice you would care to pass on?
A: I would urge karate-ka everywhere to always try to improve their skills. They should never be satisfied. They will help to keep karate strong if they are always trying to improve. I love karate and I enjoy practicing karate—especially with my students and the National Team members. I get a great deal of satisfaction from seeing them improve their techniques. I believe that at least I'm passing along this attitude, this love for the art, to all those who train with me.

"I love karate and I enjoy practicing karate—especially with my students. I get a great deal of satisfaction from seeing them improve their techniques. I believe that at least I'm passing along this attitude, this love for the art, to all those who train with me."

Yasuhiro Konishi
Over a Giant's Shoulders

AFTER THE DEATH OF GRANDMASTER KONISHI SENSEI IN 1983, THE LEADERSHIP AND AUTHORITY OF THE SHINDO JINEN RYU STYLE WAS PASSED TO HIS SON, YASUHIRO (TAKEHIRO) KONISHI. TAKEHIRO KONISHI, A 10TH DAN, CHANGED HIS NAME TO YASUHIRO KONISHI AFTER HIS FATHER'S DEATH. HE WAS BORN ON MAY 25, 1931, IN TOKYO, JAPAN. HE GRADUATED FROM KEIO UNIVERSITY IN MARCH 1955. HIS LIFE STORY WOULD HAVE READ LIKE AN ADVENTURE NOVEL. SURROUNDED IN HIS YOUNG DAYS BY SOME OF THE BEST KARATE-KA IN HISTORY, KONISHI SENSEI'S SENSE OF DUTY TO PRESERVE HIS FATHER'S LEGACY LED HIM TO SHARE HIS EXPERIENCE AND KNOWLEDGE WITH STUDENTS FROM ALL OVER THE WORLD. HIS GENTLE CHARACTER INSURES THAT HE DOES INDEED GO SOFTLY AND QUIETLY THROUGH LIFE AND ONE ONLY HAS TO SEE HIM EXECUTING KARATE TECHNIQUES TO REALIZE HE CARRIES WITHIN A LETHAL WEAPON. CURRENTLY, HE OVERSEES THE OPERATIONS OF ALL THE JAPAN KARATE-DO RYOBU-KAI SCHOOLS IN JAPAN, AND HE CONTINUES TO GUIDE THE POLICIES AND PHILOSOPHY OF THE STYLE.

Q: What can you tell us about your father, the Grandmaster Yasuhiro Konishi?
A: My father was born in 1893 in Takamatsu, Kagawa, Japan. He began his martial arts training at age 6 in muso-ryu jujitsu. When he entered the equivalent of a western high school, he began training in takenouchi-ryu jujitsu. This particular jujitsu style is known for its strong kicks and punches, which is very similar to karate. At age 13, while practicing jujitsu, my father began studying kendo as well. In 1915, he commenced studies at Keio University in Tokyo. While the average tenure at a university is four years, he remained at Keio University for eight years because of his love for kendo and jujitsu. He was Keio University's kendo team captain, and he continued coaching the university's kendo club after his graduation.

Q: How did he start training in karate?
A: My father's first exposure to "te" was through a fellow classmate (Tsuneshige Arakaki of Okinawa) at Keio University. My father found the techniques of "te" very similar to those of Takeuchi Ryu jujitsu. Though

Karate Masters

"My father, Funakoshi Sensei and Ohtsuka Sensei were the principal instructors. My father continued to instruct a curriculum consisting of kendo, jujitsu and western boxing at the Ryobu-Kan."

Arakaki was in no way a master of "te," my father found the system to be very intriguing. He quit his job and opened his own martial arts center in 1923. He called it the Ryobu-Kan (The House of Martial Arts Excellence), and he taught mainly kendo and jujitsu.

Q: Your father spent a great deal of time training and sharing knowledge with other legendary masters like Mabuni, Ohtsuka, Funakoshi and even Ueshiba Morihei. What can you tell us about his relationship with these other giants of karate-do?
A: In September 1924, Hironishi Ohtsuka, the founder of the wado-ryu style of karate, and Gichin Funakoshi, the founder of shotokan karate, came to the kendo training hall at Keio University. They approached my father with a letter of introduction from Professor Kasuya of Keio University. Mr. Funakoshi asked if it would be possible to use the training hall to practice Ryukyu Kempo To-te jutsu. During this era, it was unheard of for one martial arts school to allow a martial arts teacher from another system to teach in their dojo. Such a request would be considered a "challenge" to the dojo. My father, however, was a visionary in the sense that he saw value in cross-training; he remembered the kata demonstrations Arakaki performed during his university days, and he agreed to Funakoshi Sensei's request. With the help of my father, Funakoshi Sensei established a To-te practice club at Keio University, the first university karate club in Japan. My father, Funakoshi Sensei and Ohtsuka Sensei were the principal instructors. My father continued to instruct a curriculum consisting of kendo, jujitsu and western boxing at the Ryobu-Kan. Karate-jutsu was born when Funakoshi Sensei added karate to this mix. As yet, no names were applied to the emerging styles.

Q: Is it true that there were challenges issued at that school?
A: Yes. Groups that practiced a pure form of jujitsu did not think highly of karate, and they challenged Funakoshi Sensei. However, under Japanese

budo, one does not initially challenge the master of a particular school or style; a challenge is first issued to the senior student. If the challenger defeats the senior student, then he can challenge the master. If the challenger defeats the master, he can take the dojo sign as a trophy. All challengers were defeated by my father and Ohtsuka Sensei, as they were Funakoshi's senior students. After a challenge had been met, Funakoshi Sensei would explain karate-jutsu and highlight the mental and spiritual benefits of the style. Many listeners understood and agreed to the point that they switched styles to study karate.

Q: When did your father's relationship with Mabuni Kenwa, Chojun Miyagi and Choki Motobu begin?
A: Because of my father's open-mindedness, many well-known budo-ka visited him so they could exchange techniques. Kenwa Mabuni, Chojun Miyagi and Choki Motobu were among them. These three masters influenced my father in various ways and made definitive contributions to his emerging style. My father considered

"All challengers were defeated by my father and Ohtsuka Sensei, as they were Funakoshi's senior students. After a challenge had been met, Funakoshi Sensei would explain karate-jutsu and highlight the mental and spiritual benefits of the style."

Choki Motobu to be a martial arts genius and made every effort to train with him. Motobu Sensei's specialty was the *naifanchin* kata. As a teacher, he knew many kata, but he would only teach them when his student had mastered *naifanchin*. Through training in this kata he became famous for scooping his opponent's legs. Although physically a big man, Mr. Motobu was very light on his feet, which may be the reason why he was so successful in challenging other martial artists in kumite. In his teaching to my father, he emphasized footwork and Ki. Motobu Sensei didn't speak Japanese very well, and he relied on friends to translate for him when he taught. He was not wealthy and had difficulty supporting himself during his visits to Japan. My father organized the Choki Motobu Support Society and arranged for seminars and training sessions at which Motobu Sensei was able to collect fees. He accompanied Motobu Sensei to many training

Karate Masters

"If you train in karate in a natural way and master your body, you will expand your knowledge and experience, and establish a solid foundation for naturally living a morally correct life."

sessions so he could assist him in explaining karate's concepts and techniques.

Chojun Miyagi, by all accounts, did not talk very much. He was famous for his big hands, and he was noted for grabbing and pulling very strongly. Though my father did not train with Miyagi Sensei as much as with other karate masters, Miyagi Sensei did impact my father's knowledge of karate by presenting him with an original manuscript, *An Outline of Karate-Do*, dated March 23, 1934.

On another hand, my father trained extensively with Kenwa Mabuni, the founder of shito-ryu. Mabuni Sensei resided at my father's house for about 10 months. This was from 1927-1928. They became very close friends. Mabuni Sensei was celebrated for the wide number of kata that he knew and performed with great elegance and calm. My father developed the kata *seiryu* in collaboration with Mabuni Sensei. Kenwa Mabuni's influence in *shindo jinen ryu* is evident in the kata syllabus of ryobu-kai.

Q: How did your father decide on the name of the style he created (shindo jinen-ryu)?

A: My father believed that if you walk a morally correct path in this life, then you are naturally following the divine way. If you train in karate in a natural way and master your body, you will expand your knowledge and experience, and establish a solid foundation for naturally living a morally correct life. And so his style, on the recommendation of Morihei Ueshiba (the founder of aikido), came to be shindo jinen-ryu karate-jutsu, It means "godly, natural style, complete empty-handed way."

Q: How much did Morihei Ueshiba influence your father's art?

A: My father studied under Morihei Ueshiba, who was still teaching daito-ryu aikijujitsu at that time. He considered Ueshiba Sensei to be the best martial artist he had ever known and carried this opinion throughout his lifetime. Having already trained in karate for a number of years, my father demonstrated the kata *Heian Nidan* to Ueshiba Sensei. However, Ueshiba Sensei remarked that my father should drop such nonsense for such techniques are ineffective. This comment came as a blow, because my father believed in karate and held Ueshiba Sensei's opinions in the highest regard. He felt that karate still had much value and that he had the responsibility to develop it. Thus, he requested that he be allowed to continue training in karate, intending to develop the techniques so that it would be acceptable to the great teacher. After many months of research and training, my father developed a kata called *Tai Sabaki*. He based this kata on karate, but he incorporated principles found in the teachings of Ueshiba Sensei. Though the new kata did not contain any complex movements, it consisted of a chain of actions with no pause after each action. After Konishi Sensei demonstrated this kata, Ueshiba Sensei remarked that, "The demonstration you did just now was satisfactory to me, and that kata is worth mastering." Later, my father developed two other kata based on the principles of Tai Sabaki. The three kata became known as *Tai Sabaki Shodan, Tai Sabaki Nidan* and *Tai Sabaki Sandan*.

"After many months of research and training, my father developed a kata called Tai Sabaki. He based this kata on karate, but he incorporated principles found in the teachings of Ueshiba Sensei."

Karate Masters

"The Dai Nippon Butoku-Kai, the Japanese governing body for budo, was politically very strong; they set the standards for ranking individual martial artists and signed all certificates of membership."

Q: How did karate become accepted in Japan?
A: The Dai Nippon Butoku-Kai, the Japanese governing body for budo, was politically very strong; they set the standards for ranking individual martial artists and signed all certificates of membership. My father was already a member through kendo and jujitsu; he felt that karate would be effective in the education of the Japanese people, so he applied to the Dai Nippon Butoku-Kai for the recognition of karate. Through 1934, however, the government continued to award titles in jujitsu and judo, but not in karate. Finally, in 1935, the Dai Nippon Butoku-Kai recognized karate as a member and awarded *kyoshi* [Master Instructor] rankings to my father, Miyagi Sensei and Ueshima Sannosuke (the founder of kushin ryu). The Dai Nippon Butoku-Kai also insisted that all budo have style names, and my father encouraged the prominent karate instructors of that time to name their individual styles. Because of his diligent efforts to advance karate in Japan, as well as his high level of skill in karate, my father was assigned in 1938 as the chairman of the screening committee of the Dai Nippon Butoku-Kai that reviewed all licensing applications in karate-jutsu.

Q: What can you tell us about the kata seiryu?
A: Around 1935 my father, Ueshiba Sensei, Mabuni Sensei and Ohtsuka Sensei were training together almost daily. At this time, the top officers of the Imperial Army largely controlled the Japanese government. The commanding general of the Japanese Army asked my father to develop women's self-defense techniques. His first step in fulfilling the Army's request was to ask Mabuni Sensei to help him develop standardized training methods, and this was designed to help the students remember the techniques. Together, they developed a karate kata that incorporated the

"Ueshiba Sensei strongly felt that the kata should be modified based on the gender of the practitioner, because of the need to protect very different sensitive areas. As a result of the collaboration between three great masters, the seiryu *kata contained the essence of both aikido and jujitsu."*

essence of both of their styles. As they worked to finalize the kata, they shared it with Ueshiba Sensei, who approved some sections and advised certain changes in others. Ueshiba Sensei strongly felt that the kata should be modified based on the gender of the practitioner, because of the need to protect very different sensitive areas. Also, a woman's training was normally executed from a natural [higher] stance. The female position in Japanese society was another factor that greatly influenced the kata. At the time, a woman's life was defined by cultural customs, though both sexes wore a kimono and used *geta*. All of these factors were considered in the process of developing the kata. As a result of the collaboration between three great masters, the *seiryu* kata contained the essence of both aikido and jujitsu. This meant that it [the movement] was going with the force instead of directly opposing an opponent's attack. Ryu means willow in English, and just like a willow will bend with the wind, so should

Karate Masters

"If your instructor is old and you are young, you are going to perform karate differently. The students must understand that they need to train their bodies in a different way. They need to listen more rather than copying their teachers."

the martial artist practicing this kata. The term also implies great strength, for the willow does not break under the force of the wind. The kanji for this kata may also be pronounced *aoyagi*.

Q: Sensei, let us talk about other technical aspects of the art and how it is practiced now. Should the student try to copy his teacher at all times?
A: Not really. If your instructor is old and you are young, you are going to perform karate differently. However, students should listen to their instructor. He sure has a reason for it [explaining a technique]. The students must understand that they need to train their bodies in a different way. They need to listen more rather than copying their teachers.

Q: Kime is always applied to the physical technique, but you mentioned once that this principle goes beyond punching and kicking. Would elaborate on that?
A: In the Western world, practitioners think that kime is only related to the physical aspect of karate training. However, in Japan, kime applies to other elements of life, including culture, life, even a traditional flower arrangement! Kime is a very simple word, but it is very complex for Westerners to understand because the Japanese concept embodies much more than what it is understood in karate circles. It represents the idea of perfect balance, a perfect harmony. Kime means perfect balance and this idea goes beyond the western conception or power. So, if we understand kime as perfect balance and harmony, we'll soon realize that when we punch or kick with kime we in fact are looking to get a perfect balance and harmony in the expression of

"Japanese students don't ask questions. It is the traditional way. You look, copy and try to find the answer within your own body. If you don't understand something, you don't directly ask your teacher. You think about it, you study your teacher's movement, you listen to his explanations, and you research the subject to try to come up with the answer."

a karate technique through the body. It is a concept very difficult to express in words ... almost impossible to convey in words. When we see something well done, we say, "Perfect!" In Japan, a true master says, "Kime. Great kime!" This is a natural balance that is very hard to achieve in modern society.

Q: What is the difference between Japanese students and Western students?
A: Many. To begin, Japanese students don't ask questions. It is the traditional way. You look, copy and try to find the answer within your own body. If you don't understand something, you don't directly ask your teacher. You think about it, you study your teacher's movement, you listen to his explanations, and you research the subject to try to come up with the answer. Even if you don't get a complete and logical answer to the question, you are developing an attitude to look inside yourself for

Karate Masters

"In budo, the teacher teaches in circles. You have to 'steal' the knowledge because the knowledge won't be given to you. You have to develop your own feeling and perception of everything surrounding you."

the answer. Then, one day you may approach your teacher and explain your dilemma. He won't give you the complete answer to your question, but he will point you in the right direction. In budo, the teacher teaches in circles. You have to "steal" the knowledge because the knowledge won't be given to you. You have to develop your own feeling and perception of everything surrounding you. This is a very discriminatory method. Why? If the student is not truly interested in doing the "homework," he basically won't learn anything. They will never understand. Therefore, the master will concentrate only on those who truly are looking for the answers. Sometimes it happens that great and talented athletes never become successful in karate because of their weak mind. The problem lies in the mental aspect and not in the physical. In Japan, the traditional approach is: "Don't talk. Train." Work hard in the basic techniques and you'll find answers by yourself. You'll find your own karate.

Q: Has your training changed over the years to adapt to the modern times?
A: Definitely. My training today is not the same that it was 25 years ago. Everybody's personal training should change with his age. The body changes and training sessions should be modified to fit these changes. Some individuals suffer injures or experience physical problems that affect what they can do and how they can do it. A person can't train the same all his life. It is natural to change. When you are young, physical power is the main thing, the muscles are the main source of power and the internal organs simply provide support. When the muscles start to get weaker with age, the internal organs are the source of power. Then, the spirit needs to be strong to support this. Later on, when the internal organs get weaker because the individual gets older, the spirit carries the weight of your personal training. Remember that the techniques should be adapted to the age of the practitioner. A 20-year-old karate-ka is not going to do the technique the same way that a 60-year-old individual does.

Q: What about changing the training for the students?
A: Well, based on what I just said, the teacher should adapt the training specifically to the individual. The truth is that most of the students around the world are young individuals; therefore, the training we have these days doesn't require to be changed. For young people, the general karate training we see around the world is all right.

Q: Your approach to teaching is based on the students doing their "homework" after class. Do you think this is realistic for our modern society?
A: It may not be, but that's the way it is in the traditional approach to budo. The teacher should teach the fundamentals of the movement and make sure students get the basic techniques down, but it is up to the students to work hard. Karate is a personal quest, and it is a personal journey. Therefore, a military approach to training is not exactly the best way to go because the students will think that if they are not in the dojo with the teacher counting the number of repetitions they won't be able to train. This is not right. The students must do their own personal training without the instructor watching. Students need to understand that what they are learning from the instructor is the foundation; they need to build the rest. Unfortunately, nowadays people do not have too much time to dedicate once they leave the dojo. So, basically they need to get everything they can—as far as physical training goes—when they are in the

school because when they leave they won't train again until the next session. Karate becomes a three-days-a-week activity instead of an every day way of life.

Q: Nowadays, many well-known karate instructors combine kata from different styles in their curriculum. What is your opinion of this?
A: I understand the fact that different kata origins influenced the principles and concepts behind the forms. If a shotokan instructor thinks that it can be beneficial to incorporate a shito-ryu or goju-ryu kata into the curriculum to fill some gaps of the shotokan style, there is nothing wrong with that. Some styles have deeper bunkai study and analysis and this is a great reason to incorporate a certain kata. Karate self-defense lies in kata bunkai. Therefore, I may see a reason in doing it.

Q: Sensei, there are two basic approaches to karate technique. One is the long-distance method used mostly by shotokan practitioners and the other a short-distance approach used in other styles like goju-ryu and shito-ryu. What can you tell us about this?
A: Here we are looking at a very complex subject. Let me explain this to you. Long distance movements are good for young people because they stretch the body and force the student to move in larger ranges of motion. This approach is good in the beginning stages [of training]. The students need this long-distance approach to de-contract the body and learn how to use all the muscles in the technique. Later on, when the student has been practicing for years, his body will automatically bring into place all the muscles without needing the extra distance to perform the technique with full power and kime. When the mastery of the art grows, the movements are shorter and more economical. When defending or attacking, the fist is not chambered before defending or attacking. They [fist or foot] hit from whenever they are at that particular moment.

While sparring, it [long distance] allows a student to hit the opponent from a farther distance, which is always good for competition. What is important to remember is the fact that self-defense situations occur at short-distance. If the student has a very specific conception of what the distance should be, he may get caught by surprise. Goju-ryu and shito-ryu, because of their emphasis on kata bunkai, use a lot of close-range techniques that apply to self-defense situations. What exponents of these systems do they use in sport competition , and they use the long-distance approach! So basically, I can say that neither one is the best approach. Both are good, but it is important to understand why and when to use them. I know Funakoshi Gichin developed this long-distance approach to be used as a training method for his young students. In addition to that, he also wanted to get away from the street fighting approach that karate had at that time.

Q: What is the most important aspect of karate training?
A: In the physical aspect, it is the fundamental techniques. This is what people call the basics. Focus on these fundamental movements because they are the building block for everything else. Forget about the secrets of the "advanced" techniques. The only "secrets" are within your body, and it is up to you to unveil these and make them work for you. Make every technique perfect. True karate cannot be discovered by simply talking and discussing philosophy and technique. Only through hard physical training and dedication can we feel what the true karate has to offer. Less talk and more sweat. Put passion in every training session, keep your spirit strong and the right way will open in front of you. O

"Make every technique perfect. True karate cannot be discovered by simply talking and discussing philosophy and technique. Only through hard physical training and dedication can we feel what the true karate has to offer."

Shojiro Koyama

The Perfect Balance

Born on December 4, 1935 in Tokyo, Japan, Sensei Koyama moved to the United States in 1964 and began teaching at the Arizona Karate Association, where he remains as chief instructor today, as well as in the Physical Education departments of ASU, University of Arizona and a number of community colleges. He has been promoting karate for more than three decades by teaching as a guest instructor in many other areas of the world, including Pan-America, the Caribbean, the Middle East and Canada.

He is liberal and open-minded about his methods and does not propose his to be the only true path to karate mastery. "All the fighting disciplines have a spiritual quality about them that all practitioners should try to develop," he says. The way he explains the philosophical foundation of karate-do is refreshing and soothing at a time when martial arts in general are leading us to more combative and violent approaches.

Author of several books on karate and health and many articles for leading martial arts publications around the world, Koyama Sensei is an 8th dan, the Western Regional Director of the International Shotokan Karate Federation, headquartered in Philadelphia, and is a member of the *Japan Karate Association* Shihan Kai Instructor's Group. His remarkable contributions to the art of karate brings one to the conclusion that his has been a life well spent, and he has the right to be satisfied with it.

Q: How long have you been practicing the martial arts, and in how many styles of karate have you trained?
A: I began training in Shotokan karate in 1950 at the age of 15. I attended Hosei High School in Tokyo. In my senior year, I became the captain of the school's karate team. In 1954, I entered Hosei University, where I trained under Master Saiki and Master Kimio Itoe. By the time of my graduation, I had become the co-captain of the university's karate team, and I remained there as a team coach until 1964. I have only trained in shotokan karate. However, after so many years of karate training, I have had the opportunity to meet masters of other styles and that

Karate Masters

"To fit the Western psyche, I tend to use more explanations and come at these explanations from many different angles, which is not really the traditional Japanese teaching approach."

helped me to better understand other styles and methods of karate.

Q: How do Westerners respond to traditional Japanese training?
A: Western students are very open to absorbing Japanese culture. They tend to be open, accepting and rather obedient. However, although it appears on the surface that Western students absorb the culture, even after 40 years in the U.S., I can't be sure that they absorb the teachings at the subconscious level.

Also, when I first came to the U.S., I taught using the Japanese instructional approach. Pretty soon it became apparent that this style was not a very good fit for the Western mentality. Therefore, I can say that the aim of my teaching remains the same, but my approach to teaching it has changed and evolved throughout the past four decades. To fit the Western psyche, I tend to use more explanations and come at these explanations from many different angles, which is not really the traditional Japanese teaching approach. Japanese students are not used to as much explanation; they are more accepting of basic drilling without verbal clarification.

Q: Were you a natural at karate? Did the movements come easily to you?
A: No, I was very stiff. In the beginning, it was not at all easy for me.

Q: How has your personal karate changed and developed over the years?
A: This is a very interesting question. When I was young, I only studied and practiced my technique, and I thought that my technique would improve through this type of training. My instructors always said that I must also "Seek perfection of character" as part of my training and development or my technique would never really improve. Of course, as a youth I doubted that advice. I believed that "technique is simply tech-

nique." Now, however, I think I understand what my teachers were trying to tell me. After a lifetime of experience, I understand that hardship and struggle must be incorporated—in the form of character development—into one's training in order to improve one's performance. I watch videos of my old performances and demonstrations, and I can see a big change in my technique and myself since the earlier days. I attribute that change to the dignity, judgment and composure that I developed through my lifetime of experiences, good and bad, but especially to those that resulted in hardship and struggle. I have always said that karate is a lifetime exercise. If I continued to view karate only as a sport, as I did when I was young, I think that I would never have understood that lifetime exercise and character development actually lead to improvement in technique. This concept has to do with what it is referred to as EQ (emotional quotient or emotional intelligence). In the Oriental way of thinking, emotional intelligence, born out of a lifetime of experience both good and bad, is very important in every endeavor. This is true for karate as well.

I have come to understand that sometimes American students don't like the Oriental militaristic style of teaching. It is usually the instructor's fault that students fail to understand that the extreme concentration and focus required of a karate-ka depends on a strict code of obedience and a strict style of teaching. Otherwise, technique will never really improve.

Q: What are the most important points of your teaching philosophy?
A: For me, karate is a mission, a mission that I brought to the U.S. when I arrived in the early 1960s. For example, early on when I arrived in the U.S., I formed the Western States Karate Championship Association. The annual tournament hosted by the WSKCA has always been an excellent vehicle for translating the philosophical pillars of karate into a practical reality.

Also, my karate philosophy reflects my belief that under adverse circumstances and conditions of struggle, a person's true character emerges. This is true in life and in the microcosm of life that karate represents. For example, when a karate-ka is unsuccessful in a dan exam or tournament competition, his or her true nature is revealed quite clearly. Those people who have begun to understand the importance of character development understand that—when initially unsuccessful—patience and composure are most critical. Failure can be a very good learning experience. Many people do not understand this concept and are always quick to compliment and try to soften the blow when their student is unsuccessful. However, I believe that this soft approach will most often not bring out strength of character as efficiently as when one simply accepts failure, learns from it and commits to persevering despite of it. This mindset forms the core of educational karate and of karate as a lifetime exercise, and is, I believe, what is really meant by the first tenet of the shotokan dojo-kun: "Seek perfection of character."

Q: With all the technical changes during the last 30 years, do you think there is still pure shotokan?
A: Of course, despite all the changes on the surface, the fundamentals remain the same. These immutable basics (strong hips and body core or *seikatanden*, solid grounding, et cetera) are very, very important and always will be. That being said, it is undeniable that tournament technique is very different today than it was in earlier times. It used to be that karate opponents faced one another with a "one-punch, one-kill" frontline mindset. Now, karate competition is much more like a game. Nevertheless, basic foundations never change. Good competitors will always need to have techniques grounded in excellent basics, regardless of what current trends are reflected in those techniques.

Life is changing, becoming more complicated economically, geographically, politically... Evolution in karate technique reflects these changes. A strong "one-punch, one-kill" mentality is no longer enough. Nowadays, a successful competitor needs timing, speed and balance, and that comes from developing composure, patience and psychological grounding. Therefore, character development is most important.

Q: Do you think different ryu are important? And what are the main differences between the different shotokan methods that have appeared after the original JKA split?
A: The JKA split resulted in two distinct organizations, but I think that technically the karate in both is very similar. What differs between the two is organizational structure and management, even though basics and style remain the same. I hope that philosophically both organizations follow the guiding principles of Master Funakoshi and Master Nakayama, which form the core and foundation of traditional shotokan, regardless of organization.

Q: What is your opinion of full-contact karate and kickboxing?
A: Although beautiful in its own right, this type of karate is 100 percent different from traditional educational karate. In sports styles such as kickboxing and K-1, victory or defeat is all that matters. Winning is everything and defeat is to be avoided at all costs. In some ways, I think that it is dif-

ficult to learn and grow with that type of mindset (one is focused on nothing but winning the next match). A famous professional sports coach once said, "Winning isn't everything; it's the only thing." I don't think this type of mindset is compatible with karate as a lifetime activity. Failure is an opportunity for growth. Sometimes that growth comes many years later, when one has progressed and developed enough to comprehend the lesson in that failure. But it does come when one has the patience to wait for it. Sports karate, wherein "winning is the only thing," is not as conducive to that type of patience or learning.

"Failure is an opportunity for growth. Sometimes that growth comes many years later, when one has progressed and developed enough to comprehend the lesson in that failure."

Q: Sensei, how do you think a practitioner can combine the principle of character development as Funakoshi Gichin described and the art of karate in the 21st century?
A: Master Gichin Funakoshi wrote, "The ultimate aim of the art of karate lies not in victory or defeat, but in the perfection of character of its participants." He wrote this during the early 20th century, arguably the most aggressive and violent century in history. The generation of that time pioneered modern weapons of mass destruction and engaged in human rights violations of a scale never before seen or even imagined. Certainly, one would have hoped that the 21st century would bring a spiritual awakening and a fundamental change in the nature of human relations as the world began to look back on the tragedies and violence of the previous era. Unfortunately, it seems that human relations remain very complicated. Although the world has had the opportunity to reflect on the possibilities that face the human race in an age in which technology is capable of vastly improving life, or conversely, destroying it. Sadly, aggressive regimes continue to threaten their citizens, nations continue to wage war and terrorists attack innocent civilians. Perhaps human nature is fixed and will never change. If this is the case, it certainly seems that soci-

Karate Masters

"There are no true losers among practitioners of the martial arts, because both victory and defeat are opportunities for spiritual growth."

ety needs to pursue areas of spiritual growth or peace will continue to be elusive.

Q: Practitioners of Master Funakoshi's karate maintain that the martial arts are different from, and more spiritual than, entertainment sports. How do we differentiate martial arts from sports?
A: To put it briefly, the aim of sports is to win, conquer and dominate the opponent. Losing is "bad" and therefore value is only to be found in victory. But, as Master Funakoshi's quote so eloquently explains, the value in the martial arts, such as karate, is to be found in the lessons learned from losing as well as winning. There are no true losers among practitioners of the martial arts, because both victory and defeat are opportunities for spiritual growth. Throughout life we must all learn to face both victory and defeat with grace and spiritual grounding. Otherwise, the disappointments of day-to-day living, over a lifetime, wear us down, make us bitter and cause us to behave aggressively, discourteously and possibly even destructively toward others. Karate fosters in us the ability to appreciate the learning opportunities inherent in defeat and loss throughout a lifetime of experiences, both good and bad.

One of the most important lessons that karate teaches us is that courtesy and respect are paramount. Without courtesy and respect, the martial arts are exactly the same as street fighting. That is what Master Funakoshi meant when he wrote the 20 basic precepts of karate, in which the very first one states that, "In karate, begin with a bow and finish with a bow." Where one consistently follows this principle, one begins to appreciate that courtesy and respect are more important than "winning." By respecting and valuing our opponents, we become capable of recognizing their courage, guts, mettle and spirit, regardless of who ultimately emerges "victorious." Character development means recognizing that this "spirit" is far more important than the trophy or medal that the winner receives.

For more than four decades, I have tried to operate a tournament that reflects Master Funakoshi's and Nakayama's philosophy. At times, it can be very difficult to keep competitors and fans focused on the difference between entertainment sports and martial arts because, naturally, in the excitement of the tournament, many people are more focused on the entertainment value of the event and on carrying home the championship trophy. That, of course, is human nature. But, I will try to continue to promote the importance of the principles that underlie our art and differentiate it from other types of sports, as I have done for 40 years. That is, after all, the basis on which Masters Funakoshi and Nakayama founded the art of traditional karate.

Q: How would you describe the life and dedication of the late Nakayama Sensei to the arts of budo and specifically to karate-do?
A: Master Nakayama was the essence of modern budo. After WWII, Master Nakayama created a new budo, which we still follow to this day. It used to be that there were no tournaments, just drilling in the basics with a one-punch, one-kill mindset, albeit confined to a non-tournament setting. This type of training appealed to only a limited number of people. Master Nakayama opened traditional karate to a much broader audience and a wider market of potential students with the advent of tournament karate. However, I think that Master Nakayama might look at the ultimate destination toward which karate seems to be headed and perhaps conclude that the sports mentality has been taken to an extreme. In that regard, as the father of modern karate, he might be a bit taken aback at the direction taken by some of his "children," a direction he probably never envisioned when he pioneered modern budo.

Q: Do you think that karate in the West is on the same level with Japanese karate?
A: I'm afraid that I can't answer that question yet. My mission was to bring Master Funakoshi's and Nakayama's art to the U.S., but that mission is still a work in progress. If one considers only the technical aspects of karate as the basis for comparison, maybe the levels are the same. However, because karate is a form of lifetime exercise and education to me, I cannot judge yet how successful those who have pioneered shotokan in the West have been. The results can only be judged on the basis of how many people have truly enjoyed life as a result (at least in part) of their training. Because that is the Oriental mindset, it is difficult to

compare the Japanese "level" versus the Western "level." The basis of comparison is intangible when one looks beyond technical competence.

Q: In regards to physical capabilities, do you feel that there are any fundamental differences between Japanese karate-ka and European or American karate-ka?
A: I'd have to say that, in general, European people are stronger, but Japanese people are more technically "fine-tuned." These differences are analogous to the comparisons between Japanese and European/American technology. Japanese products such as Toyota and Sony are often thought to be more technologically refined, but European and American products are thought of as sturdier and more durable.

Q: Do you feel that you still have further to go in your studies in budo?
A: I recognize that sports, entertainment and pleasure are very important, but philosophy and education is my field, my life's work. Personally, I believe that learning and studying are essential throughout life.

Q: Japanese coaches and Western coaches have a very different method of dealing with the preparation of a sport competition. Which method do you think is better?
A: There is no better method. Let me give you an example. In the 1964 Tokyo Olympic games, the Japanese women's volleyball team took the gold medal. That year's team coach was a man by the name of Dai Matsu, whose nickname was "The Demon." The Demon was a very strict, very hard man, much like an old-time Japanese military officer or samurai warrior. Many people believed that he was so successful because he was so strict and militaristic. This year the Japanese women's volleyball coach is 180 degrees different from The Demon. However, despite his differences in coaching style, he too led his team to victory in the Asian regional trials. It is very interesting that these two diametrically opposed leadership styles, one very regimented and harsh, one compassionate and gentle, have both been effective at different times and with different teams, although it might be argued that Dai Matsu's style was ultimately more effective because this year's Japanese team did not take home the Olympic gold! I think that the reason that each style has been effective in its own time is that today's players are also very different from those of the 1960s. This difference is characteristic not only of Olympic athletes but also of young people in general. For example, today's young karate-

ka are much more recreation- and sports-oriented and much less focused on discipline. The spiritual and artistic features of karate are frequently neglected in favor of a focus on competition and showmanship. Unfortunately, when we turn completely away from the original cultural ideals or our art, we risk losing its rich and beautiful legacy, which is, of course, very sad. Perhaps even sadder is the likelihood that a focus on the sports-like aspects of karate leaves less room for the philosophical foundations that guide and enrich the life of the true martial artist.

"Today's young karate-ka are much more recreation- and sports-oriented and much less focused on discipline. The spiritual and artistic features of karate are frequently neglected in favor of a focus on competition and showmanship."

Q: Sensei, you like to talk about some elements of the Chinese philosophy and something described as "the philosophy of kai." Would you elaborate on that?

A: Of course! The Chinese have a very interesting life philosophy. A person's life, they say, is like a bamboo stick. It is organized in discreet sections rather than along one long continuous pathway, as many people seem to believe. Life can be thought of as a learning process composed of five segments or stages. Stage one, *sei-kai*, is the beginning stage, in which the very young child is focused on being and existing in the physical world. Physical needs are all that the baby knows and is concerned with, and he or she is completely grounded in the present moment. Stage two, *shin-kai*, is concerned with forming a basic self-identity, which is based in defining a life purpose. In this stage, formal education geared toward an eventual occupation is the all-consuming focus, and the young person begins to develop a future orientation. Stage, three, *ka-kei*, is the point in life in which one begins to focus on raising a family. *Ka* means house, and the person at this stage of life is concerned with hearth and home, spouse and children. *Ro-kai*, stage four, is the beginning of old age. The individual at this stage of his life is starting to focus on defining a meaning for his existence and on finding a purpose in life. A focus on the past becomes important in order to understand and find value in one's lifetime of achievements, accomplishments and experiences. However, liv-

Karate Masters

"Depending on culture and religion, one might, for example, begin to imagine what heaven would be like or might wonder in what form he will eventually be reincarnated."

ing completely in the past is dangerous at this stage because in doing so one risks losing a sense of purpose in one's continued existence. That is the reason that many people die shortly after retirement. They find themselves drifting aimlessly and failing to find meaning in their post-retirement activities. During the final stage of life, *shi-kai*, one begins to think about his or her mortality and to prepare for eventual death. This is also a time of contemplating life after death and may bring a new orientation to the future, along with this focus on the afterlife. Depending on culture and religion, one might, for example, begin to imagine what heaven would be like or might wonder in what form he will eventually be reincarnated.

The important point in this philosophy is that a person should not move aimlessly or mindlessly through these stages. *Kai* means plan or study and inherent in the name of each stage is the implication that successful negotiation of every one depends on developing and following a meaningful personal philosophy during each of these life phases. Remember too that karate follows a similar pattern of development, which elsewhere I have referred to as seasons. The individual who is, for example, exclusively and narrowly focused on competition (the middle stages of his training) will ultimately neglect the latter stages and will fail to find any purpose in the practice of his art as he inevitably retires from the tournament ring. One very productive way of finding value in the post-competition *ro-kai* stage is by teaching, for example, as a karate instructor. Through teaching and passing on what you have learned, you achieve a sort of immortality. This is what the great psychologist Erik Erikson referred to when he wrote about successful negotiation of old age through the passing on of wisdom and guidance to a new generation. Also, as Erikson said, successful negotiation of any stage depends on successful resolution of previous life stages. In this regard, a lifetime is much like a child's game of dominoes. If an earlier domino is off balance, it will impact each succeeding one in a negative way, ultimately resulting in failure of the entire chain. Remember, in everything that you do, keep in mind the Chinese philosophy of life stages and you will find satisfaction throughout your lifetime.

According to the Chinese philosophy, I am currently in the *ro-kai* stage of my life. Some people, even those much younger than I, perhaps only in their 50s or 60s, look very old and unhealthy. As they exited what they thought of as the "prime" of their lives, their physical condition declined and their functioning deteriorated. That is, of course, natural and inevitable. However, it is not healthy to merely accept this decline as the beginning of the end, without a plan for the latter stages of life. That is why *kai*, planning and studying, is so important, especially as we begin to age. That is also precisely why the practice of the lifetime art of karate is so beneficial. Supplemental exercises such as stretching, push-ups, diaphragmatic breathing and so on are excellent methods for reducing stress, increasing mental and physical flexibility, and in general, combating the deleterious effects of aging, especially depression and anxiety. Each stage is an opportunity for study, planning and finding new meaning in all of our activities, such as the practice of karate. However, this opportunity is lost when one passively and fatalistically accepts functional decline as a sign of impending uselessness and deterioration.

Q: How exactly does karate fit into this philosophy?
A: That is for each of you to decide for yourself. Each person's physical condition and capabilities are different. Some people can continue to compete into their 40s while others are no longer physically capable of competing in their 30s. I can provide you with the basic philosophical framework as articulated in the Chinese philosophy of *kai*, but you must determine for yourself how you will apply it in your own life. One principle, though, is important for everyone, regardless of their personal life stage or circumstances, and that is this: Study and planning are important and are your responsibility. Mindless existence is a waste of your valuable and unique life potential. If you think of karate as only a form of recreation to pass the time, you will not be able to use your art in pursuit of your maximum potential. Instead, use your art as a learning opportunity and a route towards character growth, and you will reap the rewards of following the philosophy of *kai* toward a successful and fulfilling lifetime of experiences.

Q: How do you see karate in the rest of the world at the present time?
A: One night I was watching CNN and saw something that I think was very sad. The reporter was showing a terrorist training camp in which the trainees were practicing karate. To me, this is a tragic misuse of a beautiful art which celebrates non-violence and prohibits practitioners from using it offensively. On the other hand, I have also seen karate instructors in universities throughout the world teaching young people that karate is not just a form of fighting but also a philosophy and form of mental, emotional, spiritual and physical discipline. That, in a nutshell, is life ... sometimes good, sometimes bad. I believe that karate, even if not always used as envisioned by Master Funakoshi, at the end of the day will continue to reflect first and foremost the principles on which it was founded, in spite of its occasional misappropriation.

Q: Do you think it helps empty-hand karate physically to train with weapons?
A: Of course, in some forms of martial arts, weapons are very important. I am training in an "empty-hand" style, and I consider myself in many ways still a beginner. If I ever finish my course of training, I will pick up weapons training. So, in answer to this question, I am not officially training in a weapons art at this time. That being said, however, I do find that it helps me with my karate basics to train in some basic kendo techniques, such as the *shinai*. I find that this sort of training is an excellent supplement to my shotokan training.

Q: What's your opinion of makiwara training?
A: Makiwara training is very important. It is very helpful in working the legs and hips. I myself still train frequently with the makiwara. As people age, they become mentally and physically weaker. The makiwara is particularly good for older people because it trains the mind and the body at the same time, requiring sharp mental and physical focus and speed training. Older people often fear becoming slower as they age, and the makiwara helps combat slowing and loss of concentration. Also, the well-constructed makiwara as an opponent is very, very difficult to beat. It helps hone a competitive edge while keeping the user quite humble.

Q: How should a teacher prepare his personal training in order to progress in the arts? What elements should be more emphasized once you reach an instructor level?

A: Technique comes from the instructor's personality and personal philosophy. If your aim is to be strong and violent, all you need is technical competence, and philosophy is not important. But shotokan karate emphasizes the first principle of the dojo-kun: "Seek perfection of character." If your personal philosophy or behavior runs counter to the dojo-kun, your technique will never really improve or reach its full potential. I already mentioned that when I was younger my instructor warned me that I was concerned with technique at the expense of attitude. I have since learned that if you improve and advance your mind (attitude), your technique will follow. Unfortunately, the reverse does not seem to be true! Personally, I recommend Zen training. Zen training focuses on good, correct posture and breathing. Of course, it is a bit dangerous when an instructor tries to teach Zen to others without first having personal instruction from an experienced leader or teacher. It is relatively easy to read a book and think that you understand the principles behind Zen. However, there can be some dangerous side effects to practicing the art improperly if you have not been correctly schooled in technique.

Breathing is also important. Proper breathing leads to composure and a calm mind, as well as to physiological benefits. Breathing control translates to mental control. The autonomic nervous system (ANS) is not under the conscious mind's control, but with good breathing, a chain reaction of physiological events takes place that ultimately leads to the practitioner's ability to indirectly control the ANS.

"Technique comes from the instructor's personality and personal philosophy. If your aim is to be strong and violent, all you need is technical competence, and philosophy is not important."

Karate Masters

"To be a sumo grand champion, one must not only win the tournament but also display a commitment to perfection of character at all times. The deportment of a true sumo grand champion reflects dignity, integrity and honor."

Q: Isn't winning what is truly important in a sport competition?
A: Not really. Let me give you an example. Sumo wrestling is a traditional Japanese martial art in which aggressive competition is very important. However, sumo differs from a pure sports activity and illustrates a fundamental characteristic of martial arts in that victory is important but it is not everything. To be a sumo grand champion, one must not only win the tournament but also display a commitment to perfection of character at all times. The deportment of a true sumo grand champion reflects dignity, integrity and honor. Because sumo champions are important celebrities in Japan, they are highly visible and must be willing to recognize and accept their obligation to display integrity and honor in all of their public behavior, in the ring and out. Therefore, non-sportsman-like displays of emotion on the tournament floor, whether one wins or loses, are inappropriate and unacceptable for a competitive Japanese sumo wrestler. It is very interesting to watch a sumo match. Even though it is physiologically unnatural to suppress the intense emotions that accompany aggressive competition, the contestants almost never engage in passionate displays. Consider how different these sumo wrestlers behave than do, for example, many professional football players after scoring a winning touch-

down. This type of moderation is also traditional among practitioners of other true Japanese martial arts such as aikido, judo, kendo, and of course, karate. Students of these activities who do not behave in accordance with principles of modesty, dignity and honor cannot truly be considered martial artists in the traditional Japanese sense. Unfortunately, it seems to increasingly be the case that modern society is so influenced by the entertainment-sports mentality that many students of karate behave more like professional football players than like dignified sumo grand champions.

Q: Do you think that the mental approach of a fighter varies if he is competing in a sport tournament or if he is fighting for his life?
A: Nobel prize winning biologist Julius Axelrod concluded that human mental states (on which all of human behavior is based) are the result of hormones acting on the nervous system. In human beings, as well as in animals, passionate physical and emotional displays are a natural reaction to the secretion of hormones such as adrenaline and testosterone that accompany aggressive physical competition. The body does not know the difference between attack by an enemy and a controlled kumite match in the ring. In both cases, the brain perceives a threat and reacts by engaging the sympathetic (fight-or-flight) nervous system and directing the release of hormones that enable the body to better react to that "threat," whether or not it is actually real. Such physiological reactions are adaptive when one faces a truly dangerous situation, however, they can lead to unhealthy physical and emotional stress when they are too frequent or too intense. The restraint and self-control displayed by practitioners of martial arts such as sumo helps moderate what would otherwise be unhealthy effects of an overabundance of stress and aggression hormones. Physiologically, this behavior helps counterbalance the arousal caused by the sympathetic nervous system by engaging the calming effects of the parasympathetic system. In contrast to the sympathetic system, the parasympathetic system decreases the heart rate and blood pressure and deactivates hormones like cortisol and adrenaline that can cause unhealthy levels of stress, and eventually illnesses such as heart disease, stroke and even cancer. In this regard, the restraint displayed by martial arts practitioners that may seem to be merely a means to spiritual growth and character development is actually physiologically protective as well.

The two-minute, single point matches of karate are very compatible with moderation of physical and emotional overreaction. The emphasis on control, spatial perception and cool-down between bouts of punching and kicking engage parasympathetic-like elements of the nervous system. This balance of an increase and decrease in physiological arousal is one of the characteristics that helps to differentiate martial arts from competitive sports. Unlike martial arts, many sports can be thought of as promoting only the arousal-supportive functions of the human nervous system, including secretion of testosterone and adrenaline. After the sports competition is over, the athlete goes home still keyed up and physically aroused. In the case of the martial arts, during the match itself, the sympathetic nervous and hormone systems are fully engaged, just like in competitive sports. However, martial artists learn to moderate these reactions as soon as the match is over, thereby engaging the parasympathetic system, cooling down more rapidly and controlling the effects of hormones such as testosterone. We have learned that an inability to control these effects can be disastrous. For example, research shows that many criminals have an overabundance of testosterone and are more likely to react aggressively to its presence.

Q: How should instructors modify their training when getting older?
A: As the instructor gets older, supplemental training (Zen, breathing, stretching, et cetera) become more important. For the older instructor, I have found that the proper ratio is 2/3 supplemental training to 1/3 technique training. This ratio helps promote the practice of karate as a lifetime exercise. Many instructors, in their youth, thought of karate as merely a sport to be won at all costs, much like professional football. And like many football coaches, such a karate instructor may allow himself to get out of shape and out of practice once he is past his physical prime. He still understands logically how to win and he can continue to teach the players to win, but he does nothing to grow in his own practice. Of course, that is OK for a sports coach, but my philosophy is that karate is a lifetime exercise, and therefore, the instructor, as he ages, must continue to train his own mind and body, over time increasing the ratio of supplemental training until he reaches that 2/3 ratio.

Q: When teaching the art of karate, is self-defense, sport or tradition the most important element?
A: I'd have to answer tradition but only when the term is used as a synonym for philosophy. Sports and self-defense, as goals, are limited. When you retire from competition or pass the physical prime of youth, sports as a goal becomes potentially obsolete. And once one has mastered self-defense techniques, one may become bored with training and quit. But

for those students who find value in learning and following traditional manners and instructor-student relationships, principles of character development and Oriental philosophy, karate becomes a lifetime exercise for the long-term and shotokan becomes a way of life rather than a temporary hobby or merely a source of entertainment. Of course, everything should be in proper balance. Focusing exclusively on tradition is difficult and must be balanced with a commitment to train in the basics and, for those who so desire, engage in competition and tournament karate.

"Focusing exclusively on tradition is difficult and must be balanced with a commitment to train in the basics and, for those who so desire, engage in competition and tournament karate."

Q: In training, what's the proper ratio of kata and kumite?
A: Fortunately or unfortunately, students today seem to like sports karate. Therefore, a focus on basics is very important. Seventy percent of training should be in the basics but not only "basic" basics. Kihon with a partner in which application, coordination and practical elements of technique are emphasized is very beneficial.

Q: Some people think it is necessary to go to Japan to train. Do you agree with this point of view?
A: This is a very interesting question. For those who go to Japan for a year or less typically are only able to scratch the surface when it comes to experiencing and understanding Japanese martial arts culture and philosophy. They may come to believe that they understand it better than they actually do, but their understanding will invariably be shallow, and, as they say, a little knowledge can be a dangerous thing! However, the exception would be the person who finds a good guide/mentor, and immerses himself in Japanese culture with that mentor's instruction and guidance.

Karate Masters

"Present life satisfaction and mental stimulation are very important. Without intellectual stimulation, a human being becomes like an animal ... the spirit withers and the body soon dies."

Q: What do you consider to be the major changes in the art of karate since you began training?
A: First and foremost, karate has become more sports-oriented. It used to be the case that technical skill, philosophy and attitude were driven by a martial arts-oriented ideology. Now, these same elements are driven by a sports mentality and ideology.

Q: Whom would you like to have trained with that you have not?
A: Master Gichin Funakoshi.

Q: What would you say to someone who is interested in learning karate-do?
A: There is a Japanese saying that states if one wants to train in the martial arts the instructor must insist that one visit the school three times before deciding. Interestingly, the Talmud (the code of Jewish religious law), requires that a Rabbi turn a prospective convert away three times before agreeing to train him for conversion. Perhaps this similarity stems from the fact that, according to budo tradition, one must commit oneself fully to one's martial art and training, much as a convert is expected to commit body, mind and soul to his new religion.

Q: What keeps you motivated after all these years?
A: Of course, I have a dream, a target destination if you will, but more important is right now, the present moment. Present life satisfaction and mental stimulation are very important. Without intellectual stimulation, a human being becomes like an animal ... the spirit withers and the body soon dies. Training provides that source of stimulation. After every training session, I say, "Thank you God. I did it! Right in this moment I was able to do what I set out to do." That is a bit of a miracle if you think about it, just like the elegant physical mechanisms that underlie all of the

body processes that we take for granted, such as simply breathing. Everyone has big dreams. For example, a novice student dreams of obtaining his black belt some day, but what you are doing in the moment is what is really important. Eventually, the little satisfactions and small moments of progress that come day by day will lead you to your goals and dreams, but today is all we ever really have. That is what keeps me motivated.

Q: Do you think it is necessary to engage in free fighting to achieve good self-defense skills for a real situation?
A: When people think bad thoughts, their actions are bad. When they think good thoughts, their actions are good. Very simple! It is dangerous for a person who trains in karate to always imagine himself in a real fight with a real opponent in the real world. Violent thoughts translate to violent actions. People often make the mistake of envisioning the makiwara or bag as a real enemy. This is incorrect. The purpose of makiwara training is focus and concentration, not imagined combat. Therefore, it ought to represent an abstract rather than a concrete concept in the practitioner's mind. In fact, when practicing with the makiwara, one's body should really operate as a machine, without thinking, and certainly without thinking about real enemies or fights. Relax, empty your mind and your reactions will come very quickly.

Actually, I always say that the dojo-kun is itself the practitioner's best defense. I don't really think about real fighting, and I believe that one should keep one's mind clear of thoughts about real-life enemies and fighting when training. Your true opponent is your own mental limitation, not another person.

Q: What is your opinion about mixing karate styles? Does the practice of one nullify the effectiveness of the other? Or, on the contrary, can it be beneficial to the student?
A: All of the different styles are beautiful in their own right. That being said, I think of mixing karate styles much as I would of mixing different cuisines and cooking styles. While prime American steak, well-prepared sushi and gourmet Italian food can be a wonderful culinary treat on their own, mixed together they would lose their unique flavors and even become somewhat unappetizing. While this may seem a ridiculous analogy, it really does illustrate my feeling about mixing styles. As always, there is generally an exception to every rule, and in the case of mixing styles, it is this: As the karate-ka gets older, and after about 30 or 40 years

of practice in one art, he will benefit greatly from supplementing his training with a softer art such as yoga or even *tai chi*.

Q: Modern karate is moving away from the bunkai in kata practice. How important do you think bunkai is in the understanding of kata?
A: Like most things, bunkai training has both advantages and disadvantages. On the negative side, for any technique, there may be another more reasonable or more efficient application or countermove than what is typically taught in bunkai training. On the other hand, if one is interested in brain stimulation, training and the right hemisphere in particular, bunkai training can be very helpful because it helps develop imagination and spatial perception.

Q: Do you have a particularly memorable karate experience that has remained as an inspiration for your training?
A: I don't really have one particular memory that stands out above all others. But what I can say is that I have been practicing karate for more than 50 years, and everyday training is still satisfying, I sleep well, my appetite is good, and I am still healthy and in good physical condition. That by itself is amazing and wonderful, and I credit my lifetime practice of karate for all of these simple satisfactions. Through everyday training, I continually find new philosophical and technical inspiration, and this is most particularly true when I am teaching or observing children and senior citizens.

Q: After all these years of training and experience, could you explain the meaning of the practice of karate-do?
A: When I was young, I used to be preoccupied with big philosophical meanings. But today, as I have gotten older, mostly I just appreciate the benefits inherent in everyday practice, ordinary training and feeling good. That, in a nutshell, is the essence of lifetime exercise.

Q: How do you think practitioners can increase their understanding of the spiritual aspect of karate?
A: Early on I trained to be strong and to get stronger still. But now, through karate, I have come to understand how to be weak, how to recover from weakness, and how to maintain my level of skill and fitness. I have come to understand and accept my weak side because I understand the importance of modesty and humility. Hard, challenging training helps cultivate modesty and humility, which naturally leads to a better understanding of the spiritual aspects of the martial arts. Therefore, keep train-

ing, don't give up and don't become discouraged by your moments of weakness. Instead, learn to value and cherish them for the ultimate spiritual growth that they will bring you.

Q: How much training should a "senior" karate-ka be doing to improve and get better at the art?
A: The how is what it is important and not the how much! Maintenance is the best target for an older senior student. When a senior student always focuses on physical improvement, he or she will inevitably become disappointed or frustrated. He should just try to maintain what he has; it is a more realistic approach. This kind of goal will provide an interesting, simulating and realistic target for the older senior student.

"For the older instructor, I have found that the proper ratio is 2/3 supplemental training to 1/3 technique training. This ratio helps promote the practice of karate as a lifetime exercise."

As the instructor gets older, supplemental training (Zen, breathing, stretching, et cetera) becomes more important. For the older instructor, I have found that the proper ratio is 2/3 supplemental training to 1/3 technique training. This ratio helps promote the practice of karate as a lifetime exercise.

Many instructors, in their youths, thought of karate as merely a sport to be won at all costs, much like professional football. And like many football coaches, such a karate instructor may allow himself to get out of shape and out of practice once he is past his physical prime. He still understands logically how to win, and he can continue to teach the players to win, but he himself does nothing to grow in his own practice. Of course, that is OK for a sports coach, but karate is a lifetime exercise, and therefore, the instructor, as he ages, must continue to train his own mind and body, over time increasing the ratio of supplemental training until he reaches that 2/3 ratio.

Karate Masters

"Ninety percent of life is composed of the ordinary and the mundane. An appreciation for the mundane is what is missing in today's karate training."

Q: Is there anything lacking in the way karate is taught today compared with those who were being taught in your early days?
A: Ninety percent of life is composed of the ordinary and the mundane. An appreciation for the mundane is what is missing in today's karate training. For example, when I was a student at Hosei University in Japan, we had no tournaments ... just basic dojo training. Our instructor would say, "Today we are going to do *heian sho-dan* 100 times." We would do it and be satisfied. Now, students always seem to be chasing the next big exciting event. Often, as a result, they have little patience for the type of ordinary practice and drilling that we did in the early days.

Q: Speaking of mundane things, you once said, "An individual has to find joy in the mundane." What did you mean?
A: Unfortunately, the vast majority of the human lifespan is spent in mundane, unconscious moments. To ignore and reject them is akin to discounting a large percentage of one's life, which, of course, is unfortunate. Those who are able to rejoice in the mundane are able to make the most of every moment of their lives, and ultimately, to cultivate their abilities to

engage the unconsciousness. To engage the unconscious does not mean to bring it into consciousness but rather to use its power to mobilize relaxation and focused concentration, and to open the mind to new experience, growth and progress. This lifelong pursuit of development is the fundamental basis of educational as opposed to sports karate.

While sport karate, which focuses energy exclusively on moments of excitement like competition and tournaments, may seem like the most efficient means of skill development, in fact, the career of the sport karate enthusiast tends to be short-lived, and within the reach of only a very few elite individuals. By contrast, educational karate promotes life-long pursuit of growth and enjoyment and is open to all, regardless of age or innate talent level. Of course, as always, balance is critical. Some degree of excitement, as is found in championship tournaments, builds a healthy competitive spirit and provides short-term motivation. Furthermore, in modern Western society, the dojo that completely rejects the sport-like aspects and entertainment value of karate is unlikely to survive for very long. However, it is our responsibility as practitioners of lifetime educational karate to pass on the importance of the mundane aspects of life and training and to cultivate the patience that allows us to tap into the unconscious power of those mundane moments. Therefore, while tournaments are valuable and exciting, the more mundane events, such as the daily practice of basics and kata, are also important.

Q: How can a parent help the karate teacher in this educational process?
A: Parents play a critical role in cultivating within their children an appreciation for the mundane, in karate as well as in all aspects of life. Children who are taught to value the ordinary learn patience and develop an understanding that real life is not always going to be like a trip to Disneyland! Many modern parents have a tendency to focus on big events such as exams and championship games. They push their children toward greater and greater achievements in high-profile or high-stakes experiences, thereby seeming to devalue the routine aspects of daily study and practice. Unfortunately, these children fail to experience the pleasure inherent in the painstaking pursuit of a goal and the personal pride that comes through perseverance itself. While success in the critical experiences of life is important, we must also offer our children, as well as ourselves, the opportunity to gain meaning from the lower-profile moments that make up the vast majority of life. These lower-profile moments form the backbone of community karate. I encourage you to

take advantage of the ordinary training opportunities that are part of the community karate experience and to recognize that they can be just as meaningful, if not more so, than competitive championship tournaments.

Q: What do you consider to be the most important qualities of a successful karate-ka?
A: A commitment to everyday training and an appreciation of the mundane. Train hard, finish, bow and say "thank you" for the opportunity to sweat. The most important quality for a practitioner of lifetime karate is the ability to find such satisfaction in ordinary training. Of course, for those students who want to participate in special events and tournaments, I say fine, but don't neglect the basic, ordinary training that makes up more than 90 percent of the practice of the art. Otherwise, you risk boredom and disenchantment in between those special events, which is quite sad. As an aside, the willingness to pass on your skill and knowledge to others as you grow and develop in your own art is also important. It is said that giving nothing to others is akin to harming them. The successful practitioner of lifetime karate is successful because he has had a satisfying life, not because he is a tournament champion or 10th degree black belt. Satisfaction comes from ability to enjoy the ordinary and willingness to pass on one's wisdom as one ages. That's all.

Q: Why do many students start falling away after two or three years of training?
A: They quit because they have no philosophy and therefore no destination or long-term plans and goals. Perhaps, for example, their only goal is to get a black belt. After accomplishing that objective, they may find themselves without motivation. It is the instructor's responsibility to help the student appreciate karate as a lifetime art rather than always seeking a particular rank or a medal or trophy. Students who seek only rank or who view karate solely as a competitive sport are likely to quit when they experience defeat, fail an exam or discover that they are not likely to be the next "Bruce Lee." Those students who understand karate as a lifetime exercise and recognize that karate follows a lifecycle much like the seasons of the year are far less likely to "fall away" after a few months or years of training.

Q: Sensei, you often speak about the four seasons of karate-do. Would you please elaborate on this?
A: I am fond of saying that educational karate differs from sports karate.

But, in what way are they different? Educational karate is a lifetime exercise. The original fundamental basis of the art is in Eastern philosophy, in particular, Zen Buddhism. This type of philosophy emphasizes peaceful self-reflection and an appreciation for the natural world. The spirituality of Zen Buddhism is based in self-knowledge and personal growth. By contrast, sports karate has more in common with certain aspects of Western culture that place a much higher value on achievement, accomplishment and external measures of success. Such a value system emphasizes a competitive spirit, which, to some extent is important, but in excess tends to preclude spiritual peacefulness.

Asian cultural symbols are often rooted in images of nature, and metaphors of the natural world are used to describe human material endeavors. So, for example, an analogy might be drawn between a person's practice of the martial arts over his lifetime and the four seasons of the year.

"Educational karate is a lifetime exercise. The original fundamental basis of the art is in Eastern philosophy, in particular, Zen Buddhism. This type of philosophy emphasizes peaceful self-reflection and an appreciation for the natural world."

Spring is a time for preparing the soil and sowing the seeds of the future. Although flowers begin budding in the spring, in general, the fruit has not yet fully ripened. In karate, spring represents kihon, the basic foundations of training. At this time, stance training, makiwara practice and fundamental techniques such as five-step sparring are essential. But, like the fruit that is picked before it reaches its peak of ripeness, the karate-ka in the spring of his training is undeveloped and not yet ready to reach his full potential. The practitioner of karate who rushes his training in order to compete in tournaments is like a green banana that is artificially ripened and rushed to market. On the surface, he may appear smooth, glossy and polished, but at the core he remains immature and underdeveloped. This type of student may be prone to injury, frustration and eventual burnout, especially when he achieves easy early victories. Then comes the summer phase. Here the basic foundations of springtime training are essential but are not, by themselves, sufficient for the student to fully

Karate Masters

"Pain and suffering are inevitable human experiences and carry with them an inherent opportunity for character development because of physical injury or defeat in competition, is an invaluable source of spiritual growth as well."

"ripen." Summertime training involves development of speed, timing and balance. At this time, the foundations that are laid during springtime preparation are further developed and augmented so that flexibility, stamina and strength reach their peak. Summer is when spring's basics are applied in kumite and kata competition. It is also a time of increased risk of injury. Unfortunately, often when a student is injured during competition, he becomes discouraged and quits training. However, the student who continues to train after suffering an injury benefits from the experience of overcoming adversity and surmounting pain. Pain and suffering are inevitable human experiences and carry with them an inherent opportunity for character development. Like an oyster that transforms a painful irritant into a beautiful pearl or the poet who is only able to create his poetry when he is suffering, the true martial artist mobilizes creative energy from his own pain and suffering. Suffering, either because of physical injury or defeat in competition, is an invaluable source of spiritual growth as well. In the world of competitive sports, where victory is everything, the winners are incapable of empathizing with the pain of the losers. By contrast, the martial artist who has experienced loss and injury develops a sense of compassion and sympathy that is typically absent in the highly competitive world of sports karate. During the summertime of karate training, victory and defeat, joy and pain, agony and ecstasy—when properly balanced—contribute to full ripening of the karate-ka's physical, emotional, mental and spiritual being.

In autumn, the knowledge that is cultivated in youth is harvested, and the practitioner uses that knowledge to form a philosophy and framework for the future. In the natural world, toward the end of summer, the turning of the leaves and the briskness in the air is accompanied by a sense of foreboding. Similarly, for the martial artist, as the physical prowess of summertime little-by-little begins to decline, there is often a feeling of sorrow or regret. The student who was at his peak a top competitor eventually finds himself beaten by a younger, stronger, faster opponent who is just beginning to enter his own "summertime" training. Jealousy, envy and discouragement are natural feelings as age takes its inevitable toll. However, those who understand the value of lifetime exercise can overcome discouragement through the pursuit of beauty and serenity in the practice of their art rather than the single-minded quest for competitive victory.

Finally, in the "winter" season, all the wisdom and skill that has been gathered in youth is ready to be shared with others through teaching and mentoring. The process of aging is accompanied by decreased flexibility and physical strength, and training becomes more difficult for most people. Those who are able to subordinate their own egos can create value by passing on their knowledge to the next generation of students. This is the time when soil must be readied for the next growing season and the seedlings cared for so that they may achieve their own full potential in the coming spring and summer. A discussion of this same basic idea can be found in the works of well-known developmental theorists like Erik Erikson. In *Identity and the Lifecycle,* Erikson suggested that those who are able to find value in their own histories and in sharing their wisdom and experience are more content as they age, and less prone to despair, depression and loneliness.

Unfortunately, many practitioners of sports karate invest 100 percent of their energy in the spring and summer of their art. They fail to recognize the value of autumn and winter and may become discouraged and lose their purpose once they are past their athletic prime. By contrast, those who recognize the value inherent in each stage of the seasonal cycle can gain much joy from participating in all phases of the natural rhythm represented by that cycle. Thus, in youth, the karate-ka is taught and coached by his respected sensei. In adulthood, he develops a style and philosophy of his own, based on the earlier teachings of his instructor. As he ages, he in turn becomes the respected teacher and gives back by passing on his own wisdom to a new generation of students. That is the natural order of lifetime karate-do.

The seasons of lifetime karate can also be compared to the pursuit of higher education. Practice of the basics and their application in kumite and kata are mandatory, like the "required courses" in a liberal arts degree. Development of one's style can be thought of as the "masters degree" stage. The "Ph.D.," the highest and most respected level, is achieved by those who pass on their experience as instructors and mentors. Success in competition and physical fitness alone are not sufficient to achieve this last level; spiritual development and the wisdom that can only be achieved with age are also necessary. Those who are fortunate enough to recognize this process will be able to enjoy a lifelong pursuit of happiness through the practice of their art. Those who do not (for example, sports karate enthusiasts who value only the spring and summer of their training careers) are likely to experience frustration and loss of motivation when they are forced to retire from competition.

In karate-do, the greatest value is not to be found in a trophy, or in fame, or the admiration of fans or in higher and higher black belt rankings. The true attainments of value are far less tangible. They come from the personal experience of the performance of the art itself, from practicing, teaching and demonstrating that art. There is a great sense of personal power and energy that comes from performing one's art. As the practitioner polishes and purifies his performance, others have the opportunity to observe, enjoy and benefit from that process as well. In sports karate, the observer may notice and be impressed by the power, strength and athleticism of the competitor. However, those who observe practitioners of lifetime karate are treated to a display of beauty that goes beyond physical power. That kind of beauty is obtainable by the lowest ranking white belt or by the oldest student in the dojo just as much as by the youthful tournament champion.

For many years I have taught college P.E. courses. One night I went to the gym where my class is usually held and found the room occupied. I opened the door to look inside and was surprised to see about 200 people participating in a yoga class! Yoga is also a lifetime exercise, but unlike karate, there is little or no focus on summertime training because there is no competitive component. As a result, yoga appeals to a broad segment of the population that is not interested in or capable of engaging in competitive sports. However, the value of the competitive aspects of training should also not be overlooked. Balance is important, as are all four seasons of the training lifecycle. But, where summer training is emphasized to the exclusion of all other aspects, eventually, the activity ceases to be an art, and becomes instead a pure competitive spectator sport like K-1 or cage fighting.

Right now, dojo enrollment seems to be at ebb, particularly relative to such activities as yoga. It is not helpful to be an alarmist, but neither is it prudent to ignore a potential problem. Because educational karate retains a core of dedicated students, it is easy to overlook declining enrollment.

Eventually, however, we may find that we have passed the "fail-safe" point and have lost our students to summer-only activities like sports-karate on the one hand and "summer-less" ones like yoga on the other. If we want to continue to pursue the opportunity to enjoy the four seasons of our beautiful art, we must make sure that we recognize the value of each of those seasons and communicate that value to our younger students. Otherwise, we risk losing those students who fail to understand that the ultimate destination of the karate-ka is not the summertime tournament but is instead a lifelong pursuit of growth, development and fulfillment throughout all four seasons of the karate-do lifecycle.

"A karate instructor is similar to a golf professsional. The entertainment value and popular interest is in the competitor, not the teacher. I am a teaching professional, not a celebrity. Popularity, notoriety and fame are simply not important to me."

Q: There is very little written about you in magazines. You obviously do not thrive on publicity like some martial artists. Why?
A: A karate instructor is similar to a golf professsional. Some golf professionals, such as Tiger Woods, are focused on competition. Others are teaching pros. The entertainment value and popular interest is in the competitor, not the teacher. I am a teaching professional, not a celebrity. Popularity, notoriety and fame are simply not important to me.

Q: Have there been times when you felt fear in your karate training?
A: When I was young, I always felt fear. But as I have gotten older and entered the later stages of my life cycle, I am no longer really worried about anything. Why are people afraid? I believe it is because they have unhealthy desires such as more and more money and more and more popularity. The possibility of not obtaining these desires makes people nervous. I am approaching the end of my life's journey. I still have aims, plans and dreams, but these are no longer guided by unhealthy desires. In my youth, of course, I had those needs, and therefore, I was afraid. I have discovered in life that the biggest enemy is fear. It is only through abandoning unhealthy desires that one can finally conquer fear. The Talmud,

Karate Masters

"Mental, emotional, physical and spiritual balance are essential to pursue perfection of character, the principles underpinning in the art of karate."

which I referred to earlier, defines one who is mighty as one who conquers evil impulses. In other words, strength of character is developed through emotional and spiritual control. This same principle is embodied in the dojo-kun, which instructs us to seek perfection of character and avoid unhealthy preoccupations.

Q: How important is the principle of balance in karate and life?
A: It is very important, and I'll try to fully explain it. Although I have lived for more than four decades in the United States, I continue to find it very difficult to explain the philosophical principles of karate to American students. While part of this difficulty is due to my own grasp of the English language, in large part it is also because the Japanese way of relating through language is sometimes very different from the Western communication style. As a result, for example, it has been virtually impossible for me to translate Master Funakoshi's teachings directly to my students. I have discovered that—rather than attempt direct translation—it is often more effective to find a similar philosophical concept in Western teachings and to use it to illustrate the ideas that Master Funakoshi expressed so eloquently in his own writings.

For example, Master Funakoshi spoke frequently about the importance of balance in all things. Mental, emotional, physical and spiritual balance are essential to pursue perfection of character, the principles underpinning in the art of karate. Many Western philosophers also discuss the importance of balance in achieving progress and character development. For example, the Talmud's discussion of achievement in the mental, physical, material and spiritual realms relates to the importance of balance. The Talmud poses four important questions that we might all ask ourselves, and they are as follows: Who is wise? Who is mighty? Who is rich? Who is honored? And then find the answers.

Q: What is the answer to the first question?
A: Wise is the one who learns from all teachers. Master Funakoshi taught that humility is essential for the development of mind and body. Of course, we may learn much from our higher ranking, experienced teachers. However, I have discovered during my years as a karate instructor that I also learn from my own students, in particular the beginning white belts. The technique and skill refinement imparted by my teachers must be in balance with the humility, enthusiasm and acceptance I am taught by my own lower ranking students.

Q: Who is mighty?
A: The one who conquers evil impulse. Here, the Talmud is teaching us that strength of character is developed through emotional and spiritual control. This principle is also embodied in the dojo-kun, which teaches us to seek perfection of character through control and balance in physical manifestations of emotional reactions. A reaction that is too weak leaves one vulnerable and in the position of a victim. A reaction that is too strong is a sign of lack of control and foolhardiness. Again, balance is the key.

Q: Who is rich?
A: The one who is satisfied with his portion. Karate is a lifetime exercise. As we age, our physical abilities change and may not be as impressive as they once were. At the same time, often our spiritual development accelerates, as we grow older. If we are able to accept these changes, we are not disappointed by the loss of physical stamina. When we recognize that the losses are more than balanced by the gains, we remain content with our portion and we are able to continue to gain satisfaction from all areas of our lives. If we fear aging and resent or deny the changes that accompany it, we become discontented, frustrated and ineffective in our practice of karate … or in any other life task.

Q: And finally, who is honored?
A: The one who honors others. The principle of respect for others is, of course, the underlying tenet of the dojo-kun. We are respected only to the extent that we respect others. This balance of respect is illustrated by the formal code of conduct karate students practice in the dojo. Ritualized interactions between students and teachers reinforce the importance of this balance of respect, which, in Eastern society, reaches far beyond the dojo walls.

Karate Masters

Q: What are your thoughts on the future of karate-do and what's your opinion about karate entering the Olympic Games?
A: The Olympics provide a wonderful opportunity for the world community to get together in a common endeavor. This is a beautiful thing. The top, most elite athletes perform in front of the entire world and are treated like heroes by millions of people. Kids dream about going to the Olympics some day. Unfortunately, Olympic-level talent and the dedication that it requires are not the norm, of course. Five-year-old kids train 10 hours a day honing their skill, which is amazing and beautiful. Mankind benefits tremendously from that kind of icon. But to focus on the Olympics as an ultimate goal for the vast majority of people in any sport would be ridiculous. As it happens, something like 80 percent of school-aged athletes drop out by the time they graduate high school, largely because they had unrealistic dreams and become disenchanted. So, symbols and icons such as the Olympic athlete are very important, but it is also extremely important not to forget the principle of lifetime exercise. Regardless of whether karate ever becomes an Olympic sport, the majority of practitioners will ultimately focus on the lifetime exercise aspects of the art. Don't quit and keep training. That is the essence of karate-do.

Q: Sensei, what is the value of non-competition practice of karate?
A: Today, unfortunately, many people get caught up in unrealistic Hollywood-influenced expectations of performance and assumptions that—with enough time and practice—they will ultimately become champion martial arts competitors and recipients of higher and higher black belts. It seems obvious that without an extraordinary level of talent and natural ability that it is unrealistic to expect to receive such things. Imagine, for example, that every weekend golfer truly believed that with practice and determination he or she could become the next Tiger Woods. Golf courses would soon empty as avid but ordinary golfers became discouraged and disappointed. Of course, most leisure golfers understand that they will never be Tiger Woods and are satisfied with the enjoyment and pleasure they gain from the activity itself. Karate practitioners must likewise understand that not everyone can become a champion and that happiness can come from enjoyment of the art rather than from certificates, belts, awards and trophies.

There are many benefits that come from participation in sports. For an elite group of athletes who possess a rare combination of talent, single-minded determination and luck—Tiger Woods and Michael Jordan—

money, fame and recognition are possible. For most of us, the benefits that we can expect may be somewhat less ambitious, but they need not be any less meaningful. For example, a second group participates in sports activities for purposes of physical fitness and the pleasure that comes from being strong and in good shape. Most of this second group is comprised of healthy young people, a few of whom, with great effort and practice, may some day become elite athletes and champions. A third group participates in sports activities for purposes of physical rehabilitation (to recover from an injury or reduce the risks of chronic illness, high blood pressure, et cetera). A fourth group consists of older people who desire to stay in shape, stave off the aging process and avoid depression and inactivity. In this regard, karate is similar to other sports. Sometimes it seems that everyone thinks they will eventually become Bruce Lee, but of course, it is more realistic and less frustrating to understand what type of exercise is important and which of the four groups is the best fit. Otherwise, where the focus is on tournament performance, many people become quickly discouraged and quit training. Likewise, where the focus is on chasing ever-higher belts and ranks, disappointment, frustration and impatience are common. Internal pleasure and happiness are lost in the quest for external symbols of achievement and glory.

"Regardless of whether karate ever becomes an Olympic sport, the majority of practitioners will ultimately focus on the lifetime exercise aspects of the art. Don't quit and keep training. That is the essence of karate-do."

Of course, those individuals who truly have the skill and drive to succeed competitively should not be discouraged from challenging themselves to do so. These individuals may achieve "Tiger Woods" success with lots and lots of practice, sweat and effort, and not a little luck. But, the vast majority of us risk appearing to be ineffective if we focus on glory rather than on development of our art for its own sake. Do not let this dismay you, however. Remember, there are many paths to ultimate happiness. Most of these roads do not end with a tournament trophy. Karate should be thought of as a lifetime exercise. Remember, even champions eventually retire and must seek pleasure in the more ordinary benefits enjoyed by members of the other three groups of sports participants.

The great Greek philosopher Socrates said, "Know thyself." Thus, seek happiness through understanding your real objectives, analyzing your abilities and needs, and deciding in which group of karate practitioners you truly and realistically belong. It is my responsibility to educate the current generation of karate-ka about the discouraging results of succumbing to the American celluloid image of martial arts and the importance of finding one's true path and true goals of training.

For example, championship fighters may not focus on learning the 26 shotokan kata (and in fact, may not even know most of the kata at all). It is up to the larger majority of us—those who view karate as a lifetime exercise meant to challenge the mind, body and spirit—to study the intricacies of these beautiful traditions and pass our learning on to each new generation of karate-ka. If we think of the trophy, the tournament title or the fifth dan certificate as the ultimate "work product" of karate society, most of us will feel that, our karate seems to be purposeless. We should not fall into the trap of believing this to be the case, however. According to Master Funakoshi, perfection of character and improvement in body and soul, not a tournament trophy, should be the ultimate goal of the practice of karate. Many benefits may be discovered along the journey toward self-improvement but it is only when one ceases to focus on external symbols of success and instead looks toward more meaningful goals of internal happiness that physical strength and spiritual fulfillment can be attained. We must avoid fixating on championships and glamorous tournament performances; otherwise, we risk spinning our wheels, forever chasing an unobtainable goal.

Q: What do you think are the main reasons why people come to your school, and how do these motives affect their progress in the later years of their practice?
A: Just recently, I distributed a questionnaire at the dojo to collect student opinions about our training program and the quality of instruction. Preliminary results indicate that, in general, students are very satisfied with training in kihon (basics) and in karate's philosophical principles. Furthermore, many students rated kihon, kata and mental/spiritual development as the aspects of training most important to them at this time. These results greatly encourage me because they suggest that the areas rated most highly and deemed most important by my students are, in fact, the very ones upon which I focus my teachings, and those that are most essential to Master Funakoshi's and Master Nakayama's basic principles of shotokan. I do not believe that the survey results are mere coincidence, rather that they are a reflection of my students' understanding of the critical role of basics in shotokan karate. This being the case, it seems

that I have succeeded in passing on to my students some of the most important teachings of Masters Funakoshi and Nakayama.

Q: Why have you chosen to refocus your teaching on the basic skills rather than on more flashy or intricate techniques and applications, even though some people may consider the basics less interesting?
A: Unlike in most other sports or activities, *kime* and *Ki* (spirit) must also accompany the practice of these techniques; otherwise, improvement will be elusive. Therefore, you must understand the importance of this type of basic training and believe in the benefits you will receive from it. In karate, the focus of basic training is development of the body's core, known in Japanese as the *seikatanden*, and its connection with the hips and legs. The triad of the seikatanden, hips and legs forms the fundamental body structure on which all stances and techniques depend. If I were to focus in class on more fancy and elaborate techniques, students may find class more exciting; however, the benefits to the fundamental body structure would be more limited. By focusing on the basics, over the long term, one begins to appreciate the improvement in one's form and will notice the positive effect that a stronger, better developed fundamental body structure has on one's ability to perform the more elaborate aspects of karate. In time, I guarantee that the development of fundamental body structure will, in turn, be reflected in a stronger, healthier mind, body and spirit, as well as in better karate!

In addition to a renewed focus on basics, I also provide more training in kata, both because my students have expressed an interest, and because I believe in the maxim that "knowledge is power." The more you know, the more you will desire to learn, the more interested in your art you will become, and, paradoxically it may appear, the greater will be your commitment to the basics. In shotokan karate, we have 26 kata. Of course, I do not expect to learn all 26 kata to perfection; that would be impossible. But kata, performed with grace and Ki, can ignite the imagination, inspire the spirit and provide meaning to one's practice of karate, as well as foster an appreciation for solid fundamental techniques.

Q: How does the concept of knowing yourself affect a karate-ka's training and his personal development as a human being?
A: There are four different kinds of people. Members of the first group never even ask for advice or instruction. Everything they do has to be done "my way or no way." Often, they act without thinking at all, and certainly without considering other more qualified opinions. Members of

Karate Masters

"People live their lives according to many different styles. As the philosopher Victor Frankl observed, 'Suffering gives meaning to life.' Without pain, one cannot fully appreciate pleasure."

the second group may ask for advice, and when they receive it, they hear it but do not listen to what they hear. While they may solicit expert opinion, they continue to do things their own way, never changing in response to the suggestions they receive. The third type of person solicits advice and then incorporates it in its entirety, but without critically evaluating it or tailoring it the specifics of his situation. The fourth and final group is the one I think of as superior. Members of this group seek qualified advice, listen to that advice, evaluate it and then incorporate it selectively and thoughtfully into their unique situations.

Many students exclude themselves from membership in the third or fourth group of people, not because they are unwilling to heed advice, but simply because they fail to ask for it! Of course, many students are reluctant to ask for instruction because they are intimidated, shy or overly reserved, or they do not want to interrupt their busy instructor. However, with the proper modest and respectful approach, an interested student can and should request assistance, feedback or advice. A smart student looks for an opportunity when the instructor is free and approaches the instructor with a well thought-out question. Once the student receives a response, it is his responsibility to make use of it. By pondering the response and incorporating it thoughtfully along with other qualified advice and instruction, the student gains membership into the most superior of the four groups.

People live their lives according to many different styles. As the philosopher Victor Frankl observed, "Suffering gives meaning to life." Without pain, one cannot fully appreciate pleasure. And without personal suffering, one is less capable of feeling true compassion or empathy. Suffering makes philosophers out of all of us, even those who have gone through life mostly thoughtlessly.

After more than 50 years of karate training, I believe that I understand how suffering can lead to philosophical growth and character development. Socrates said "Know thyself." Examine yourself, and critically evaluate what kind of person you are. Do you have a philosophy? Do you appreciate the ordinary as well as the extraordinary? Use the pleasure and pain your karate training brings you to help you increase your self-knowledge and enjoyment of life. Do not wait for bad news or tragedy to make you into a philosopher. Live each moment as if it is the most important one of your existence, for "right now" is all we really have. The past makes us what we are, but we cannot change it, nor can we predict the future. The present is what is important because it is where we learn from the mistakes of the past and plan for whatever the future may bring.

Q: Sensei, is there anything else you would like to add?
A: I came to the United States more than four decades ago with a mission to spread Master Funakoshi's and Master Nakayama's philosophy and teachings. That mission remains a work in progress, and I will never give up, no matter what circumstances may bring. It is my life's work, my passion and the *raison d'etre* for my dojo. I hope that you will make it your mission as well, so that we may pass the baton on to the next generation of karate-ka, and ensure that we and generations of the future may continue to benefit from the beauty that is Master Funakoshi's karate. I have managed to survive as a karate instructor in the U.S. for over 40 years now. Not only have I survived, but I have been fortunate to be given the opportunity to serve the community through promotion of the art of shotokan, as well as through the charitable work that the Western States Karate Championship Association promotes, year after year. That in itself is a miracle which provides me with much satisfaction. This miracle is the result of the combined effort and commitment of many, many dedicated people over the years. I am just an ordinary man, but as a group, we have been able to accomplish extraordinary things because so many people have joined together and operated as a team for so long. I am very proud of what we have accomplished. As you may know, my own personal belief is in the Eastern notion of reincarnation. If I can be of service to others in this lifetime, perhaps someday when I pass over into the next, I will be privileged to encounter the great Masters such as Master Funakoshi, Master Nakayama, and Master Itoe, and the many other great individuals that pioneered the beauiful art of shotokan karate. O

Akio Minakami

A Warrior's Journey

Born and raised in Tokyo, Japan, Shihan Minakami began his formal martial arts training at 7. He belonged to the Jujitsu/Kodokan Judo School under Takagi Sensei. Takagi Sensei was a 9th-degree Kodokan black belt. Minakami moved to the United States in 1963. During his first years in America, Shihan Minakami made a name for himself as an outstanding karate man. By age 21, he was the first man ever to win both kata and kumite at the All-Hawaii Championships.

His most outstanding accomplishments include winning five gold medals at the Hayashi-Ha Shito-ryu Kai International Championships and five gold medals at the All-Japan Karate Championships. He was also the first man ever to win five gold medals at the AAU National Championships.

In 1983, Minakami received his *Shihan certificate* from both Hayashi-Ha Shito-ryu Kai and from the Federation of All-Japan Karate-do Organization (FAJKO). Shihan Minakami was the first to receive a unanimous passing grade, meaning all 11 masters (representing the four major styles) on the examining board gave him their approval. This is an amazing honor for which he will always be known. In 1985, Shihan Minakami founded the Minakami Karate Dojo. It was his goal to teach traditional Japanese karate and pass his knowledge onto dedicated students who would learn and enjoy the techniques, as well as attitudes, of the true martial artist. He is quick to make every opportunity a blessing for karate and is dedicated to improving the art and creating more interest in it. "Nowadays, karate is available to everyone who really wants to learn. I can't take it with me, and I want to leave something of value behind," he says with a smile on his face.

Q: How long have you been practicing the martial arts?
A: My father is a martial artist and naturally I played and wrestled with him as a boy. Our house was only 50 feet away from the Judo Dojo in Koenji, Tokyo, and I grew up listening to good *kiai* every evening. On August 12, 1956, following an interview by Kiyokazu Takagi Sensei, I enrolled at this dojo. Takagi Sensei was a Kodokan 9th Dan. Before the war, he was Shihan

Karate Masters

"When I was 28 and a fifth-degree black belt in karate, I wanted to broaden my martial arts practice—not only to become a stronger fighter—but also to become more skilled in natural movement and discover greater wisdom and spirituality."

at the Military Academy. After the war, he was Shihan at the Tokyo Metropolitan Police Department. He explained to me that the martial arts are not for fighting but to discipline one's self to become a good citizen. He said that our spirit must be strong enough not to be drawn into petty quarrels, even if it means running away. He used to say, *"Kunshi ayaukini chikayorazu,"* which means that a wise man never courts danger and *"Kichigai nihamono,"* which means that a crazy person with a weapon is dangerous. I was 7 years old and just wanted to learn how to fight. It's funny, but the older I get, the more I understand what he meant. Now I teach the same way.

Q: In how many styles of karate or other methods have you trained?
A: I practiced karate at the JKA when the headquarters were in Suidobashi, Tokyo. I also practiced kyokushinkai and met Oyama Sensei. I had seen his book, *What is Karate?*, and I thought he was going to be big. I was surprised to find that he was short. He was a powerful man, friendly and humble. I learned *tekenjutsukai* from Mr. Bingo in Hawaii. I also practiced with my friend's uncle, Professor Chow, the founder of American kenpo. I remember him pounding a huge flagpole and making it ring loudly with each hit.

In 1965, I met shito-ryu instructor Chuzo Kotaka Sensei. I had never seen a front kick like his. I thought that no one could withstand his kick without being hurt. I wanted to learn this kick from him so I joined his dojo. In 1974, Kotaka Sensei introduced me to his teacher, Teruo Hayashi Soke. I have been with the Hayashi-Ha Shito-ryu Kai ever since.

When I was 28 and a fifth-degree black belt in karate, I wanted to broaden my martial arts practice—not only to become a stronger fighter—but also to become more skilled in natural movement and discover greater wisdom and spirituality. Luckily, I found Nobuto Omoto Sensei, 7th dan in kendo. He was a graduate of the Budosenmongakko in Kyoto, which was shut down right after General McArthur occupied Japan. People say that this was the last samurai school. Omoto Sensei explained that the *kuden* or verbal teaching between the student and the teacher at the *Budosenmongakko* was usually done in a relaxed, private situation. Omoto Sensei said that he learned a lot of the inner teachings of the martial arts when he was serving tea to his instructors in their office.

When I put away his *bogu* after each class, Omoto Sensei would talk to me about how to be a samurai. He did not talk just about fighting. He also talked about *bushi no tashinami* or the etiquette and knowledge of a martial artist, including taking care of equipment, sewing, cooking, singing and even partying.

Also, I am a good friend with Toshihiro Oshiro Shihan, and I have been lucky enough to meet his teacher, *yamanni-ryu* Master Chogi Kishaba Sensei. I have had the opportunity to talk to him many times about the martial arts.

I have a black belt in Kodokan judo from Kiyokazu Takagi Sensei, a 3rd Dan in kendo from Nobuto Omoto Sensei, a 5th Dan in *yamanni-ryu bojutsu* from Chogi Kishaba Sensei, an 8th Dan in hayashi-ha-shito-ryu kai from Teruo Hayashi Soke and a 7th Dan from the Japan Karate Federation.

"There were no styles before Funakoshi Sensei, Mabuni Sensei, Otsuka Sensei and Miyagi Sensei. The original ryu-kyu bujutsu—*which includes what we now call sumo,* bo, sai, nunchaku *and empty-hand fighting—was originally called simply "te" or "ti" in Okinawan pronunciation."*

Q: With all the technical changes during the last 30 years, do you think there is still "pure" shotokan, shito-ryu, goju-ryu, etc? What is your opinion about mixing karate styles?

A: There were no styles before Funakoshi Sensei, Mabuni Sensei, Otsuka Sensei and Miyagi Sensei. The original *ryu-kyu bujutsu*—which includes what we now call sumo, *bo, sai, nunchaku* and empty-hand fighting—was originally called simply "*te*" or "*ti*" in Okinawan pronunciation.

We all study how to kill a person as quickly and efficiently as possible. If someone is doing this better, it seems foolish to say, "I won't do it; it's not in my style." We all have a body, two arms, two legs and so forth.

Karate Masters

"If you see something that works, take it and make it yours. No style is better than the others, but the person practicing and the person teaching make a difference."

And we have books, DVD, TV, seminars and are more informed than ever. So forget about style and be smart!

Karate should become better with time. If nothing changes, then you must wonder about the teacher's practice. Isn't it the same with electronics or cars? Don't they get better every year? Open your mind and look at things around you. If you see something that works, take it and make it yours. No style is better than the others, but the person practicing and the person teaching make a difference. Sadly, I have seen many people who think that their style is best ... people with a limited outlook. We should always stay open-minded and be aware. Be a martial artist.

For instance, Sean Roberts Sensei leads my dojo in Hawaii. His background is in shotokan from Enoeda Sensei, but he incorporates my karate and teaching into his shotokan. Although I don't know the sequences of shotokan kata, I still can help Roberts Sensei with how to kick, punch and move more naturally. He endeavors to blend his karate experiences with my karate teaching.

Q: How would you describe the life and dedication of your teacher, Soke Hayashi Teruo, to the arts of budo?
A: There was a time when Hayashi Soke visited Okinawa so he could learn from a particular master. At first, he was not accepted as a student. He was monzen-barai or kicked out at the gate. Thus, he slept under a bridge to hide from the weather. He tried again day after day. He didn't give up until finally he was accepted. Soke knows how to be at the bottom as well as at the top of his field. I don't think many teachers in mainland Japan have done things like this.

Back in the early 1970s, Soke put less emphasis on the aesthetics of the techniques. Nevertheless, his karate was extremely dangerous. Later, when he became chief referee at the Second World Championship in Los Angeles in 1974, he began to emphasize more "modern" or athletic karate that was safer and easier to learn. Tournament karate has since flourished around the world.

Soke disguised his natural movements to superficially look like "modern" karate. Just six months before he passed on, I was privileged to have private lessons with him. We worked out together strenuously for three hours a day, five days in a row. His karate was fast, strong and precise. It would have been impossible for him to move like this at his age without natural movement.

"Competition karate has many regulations and is safe. It is a sport enjoyed by many people, especially kids. As long as it is fun, then it is a good thing."

Soke always allowed us the freedom to try different ways to learn natural movement. As a result, our training methods changed and even our kata changed over time. When we went too far astray, Soke would make corrections. Many times we may not have understood his adjustments right away, but it was inappropriate to ask for further explanation without first trying. After a few years of effort, if we had to question, then we went through the chain of command. Tadashi Hashimoto Sensei headed the Hayashi-ha technical department, and he usually answered for Soke. He researched natural moves more than anybody else in the organization, and his karate is very dangerous.

Q: Karate is nowadays often referred to as a sport. Would you agree with this definition or do you think it is only budo?
A: Of course, karate can have a sporting element. Competition karate has many regulations and is safe. It is a sport enjoyed by many people, especially kids. As long as it is fun, then it is a good thing. However, if poor etiquette and rude conduct should emerge, then we should stop hosting tournaments.

I don't believe that most people appreciate budo, which should be distinguished from *bujutsu* or fighting techniques. Budo is to empty one's

Karate Masters

"Awareness and control of breathing are important if we are to be present in what we are doing. This is why the samurai practiced so much zazen or sitting meditation. It is an essential part of budo. It is not for relaxation. It is to control the mind, and this is difficult!"

self through the martial arts ... to be fully present here and now with no extra thoughts in mind. Just deal with whatever you are doing now and that's all. This is challenging because we are thinking animals. It is like reading a book and not remembering what you've read. The mind is easily distracted.

Awareness and control of breathing are important if we are to be present in what we are doing. This is why the samurai practiced so much *zazen* or sitting meditation. It is an essential part of budo. It is not for relaxation. It is to control the mind, and this is difficult!

Q: How do you see the state of karate in the world at the present time?
A: Competition kumite has been similar in every style for a long time, as competitors adopt the movements of the champions. The same evolution is happening now even in kata tournaments. I went to the All-Osaka Championship. I was surprised to see the competitors all doing the same kata from the JKF. I couldn't tell the difference in styles like before.

My friend Oshiro Shihan is an excellent shorin-ryu and yamanni-ryu teacher. Each year he is invited to Europe to teach—and not only in shorin-ryu dojo. These days I think that many people appreciate that karate skill is beyond any particular style. Such open-mindedness is important and promotes development. For example, the late, great Enoeda Sensei gave me permission to teach at some of his European shotokan dojo. I really respected his open-mindedness.

Q: Do you think that karate in the West is at the same level with Japanese karate?
A: There used to be a big difference because the Japanese were smaller in stature. But now, because of the change of diet, Japanese people are taller and larger than in the past. In terms of competition, everyone is the same. However, I think that the general skill level is much higher in Japan. In the

U.S., maybe 30 people out of 100 look good. In Japan, 80 out 100 look good. It comes from the educational system and the culture. In Japan, the people tend to think more alike. Everybody is going in the same direction. In America, there are so many different cultures and so many different ways of thinking. Everybody is going in a different direction. If the American educational system were different, American karate could be different.

Q: Some people think it is necessary to go to Japan to train; do you agree with this point of view?
A: No. Nearly all karate populations blindly follow their teacher and do not recognize good karate. This is equally true in Japan as it is in the rest of the world. So, while there are many good traditions that can best be experienced in Japan, it is not necessary to go to Japan to learn karate dogma. Take advantage of wisdom that is all around. Learn from other's kindness. Be hard on yourself and be kind to others, wherever you are. This brings discipline to your practice and harmony with fellow human beings. Eventually, with a good heart, you are able to make your own traditions and culture. With good culture and experience, you will develop wisdom and the ability to see good karate.

"Learn from other's kindness. Be hard on yourself and be kind to others, wherever you are. This brings discipline to your practice and harmony with fellow human beings."

Q: What are the most important points of your karate philosophy?
A: Be self-reliant. Karate training is for you and for no one else. Make yourself strong and be smart. Avoid violence whenever possible but fight without fear if you must. In an emergency, there is no one to rely on but you.

Kanto no seishin means to do your best with all your vitality. Have a fighting spirit and a good kiai.

Karate Masters

"Karate is a life-long endeavor that can bring us happiness. If it doesn't, then we should look for something else to make us content. Either way, keep smiling. If your practice is too serious, then it is no fun and you won't want to practice."

Fukutsu no seishin means to never give up, even when the going gets tough. To quit is to die.

Hissho no seishin means to have a sure-win feeling no matter what. Even when faced with a superior opponent, you still have a chance. Keep in mind that he is not perfect and you will find a way to win. Without this confidence you will surely bring defeat upon yourself. Even if you were to lose, you did your best. Like the ancient warriors said, "That which burns to ashes has no regrets."

Be calm. Keep a cool head no matter what. We realize our potential with a calm mind.

Be strong. Keep a good spirit to withstand anything and persevere.

Be proud. Not better-than-you proud but afraid-of-nothing proud.

Be happy. Karate is a life-long endeavor that can bring us happiness. If it doesn't, then we should look for something else to make us content. Either way, keep smiling. If your practice is too serious, then it is no fun and you won't want to practice.

Make mistakes in training and in life. It is OK to make mistakes. It is necessary to make mistakes. Learn and try not to make the same mistake again.

Be sincere. Don't waste time doing things half-heartedly.

Be patient. If you want to prepare fast food, it may take you a couple of weeks to learn the ropes. However, if you want to be a good French chef, it will take many years and you never stop learning. Karate is the same. There is always more.

Q: Do you feel that you still have further to go in your studies of karate and budo?
A: In college, you take classes, get a degree and then you're done. In

budo, or spiritual training through the martial arts, there is no graduation. There is no end to experience and wisdom. If you go deep into budo, it is no different to the Chinese Dao and the Japanese Zen. It teaches us to do good and not evil—like religion.

Even physically, as we grow older and weaker, we still have the opportunity to discover and develop natural movement. There can be no such thing as a perfect kata. We can go deeper and deeper into one kata and continue to uncover hidden skill. This too is a never-ending process.

Q: What is it that keeps you motivated after all these years?
A: I make every effort to empty myself through the ryu-kyu martial arts. It keeps me more aware of how vast nature is and how small I am. Hayashi Soke describes karate as being full of *gokui* (secrets) and students need to be wise enough to figure them out. Karate is a beautiful art. The deeper you go, the better it gets. There is so much to learn and each small moment of discovery is blissful and ecstatic. So I keep trying. I find it spiritually rewarding and definitely worth the effort.

"There is no end to experience and wisdom. If you go deep into budo, it is no different to the Chinese Dao and the Japanese Zen. It teaches us to do good and not evil—like religion."

Karate is a personal experience in nature that needs nothing and no one else. It is always freely available, here and now! I feel lucky to be alive and to be able to practice karate. I feel grateful to my parents for bringing me into this world.

One day we were at a park in front of a huge pine tree. My teacher, Hayashi Soke, told me not to become like this pine tree. It was straight and tall. He said it was tasteless. Become like the pine tree on a beach that is weather-beaten and has character. I relate to this because I have been living in the United States and so, for the most part, I am self-taught. I have made and continue to make many mistakes. But this is who I am. I developed my own character like Soke's pine tree.

Karate Masters

It is not always easy. I remember having a bad financial problem and being depressed. Soke Hayashi came up to me and asked why I was so depressed. When I explained the reason, he started to laugh. He told me not to feel sorry for myself. There are people in this world who are without food and very ill. You are not sick and not starving. Just work hard and you will recover in no time. So practice with good spirit and kiai! Soke helped me to realize that depression is all in the mind. I thank Soke Hayashi for his inspiration.

Q: How do you think a practitioner can increase his understanding of the spiritual aspect of karate?
A: We are born into this world with pure, uninhibited feelings. Whether a boy or a girl, we don't cry half-heartedly. We are completely free and confident. We don't care what people think of us. We just do our own thing. We cry with all of our might. Our first kiai is the loudest. As we grow up, we change slowly according to our experience. By observing our surroundings and through our intelligence, we learn how to act. Don't be an actor. Don't act cool. Don't act tough. Be true to your original self. Be true to your heart. Live like your baby-time kiai ... with no hesitation and with all your might. Abandon small-minded images of who you want to be. Don't waste time pretending to be somebody that you're not. Just get on your life now! This is genuine confidence. This is your true self. Like a baby, you are free. Be patient. Re-discovering our original confidence is a life-long task.

Q: Soke Hayashi was an expert in the weaponry art of kobudo. Do you think it helps empty-hand karate physically to train with weapons?
A: Our body is the same whether we are holding a weapon or not. The stances, steps, direction changes and upper body movements for kobudo are just the same as for empty-hand. It should be no surprise then that weapons give you clues to understanding natural movement and hidden fighting techniques. Both weapons and empty-hand should be practiced to fully appreciate ryu-kyu bujutsu. Even the founder of shotokan karate, Funakoshi Gichin Sensei, practiced weapons.

Also, if you practice weapons you don't need to lift weights or do most other types of supplemental training. Using weapons strengthens the body, legs, arms and grip, all of which are necessary in fighting.

Q: What's your opinion of makiwara training?
A: Target training is important to make sure our joints are correctly aligned, stable and coordinated with our breathing at the moment of impact. This we can do with makiwara, punching bags or even portable targets. Each practitioner should use whatever works for him. I prefer to use punching bags that allow me to hit with all my might without risk of injury.

Q: What advice would you give to students on the question of supplementary training?
A: Stretching must be done every day. I like running for fun. Weight training should be done only *hodo-hodo* or moderately. Too much muscle will prevent you from being able to move smoothly and naturally. None of these are necessary if you practice weapons such as bojutsu or *saijutsu*.

"Target training is important to make sure our joints are correctly aligned, stable and coordinated with our breathing at the moment of impact. This we can do with makiwara, punching bags or even portable targets."

Q: To achieve good self-defense skills for a real situation, do you think it is necessary to engage in free fighting?
A: Free fighting and self-defense are completely different. Free fighting has rules. Self-defense has no such limits. In self-defense, just think, "What can I do?" at every moment. Do whatever it takes. For example, you could even throw a teapot to distract your opponent and then poke him in the eyes.

Karate Masters

"Kata teaches us how to naturally move our bodies from point A to B. When done correctly, such natural movement is delightful. Nothing compares; it feels like bliss."

Q: Do you think bunkai is important in the understanding of kata and karate in general?

A: Kata teaches us how to naturally move our bodies from point A to B. When done correctly, such natural movement is delightful. Nothing compares; it feels like bliss. This is the true wisdom left for us in kata by the ancient ryu-kyu warriors. It is up to us to discover, temper and polish this wisdom. Furthermore, natural movement will stimulate and unclog the meridians in our body and therefore bring us good health and great Ki or universal energy. Movements that use just muscles and tension will strain the body and, sooner or later, cause injury, especially in older age. By comparison, bunkai is easy. Knowing the bunkai is not enough. If the movement is not expert, then the art will be at a low level.

Q: To progress in the arts, how do you think a sensei should prepare and schedule his personal training?

A: First, we should practice our conduct 24 hours each day. Physically, we must train in class with the students, not necessarily the whole class, but at least here and there we need to show the students what to do. When demonstrating, it is important to move well.

We should learn from books. We should study other martial arts. We should scrutinize old photographs of ryu-kyu teachers, but it is important to be selective because not all famous teachers are highly skilled. We must solve many puzzles. Why did they practice kata in preparation for combat? Is our kata suited for combat? Can we find similar movements in other Japanese martial arts? For example, kendo and *kenjutsu* can help us to understand how karate developed from te. Their kata are far more natural and suitable for combat than the karate kata that we see in tournament these days. Why? The master will keep researching, whereas a novice will be satisfied if he can take a step. There are endless secrets in how to take one step, so how can we master it in one lifetime? Never give up; research in one skill extensively. Keep scrutinizing and analyzing kihon and you will be an expert in the *jutsu* or art some day.

There is no limit to the secrets hidden in the kata. I am not talking about *bunkai*. I am talking about natural movement, such as how to take one step forward or make one turn. Often, this requires a very sophisticated level of kihon or basics. For this reason, kata is important. We should practice kata. Being a sensei will take a lifetime. Isn't it nice to have a lifetime's work?

Q: What do you consider to be the most important qualities of a successful karate-ka?
A: For me, success as a karate-ka is measured not by how famous you are or how many students you have, but by the quality of your movement. How much did the person research natural movement? We must realize or become enlightened to a better way and find out the secrets. This is not easy. If a person is enlightened to the natural moves, the person is successful in karate.

Q: What do you see as the most important attributes of a student?
A: A good student will do his or her homework. He does not practice only in the dojo. He takes responsibility for his own development and does not expect only to be taught. If he wants to learn, he has to make an effort. Nobody has to teach him anything.

Q: Whom would you like to have trained with that you have not?
A: I would like to have studied Zen and sword under Tesshu Yamaoka. He was the Emperor's bodyguard after the Meiji restoration in Japan. He was a highly spirited person and the way he thought and trained would have given inspiration to my soul.

I would like to have studied Zen under Takuan Soho Osho, and he

Karate Masters

"Karate should be recognized as representing the emptying or abandonment of extra thoughts and the awareness of what we are doing now. We develop this attitude in our training in te and carry it into all our learning and life."

was also known as a Takuan priest. He had no training in swordmanship, but he knew about the human mind. He was very wise, and he could lead you in the right direction. He taught Munenori Yagyu, the Shogun's martial arts teacher, how to free his mind.

I would like to have studied under Musashi Miyamoto. His famous book *Gorin No Sho* or the *Book of Five Rings*, is a good technical martial arts book and highly recommended.

These three people have already passed on, but I am still learning from them indirectly, through their words. I have read their books many times, especially when I'm down or confused in my life. Their books give me Ki or energy and direction. I am here now, free and I can do anything I wish. All my suffering is delusion. It will pass and be forgotten in time.

Q: What is your thought on the future of karate-do and what's your opinion about karate entering in the Olympic Games?
A: Olympics or not, karate can develop much further in the future. My hope for the 21st century is that karate becomes more widely understood for its philosophy and as a way of living. Karate should be recognized as representing the emptying or abandonment of extra thoughts and the awareness of what we are doing now. We develop this attitude in our

training in *te* and carry it into all our learning and life. This way, moment to moment, we live life to the fullest. That which burns to ashes has no regrets!

Q: Anything else you would to add for the readers?
A: While I was preparing my answers for this interview, my teacher, Soke Hayashi Teruo, passed on to the next world where we all have to go some day. I experienced impermanence in a very strong way.

During my last visit to see him, we practiced Monday through Friday for three hours each day. We worked with vigor and vitality—training with all our might. We performed kata together at full speed many times so that he could teach me the slow and fast parts of the kata at the same time. He left the *tatami* two to three times, for about five minutes at a time, and that is all the rest he took.

Two weeks later he was admitted into the hospital and never came out. He passed away six months later. During this time, only his family and two of his disciples knew where he was. His wish was not to show his ill self while lying down. This is the samurai teaching of not showing your sleeping face to your retainer. Now that he is gone, we remember him only as a strong warrior. He was truly a 21st century samurai. O

"There is no limit to the secrets hidden in the kata. I am not talking about bunkai. I am talking about natural movement, such as how to take one step forward or make one turn."

Anthony Mirakian

The Legendary Pioneer

ANTHONY MIRAKIAN IS CURRENTLY THE MOST ACTIVE SENIOR MEIBUKAN INSTRUCTOR. HE STARTED HIS GOJU TRAINING UNDER MASTER TOGUCHI AT THE SHOREIKAN DOJO IN THE EARLY 1950S WHILE STATIONED AT THE KADENA AIR FORCE BASE IN OKINAWA. HE ALSO TRAINED THERE WITH OKINAWAN KARATE MASTER RYURITSU ARAKAKI. WHEN ARAKAKI SENSEI NOTICED MIRAKIAN'S PASSION AND COMMITMENT TO THE ART, HE ADVISED HIM TO TRAIN UNDER THE FOREMOST GOJU-RYU KARATE MASTER ON OKINAWA, GRANDMASTER MEITOKU YAGI, THE TOP STUDENT AND SUCCESSOR OF THE LATE FOUNDER OF GOJU-RYU KARATE, GRANDMASTER CHOJUN MIYAGI. MIRAKIAN WAS THE FIRST WESTERNER GRANDMASTER MEITOKU YAGI TAUGHT AND THE FIRST TO RECEIVE A BLACK BELT FROM HIM. MIRAKIAN SENSEI LEFT OKINAWA AND RETURNED TO THE U.S. IN NOVEMBER OF 1959. ONCE HE GOT ESTABLISHED IN THE EARLY 1960S, HE STARTED TEACHING MEIBUKAN GOJU-RYU IN THE PUREST FORM IN THE BOSTON AREA. IN 1990, DAI SENSEI YAGI PROMOTED MIRAKIAN SENSEI TO *KU-DAN* [9TH DAN] *HANSEI*. HE IS THE ONLY NORTH AMERICAN OUTSIDE OF OKINAWA THAT HOLDS THIS RANK AND TOP HONOR.

SENSEI MIRAKIAN'S ACADEMY IN WATERTOWN, MASSACHUSETTS, IS THE NORTH AMERICAN HEADQUARTERS OF THE MEIBUKAN GOJU-RYU KARATE-DO ASSOCIATION BASED IN KUME, NAHA CITY, OKINAWA. IN 1972, GRANDMASTER YAGI APPOINTED MIRAKIAN SENSEI THE OVERSEAS GENERAL MANAGER OF THE MEIBUKAN ASSOCIATION. HIS DOJO OFFERS OKINAWAN GOJU-RYU KARATE TRAINING IN ITS PUREST FORM. MIRAKIAN SENSEI IS A TRUE AND EXCELLENT EXAMPLE OF THE BENEFITS OF LIFE-LONG KARATE TRAINING.

Q: You arrived in Okinawa in the early 1950s. How would you characterize Okinawan karate in that era?
A: This was "The Golden Age" of Okinawan karate. It was during this time that karate training first became available to Westerners, which caused a great impetus in the propagation of Okinawan karate to the Western world. During these years, Okinawan karate was taught in a traditional way as an art form of self-defense. The karate masters upheld the old karate values and standards and placed great emphasis on *dojo-kun* (etiquette). They took pride in patiently teaching their national art to Westerners, as well as

Karate Masters

"Because Okinawa was alternatively dominated by China and Japan, Okinawans were forced to develop unarmed martial art techniques to defend themselves against larger and stronger armed foes."

Okinawans. Karate was presented in a dignified, strict manner. To a Westerner, it appeared fascinating, challenging and mysterious.

Q: Do you think something has been lost, as karate has been modernized?
A: Yes. Unfortunately, much of the essence and spirit of traditional karate has been lost. Since the advent of karate championships, many practitioners are competing to win at any cost. This approach is not the traditional aim of Okinawan goju-ryu karate-do.

Q: Why Okinawa? How could an island so small and remote have produced the world's best-known martial art?
A: That's a very interesting question. Okinawa had the perfect chemistry to develop the art of karate. The Okinawans had the time to devote to the martial arts. Theirs was a quiet and simple agrarian and fishing society, without distractions. Because Okinawa was alternatively dominated by China and Japan, Okinawans were forced to develop unarmed martial art techniques to defend themselves against larger and stronger armed foes. Also, they were forced to look inward and develop an inner strength that characterizes the art. Okinawans are a civilized and peace-loving people, and these traits are reflected in the unique moral foundation of their art.

Q: When you first arrived in Okinawa, how did you find a karate school?
A: Accidentally. A friend and I hired a taxi and asked the driver to take us to a karate school. He took us to a judo dojo. One of the students there directed the taxi driver to take us to the district of Nakanomachi. When we arrived, the school turned out to be the *Shoreikan* goju-ryu karate dojo of Grandmaster Seikichi Toguchi.

Q: What was Grandmaster Toguchi's school like in those days?

A: The training at Grandmaster Toguchi's school was intensive. We trained six days a week. The only day off was Monday. The training started at 6 p.m. and lasted until 10:30 p.m. The calisthenics alone lasted an hour and a half. These were hard, demanding calisthenics that were performed in 85- to 100-degree heat and extremely high humidity. We would do all sorts of stretching, loosening-up exercises and strength training. The assistants to Toguchi Sensei were very demanding.

"I would say that many of the brown belts that I saw then would have to be considered the equivalent of fourth- or fifth-degree black belts today."

They expected 100 percent effort from us. There were about 40 students in the dojo. The school was perhaps 25 feet wide and 45 feet long, and it had a patio where we could work out. The makiwara were all outside. Toguchi Sensei supervised all the workouts. He was the only black belt in the dojo, but he was assisted by some of his advanced brown-belt students. They led the calisthenics and the basic drills.

Q: I take it that a brown belt in those days was the equivalent of a higher rank today?

A: Yes. At that time, in the 1950s, a brown belt was a highly respected rank. Some of the Okinawan brown belts were powerful and very skilled. I would say that many of the brown belts that I saw then would have to be considered the equivalent of fourth- or fifth-degree black belts today.

Q: What was the training for beginners at Grandmaster Toguchi's dojo?

A: The beginners were trained at a very slow pace. Black footprints, extending 15 or 20 feet, were painted on the dojo floor. There were two sets; one for Okinawans, and one for the larger American servicemen. For three or four months, we trained by walking back and forth on the footprints, trying to learn *sanchin* stepping. We also learned basic techniques

Karate Masters

"Advanced students weren't allowed to take advantage of a lesser student. They were there to help the junior students in a strict but friendly environment. There was a feeling of mutual respect and brotherhood in the dojo."

like punching, blocking, kicking and striking. The training was very repetitious. The kata we practiced were basic *gekisai ichi* and *gekisai ni*. We practiced these for a long time. The pace was slow, but it was physically intense. No idle talk was allowed, no socializing, no taking it easy.

Q: Did the seniors "lean" on the junior students and push them around, as one often sees in dojo outside Okinawa today?
A: That wasn't allowed. Advanced students weren't allowed to take advantage of a lesser student. They were there to help the junior students in a strict but friendly environment. There was a feeling of mutual respect and brotherhood in the dojo. In later years I noticed that this was part of Okinawan culture. They take great pride in the teaching of karate. Karate is their national art and heritage, their cultural contribution to the world. They take pride in presenting it in a civilized and dignified manner. There was no reason or excuse for needless injuries, brutality or reckless wild actions.

Q: What kind of kumite did you practice?
A: We practiced prearranged sparring [*yakusoku* kumite]. We practiced one-, three- and five-step sparring, as well as *kata-bunkai-kumite*. There was no free-fighting. When you practiced with the advanced Okinawans, you had to remain alert, because they were fast, strong and skilled; they also had control. The attitude was very serious. The students practiced kumite as if their lives depended on it, as if a mistake could be fatal.

Q: Was makiwara training part of the regular workout?
A: It was optional, but most students did a lot of it. It was common for Okinawans to have a makiwara in their back yards. The makiwara were very abrasive. The hitting surface was made of rice straw ropes and it frequently would cut your knuckles. One of Grandmaster Toguchi's most

advanced students was an Okinawan named Sakai. He wasn't large, but he was extremely powerful. He used to work out seven days a week. He would get up at 6 a.m. every day and punch the makiwara hundreds of times. During practice one day, he cut his knuckles and bled so profusely that he fainted. His wife had to come and throw a bucket of cold water over his head to revive him. He developed thick calluses on his hands, and he had devastating punches and strikes.

"It was common for Okinawans to have a makiwara in their back yards. The makiwara were very abrasive. The hitting surface was made of rice straw ropes and it frequently would cut your knuckles."

Q: Was there a moral code you were supposed to abide by?
A: Yes. Toguchi Sensei was very strict in not allowing his students to misuse the art. There was an American student there who got into a fight with three other servicemen in a bar. He beat them up badly. Later, he bragged to one of the Okinawan brown-belt students that goju-ryu karate techniques were very effective in actual combat. When Sensei Toguchi heard of the incident, he became very upset. The serviceman was told to never show up in the dojo again. Also, there were a couple of skillful Okinawan karate students who fought with some Okinawans in the villages. Toguchi Sensei expelled them for misusing the art of karate.

Q: Are any of your fellow students at Grandmaster Toguchi's dojo still practicing karate?
A: Yes. Today, several are masters in their own right. Masanobu Shinjo Sensei and Zenshu Toyama Sensei were both green belts at that time. Today, both are highly ranked, highly respected masters. And Katsuyoshi Kanei Sensei, president of the Jinbukan Goju-ryu Karate-do Association, was also a student there. He is a very strong goju-ryu karate and kobudo master and a fine gentleman.

Q: Who was your second karate master?
A: Ryuritsu Arakaki Sensei. We met for the first time in Toguchi Sensei's dojo. He was an architect, a man in his mid-forties. He was a seventh-

Karate Masters

"Today, several are masters in their own right. Masanobu Shinjo Sensei and Zenshu Toyama Sensei were both green belts at that time. Today, both are highly ranked, highly respected masters."

degree black belt master who had studied with Chojun Miyagi and Seiko Higa. I was fortunate that he befriended me, and he treated me as a protégé. I would visit his house on Sundays and eat dinner with his family. It was a great privilege to be invited into an Okinawan home. We would talk about the history of Okinawan karate, Chojun Miyagi and his training in China, and the old masters. He took me around to various dojo and introduced me to many great masters. I would never have had the opportunity to meet them on my own. One day he took me aside and said, "I can see that you have a great passion and desire to train in goju-ryu karate. You should train with the foremost authority on goju-ryu in Okinawa, Grandmaster Meitoku Yagi; he is the top, senior student of Chojun Miyagi." I was reluctant to do that, as it was at least an hour's bus ride from my base to the Yagi dojo, but Arakaki Sensei was insistent. He said, "You must train under him."

Q: How were you introduced to Grandmaster Meitoku Yagi?
A: Arakaki Sensei approached Grandmaster Yagi and recommended me to him. We visited him on a Sunday afternoon. I remember that day vividly. When we arrived, Grandmaster Yagi was in his dojo drilling holes in the wooden nametags that he hung on the rank-tag rack. His dojo was next to his house and there was a small fenced patio for outdoor workouts. He offered us tea. My first impression was that he was a very serene master. I said to myself immediately, "Here is a man of great physical, mental and spiritual powers." I sensed that I had met a great master. After asking me questions for an hour, with Arakaki Sensei interpreting, Grandmaster Meitoku Yagi asked me to demonstrate a kata. When I finished, Grandmaster Yagi turned to Arakaki Sensei and said that I had a build like the great Chinese kempo masters … like a spider. At that time I had a very sinewy body. I weighed about 150 pounds and I was 5 foot 11. He said, "I will accept Mr. Mirakian as a student, and all I expect in return is a

few words of gratitude." I was immensely happy. It was a great honor to have been accepted by Grandmaster Yagi, because Grandmaster Meitoku Yagi was highly respected among the inner karate circles in Okinawa.

Q: Did Grandmaster Meitoku Yagi have other Western students at his Meibukan dojo?
A: No. I was the only one, and I was the first Western student that he taught. There were about 15 or 20 Okinawans. As soon as I started training in his dojo, I could sense that the karate techniques and kata were practiced in a very natural way. Each student did kata according to his own physique and abilities. It wasn't as if someone handed you a suit and said, "Wear it, even if it doesn't fit you." Although the karate students were not allowed to change the basic techniques, there was more flexibility than in other dojo. A tall student, for instance, wouldn't be required to go so deep into *kiba-dachi* or *zenkutsu-dachi* that he lost mobility.

"My first impression was that he was a very serene master. I said to myself immediately, "Here is a man of great physical, mental and spiritual powers." I sensed that I had met a great master. After asking me questions for an hour, with Arakaki Sensei interpreting, Grandmaster Meitoku Yagi asked me to demonstrate a kata."

Q: What was the training schedule at the Meibukan dojo?
A: Grandmaster Yagi held four-hour karate training sessions Monday through Friday. Although the formal workout started at 7 p.m., the students would arrive earlier than that to work out on their own. I would arrive two hours before the workout to stretch, do calisthenics, hit the makiwara and work with traditional Okinawan training equipment. Grandmaster Yagi was the superintendent of the Custom's House. He would come home from work in a suit. If you saw him in the street, you would take him for a university professor. He was about 5 feet 8 inches tall, he weighed a solid 180 pounds, and he had broad shoulders and very powerful hands and arms. He would come home at seven—and without eating supper—put on his gi, and the formal training would begin.

Karate Masters

"Although the karate students were not allowed to change the basic techniques, there was more flexibility than in other dojo. A tall student, for instance, wouldn't be required to go so deep into kiba-dachi or zenkutsu-dachi that he lost mobility."

Q: What kind of training equipment was used at the Meibukan dojo?
A: There was a makiwara, *chishi* (strength stones) of about 5 to 10 pounds, stone jugs for developing a strong grip, free weights and a heavy punching bag. There was a homemade barbell, which was made from two railroad wheels that weighed perhaps 100 pounds. These wheels had probably been used years before on the small railroad cars that ran through the sugar cane fields. But in the *honbu* (headquarters) dojo, there wasn't an emphasis on lifting heavy weights. My impression was that Grandmaster Yagi felt that excessive weight lifting would cause flexibility and speed loss. He stressed that punching against the makiwara was the best way to develop devastating power.

Q: What was the atmosphere like at the Meibukan dojo?
A: A very subtle spirit pervaded the dojo. When you stepped inside, it was as if you stepped into another era or another time. It was as if you were going back to the *Shaolin* monastery 1,000 or 1,500 years ago. There was something mystical there, very difficult to express in words. A person had to be attuned to perceive this mood. There was also very little speaking allowed. There was no socializing, no idle talk, no ego, no flexing of muscles or physical vanity. That would have been contradictory to the concept of the dojo, and none of it was allowed. The karate training consisted of a blending of physical, mental and spiritual elements harmonized in a very smooth way. There was no harshness. The grandmaster led the class in a strict and disciplined way, but he did it with a friendly attitude. The karate students felt very comfortable being taught by Grandmaster Meitoku Yagi.

Q: How was the formal workout structured?

A: The formal training started at 7 p.m. and ran to 11 p.m. Grandmaster Yagi would lead the workout with the assistance of his senior student, Sensei Yushun Tamaki, one of the finest karate instructors I have ever met. To begin, all of the students would line up in complete silence. We would begin by going through all the goju-ryu kata to *suparimpei*, one after the other. This practice was done very seriously, with tremendous concentration; the mind wasn't wandering, and there was no wavering of the eyes. Once the student was training in the dojo, he had to be in command of his mind and in complete control of himself. Everybody responded to the commands at once. Everything was a drill in unison. There were no stragglers. We would always end the training with *sanchin* kata and *tensho* kata. Sometimes we would begin with sanchin as well.

"The karate training consisted of a blending of physical, mental and spiritual elements harmonized in a very smooth way. There was no harshness."

Q: How were you taught the kata at the Meibukan dojo?

A: Grandmaster Meitoku Yagi would usually take me aside and teach me the movements of the kata once. While he was performing the kata, I would follow him. It was a great honor to be taught by the grandmaster, and it was taken as a sign of respect that you would give absolute concentration and learn the basic movements on the first try. I watched like a hawk. There's a saying in Okinawa that the master speaks only once. The kata were taught in a systematic and logical way in the Meibukan dojo. Yushun Tamaki Sensei led the karate class in the practice of the kata, and the students followed him. When we went through the kata for the first time each evening, no corrections were made. But as we kept practicing the kata over and over, Grandmaster Meitoku Yagi and Yushum Tamaki Sensei would make the necessary corrections to each karate student. The kata were taught slowly and patiently, step-by-step to the karate class.

Karate Masters

"To begin, all of the students would line up in complete silence. We would begin by going through all the goju-ryu kata to suparimpei, one after the other. This practice was done very seriously, with tremendous concentration; the mind wasn't wandering, and there was no wavering of the eyes."

Generally, once a student was shown the kata, he was expected to correct the movements himself. When I was learning the tensho kata, I didn't realize it but I had been practicing a wrong move for one to two months. Finally, after paying closer attention to some of the advanced students practicing the tensho kata during one of the workouts, I noticed the right movement of the hand and corrected it myself. This was a very difficult technique to learn, because it was performed fast. Leaving a person to discover and refine techniques by himself has a great built-in value. A student who has to do this becomes highly observant, one of the most important factors in mastering karate. You must remember that there is a Buddhist tradition in Okinawa: To make spiritual progress, you must search for yourself.

Q: Were the students asked to perform kata in front of the class?
A: Twice a week or so Grandmaster Meitoku Yagi would have us sit down quietly on the sides of the dojo, and one by one we would perform kata. The atmosphere in the dojo was so calm that you could hear a pin drop. We would get a chance to see every student's kata and see the strengths and flaws. We benefited from the relaxed contemplation of each other's kata. There was never any praise given.

Q: Did Grandmaster Yagi perform kata in his dojo?
A: On occasion. They were the finest kata I have ever seen in goju-ryu karate. It was beauty in motion. The perfect balance of hard and soft. He had tremendous power, control and speed. I remember his sanchin in particular. It didn't have the extreme tension you see in some practitioners, but when he tensed his body, it was impressive and deceptive ... like tempered steel covered by velvet.

Q: What followed the kata in the workout?
A: After we finished going through the kata, we would practice many different types of kumite that had been adapted from the breakdown of the kata. We would also practice combinations of striking, punching, kicking, blocking and counterpunching. We would practice many patterns, such as *jo-chu-gae, chu-gae-jo* and *gae-jo-chu*, and do many different techniques in a very fast, sequential manner back and forth across the dojo floor. Then we would practice *ippon-kumite* at close range. When we

"Leaving a person to discover and refine techniques by himself has a great built-in value. A student who has to do this becomes highly observant, one of the most important factors in mastering karate."

did this, there was one arm length between the attacker and defender. At this range, given the skill and speed of the students, there was no margin for error. We paid close attention. We had to develop lightning-fast reflexes or we would get hit. The emphasis was on watching the pupils of the opponent's eyes. We watched closely enough so we could always see the punch telegraphed by the eyes. This was a form of active meditation, and this is much better than sitting meditation. The outside world did not exist, and we couldn't worry about the past or future. Only the split-second counted. This made the mind very strong; it developed tremendous power of concentration. We practiced against various students, so we constantly had to adjust and readjust according to the makeup of the opponent. I was a weapons technician in the U.S. Air Force. Every day I had to move three to five tons of heavy equipment by myself. And then I trained in karate four to six hours per night, five nights a week. This schedule made me very strong. But even with my strength and good training I had difficulty in blocking the punches of some of the Okinawan students. In three-step sparring against Mr. Tamaki, I was able to block his first punch and his second. On his third punch, however, he had so much momentum and power that most of the time I had to just get out of the way or get hit. There would be many repetitions of techniques, hundreds of punches, strikes, blocks, kicks. The workouts varied from day to day,

Karate Masters

"We would get a chance to see every student's kata and see the strengths and flaws. We benefited from the relaxed contemplation of each other's kata. There was never any praise given."

but we always did the basics, covering the same techniques again and again and again. There was a heavy emphasis on fundamentals, such as kata and sanchin. To develop a good stance, strength and balance, we practiced *kake-uke* on most evenings. This was not practiced as a full strength tug-of-war, as seen in some dojo today. Instead, it was done in a softer, systematic balanced way. I believe this is one of the best goju-ryu karate exercises. I remember many times practicing against Mr. Tamaki. When I tried to exert too much strength on the palm of his hand, he would sense that I was rigid and off balance and sweep me to the floor. I had apprehension at first, and my mind wasn't as calm as it should have been. Eventually, I learned that if I remained calm, without any preconceived ideas, I could sense when he was going to try to sweep me and just lift my foot. This taught me a fundamental principle that you have to relax both your body and mind to detect changes in your opponent. Kake-uke was originally used to pair highly skilled practitioners for kumite. If one student could not move the arm of another student in kake-uke or could not hold his stance, he would not be allowed to engage in kumite with that student. The feeling was that if he couldn't handle the other student in kake-uke, he would not be able to block his punches either. Thus, he could be seriously injured.

Q: Your students practice the arm-toughening drill called *kotekitai.* **Was that practiced at the Meibukan honbu dojo?**
A: No. That has been introduced in the Meibukan dojo in the past 20 years. This arm-pounding exercise originated in Taiwan, from Taiwanese kempo. Before that, the students would toughen their arms by practicing forearm strikes on the makiwara, by hitting their forearms against the trunks of the banyan tree and by blocking each other's punches.

Q: How did the workouts end?
A: Every workout ended with sanchin. Before sanchin, however, we practiced the exercise that I call the flexible horse. Each of us would count to 100. Usually there were 20 or more students, so we did at least 2,000 flexible horses. It was hot and humid there, especially in the summer. So, by the time we finished, we were soaking wet. Sweat would run down our faces, into our eyes and cover the floor. I wouldn't dare wipe the sweat from my eyes. If I did, all of the Okinawan students would give me dagger looks as if to say, "You are doing something that is improper. Can't you take a little physical punishment? Don't you have the mental fortitude to ignore discomfort?" After *zazen* (sitting meditation) and bowing to the master, we would take off our uniforms and go outside to dry off. The China Sea was only a half a mile from the dojo, and sometimes there would be a cool breeze. In about 10 minutes, it would dry our shorts and we would be able to put on our clothes. Then I would walk three miles to the bus terminal and ride the bus home.

"To develop a good stance, strength and balance, we practiced **kake-uke** *on most evenings. This was not practiced as a full strength tug-of-war, as seen in some dojo today. Instead, it was done in a softer, systematic balanced way."*

Q: You are known for conducting hard, demanding workouts in your dojo that lasted many hours. Were the workouts in Okinawa harder when you trained there?
A: Although the karate workouts at my dojo are very intensive, the training in Okinawa was even more rigorous. They were continuous workouts. There was rarely a break. When karate practitioners talk about the training in Okinawa in that era, they always talk about how hard it was physically. They

Karate Masters

"The students would toughen their arms by practicing forearm strikes on the makiwara, by hitting their forearms against the trunks of the banyan tree and by blocking each other's punches."

talk about the many hours of daily training, the relentlessness of the workouts, the endless repetition of techniques. But many students never grasped that it wasn't the physical element that was most important. It was the way the training was conducted; it was the mental intensity that counted. When you trained in the dojo, nothing else mattered. The emphasis in the dojo was on developing tremendous powers of concentration in a relaxed environment. The goal was to develop the mental concentration and physical power to be able to move in and stop an opponent with a single technique—one punch, one kick.

Q: What was Grandmaster Meitoku Yagi's approach to makiwara training?
A: Grandmaster Yagi felt that makiwara training was the best method to develop a devastating punch. The makiwara were on the patio of his dojo, which was surrounded by a seven-foot fence for privacy, so no one could view the workouts from the outside. There were six makiwara. How much you hit them was left to your own discretion, but most of us practiced diligently. The makiwara were about three feet from the fence. One of the students would tie a stick to the top of the fence and suspend a string with a stone attached to the end of it, like a plumb line. The makiwara all had a certain amount of give ... usually a few inches. The student would position the string so the stone hung perhaps three inches behind the makiwara. Then we would hit the makiwara and try to move the stone. When we were able to move it easily, we would move the string farther back. Then we had to put more power in the punches.

Sometimes Grandmaster Meitoku Yagi would practice very short punches on the makiwara. He would stand with his feet parallel in front of the makiwara and throw one-inch punches. That makiwara was made of seasoned pine and it had little give. I punched this makiwara on occasion, but I had difficulty in bending it. One night I was going to hit it, and I couldn't find it. When I noticed it, I asked Mr. Yushun Tamaki, Grandmaster Meitoku Yagi's top student, what had happened. He said that Dai Sensei had come out the evening before just as it was getting dark. He positioned himself in front of that makiwara, made a loud sound like "Unh!" and broke the makiwara with a blow of just one inch. Still I wonder all these years later what sort of an awesome punch that must have been to break off the makiwara from that very short distance. When Grandmaster Yagi's son, Sensei Meitetsu Yagi, visited my dojo in Watertown, Massachusetts, several years ago, he said that his father had developed 100 percent of his internal power over his many years of training.

"Although the karate workouts at my dojo are very intensive, the training in Okinawa was even more rigorous. They were continuous workouts. There was rarely a break."

Q: Is it necessary to develop callused hands in makiwara training? Some old pictures of Grandmaster Chojun Miyagi, for instance, show that his knuckles were unblemished.

A: You can practice on the makiwara and not develop callused hands. However, the tops of most makiwara in Okinawa were wrapped with 8 to 10 inches of rice straw rope and this would cut into the knuckles, leading to heavy calluses. But there are other ways to construct a makiwara. Sometimes they would cover the top with a blanket and this arrangement would not cut into the knuckles. It is possible to have normal-looking hands and still develop a powerful karate punch. Many people misunderstand makiwara training. They mistakenly believe that the goal is to beat the hands and develop huge calluses, but the real emphasis is on strengthening the hands and wrists, so the wrist will not buckle if you have to hit someone. Also, makiwara training encourages good stances. If your stances are weak, your punching techniques will also be weak. The makiwara exposes this. We did not hit the makiwara an equal number of times with each hand. I was told that if you are right-handed, you should

Karate Masters

"Sometimes Grandmaster Meitoku Yagi would practice very short punches on the makiwara. He would stand with his feet parallel in front of the makiwara and throw one-inch punches. That makiwara was made of seasoned pine and it had little give. I punched this makiwara on occasion, but I had difficulty in bending it."

hit the makiwara three times as often with your left hand and vice-versa for left-handers. For example, being right-handed, if I hit the makiwara 500 times with the right fist, I would strike the makiwara 1,500 times with the left fist. This way a student develops ambidextrous power.

Q: In the practice of kata, was there much discussion of the meaning of particular moves and their applications?
A: There was very little explanation of the meaning of the kata, and there was no discussion of terminology. There was very little talking at all. The emphasis in the training was on doing rather than discussing. Some of the simple applications of the kata were obvious to us. Sometimes Grandmaster Meitoku Yagi would ask Mr. Yushun Tamaki to attack him, and then he would demonstrate an application. Many times, however, the applications were left to the student's imagination and inquisitiveness. This is a logical approach that forces students to think. Some of the techniques in the kata are obvious: a strike here, a block there, a counter there. However, many of the applications are very difficult to figure out and are sometimes the opposite of what a karate-ka thinks. There can also be many applications from a single technique. I was told that masters in China would intentionally keep the advanced applications of their techniques secret, so masters from other styles would not learn their hidden fighting techniques. Someone once asked Grandmaster Yagi if goju-ryu karate had any *gokui* or *hiden* as other martial arts did. *Gokui* are the deep innermost secrets that can be understood only by those who have been training for a long time. Hiden are those secrets passed down and taught only to special students. The grandmaster replied that there were no formal gokui or hiden in goju-ryu karate. He did say, however, that every kata had *nanjiru gokuden* or secrets that you

learned yourself. These could only be understood by trial and error. He said that the effort was more important than anything else. The long repeated efforts are the secrets. You learn by yourself, under your teacher's tutelage, little by little, through long repetitive training and hardship. He also pointed out that a beginner and an advanced student, when seeing the same technique or application, will understand completely different things.

My feeling is that an inexperienced student (with only a few years of training) should not worry about applications. Instead, he should work on basics. For someone who has been studying longer, say eight or 10 years, it is healthy to ponder the meaning of the karate techniques. But one shouldn't lose any sleep over it. In an actual fighting situation, it is not the conscious applications that count; it is the spontaneous subconscious reflex reactions that count.

"There was very little explanation of the meaning of the kata, and there was no discussion of terminology. There was very little talking at all. The emphasis in the training was on doing rather than discussing."

Q: What do you mean by that?
A: Karate is not a purely physical art. It has physical, mental and spiritual aspects. The philosophy of Okinawan karate—and goju-ryu in particular—is that in training the body the practitioner is also subconsciously training the mind. This is the tremendous richness that exists in true karate. As the body trains naturally, so does the mind. For a beginner, all the movements are mechanical and must be done consciously by repetition. The conscious and subconscious minds clash with each other. The student has to learn by highly repetitive efforts. There are no short cuts. The student has to think about keeping the footwork right, the body straight, the shoulders down, the eyes looking forward and the breathing regular. After two or three years of this training, the movements become less mechanical. After 10 or 15 years, the movements become effortless and automatic. In the case of an attack, the practitioner will react spontaneously. The subconscious mind will take over, and the movements will be lightning fast. If the reactions of the practitioner are conscious, they will be

Karate Masters

"The long repeated efforts are the secrets. You learn by yourself, under your teacher's tutelage, little by little, through long repetitive training and hardship."

too slow and to the point of being mechanical. In the advanced practitioner, there is no differentiation between blocking and striking or offense and defense. It is all included in one movement. This is the by-product of years of training the mind as the body is conditioned.

Q: What was Grandmaster Yagi like when he was in the dojo? Was he approachable?
A: I would say that he had a certain amount of approachability, but—out of respect—I would not approach him often. If I asked a question about an application, for instance, he would often stop and call his senior student, Mr. Yushun Tamaki, and explain the particular movement. But sometimes he would not explain anything at all. Everybody respected him. There was a great esprit de corps, and there was also a sense of good, harmonious human relations. The dojo was not run in a high-handed manner. In some other dojo, I noticed, the masters kept aloof from the students and would get highly annoyed if someone asked about an application from a particular kata.

Q: Was free-fighting practiced at Grandmaster Meitoku Yagi's dojo?
A: No. Grandmaster Meitoku Yagi was, and is still, very much opposed to free-fighting. There has never been free-fighting in traditional Okinawan goju-ryu karate-do. There have been some experiments, but they have been dropped. Chojun Miyagi himself tried the idea of freestyle sparring with protective equipment more than a half century ago, but he cast the idea aside because he felt there wasn't any equipment that could cover all the vital areas.

Grandmaster Meitoku Yagi felt that the emphasis in goju-ryu karate should be karate-do ... karate as a way of life. He said that there was a spirit of budo in karate that is different from the spirit of sports. Grandmaster Yagi felt that free-fighting takes the true essence away from karate-do. In free-fighting, karate becomes a sport, and true karate-do is not a sport. That is why free-fighting was taboo. It detracts from karate-do, brings bad feelings into the dojo and students suffer injuries. We practiced very spirited pre-arranged kumite in Grandmaster Yagi's dojo, but we did not engage in free-fighting.

Q: Don't you think it is necessary to engage in free-fighting to achieve good fighting skills in the street?
A: No. Let's say a person has been practicing karate-do very diligently for five to 10 years. After so much practice, a student should have developed good strong techniques, fast reflexes and he should be able to defend himself against any unprovoked attack. Free-fighting can hinder the development of good karate techniques, especially in Okinawan goju-ryu in which the emphasis is on ending a fight with a single devastating technique. Fighting in a ring and fighting in the street are different situations. Many techniques are not allowed in free-fighting. Because of this, free-fighting can actually limit the practitioner. Okinawan karate is meant to be a lifetime practice. Grandmaster Meitoku Yagi still practices everyday at age 78. A student who regularly engages in free-fighting is unlikely to be able to practice karate for more than a few years. I don't allow free-fighting in my dojo.

"If the reactions of the practitioner are conscious, they will be too slow and to the point of being mechanical. In the advanced practitioner, there is no differentiation between blocking and striking or offense and defense. It is all included in one movement."

Q: Are any of your fellow students at Grandmaster Yagi's school still practicing today?
A: Yes. Several have become distinguished masters. The most prominent student in Grandmaster Yagi's Meibukan dojo was Yushun Tamaki. Today, he is a ninth-degree black belt master. He has retired from the dojo, but he still practices daily. He is the true embodiment of what a karate master should be. He is highly skillful, he is tremendously powerful, and he is polite, humble, unassuming and hard working. His kata and technical skills are exceptional. Both of Grandmaster Yagi's sons were students at the dojo when I was there. The younger son, Meitetsu Yagi, was about 9 or 10 years of age in those days, but he was already a highly spirited student. He is an eighth-degree black belt master today … a strong, skilled

Karate Masters

"In free-fighting, karate becomes a sport, and true karate-do is not a sport. That is why free-fighting was taboo. It detracts from karate-do, brings bad feelings into the dojo and students suffer injuries."

and energetic karate-ka. He has a dojo in the village of Nagata. He came to teach in my school in Watertown, Massachusetts, several years ago. My students became familiar with his favorite English word: "Endure!" He would repeat this throughout his demanding workouts. The older son, Meitatsu Yagi, was in his early teens when I first trained with him. He was slender, and his movements were fluid and strong. Today, he is a ninth-degree black belt master and was inaugurated as the chairman of the All-Okinawan Goju-ryu Karate-do Association on June 25, 1989. He is a powerful master with beautiful kata. He also came to teach at my dojo several years ago. Sensei Meitatsu Yagi has always been a very strict and powerful karate master. In addition to being the chief instructor at the Meibukan Honbu (headquarters) Dojo in Kume, Naha City, Okinawa, he is also the president of the Okinawan Meibukan Goju-ryu Karate-do Association. Sensei Meitetsu Yagi is the vice-president and Grandmaster Meitoku Yagi is the chairman of the Association.

Q: One reads a lot of conflicting information about the practice of sanchin. No other kata seems to cause as much confusion. How was sanchin presented to you in Okinawa?

A: Sanchin is the kihon kata, the basic kata, of Okinawan Goju-ryu. It has many purposes. One of them is to train the practitioner in bringing forth strength. According to Chinese masters, the human psychic/psyche center dwells in the *tan tien*, one and a half inches below the navel. This is referred to in many Chinese Taoist texts as the spiritual cauldron. Sanchin emphasizes strengthening of the *jan tien*. The karate-ka who practices sanchin for many years will develop a strong physique and tremendous power through enhanced flow of Ki, the immaterial substance of life and energy. Sanchin will calm a student, develop composure and enhance self-control. It also has many physical benefits, such as controlled breathing and the ability to withstand an opponent's attack. It's very important in the development of fighting skills. If a person pants and loses control of his breathing, he will lose control of his techniques and ultimately of himself. Another purpose of sanchin practice is to harden the entire body through dynamic tension breathing. I remember a demonstration in Okinawa more than 32 years ago by a master who had an extremely powerful sanchin. His breathing sounded like the roar of a lion, and he exuded tremendous vitality and power. I asked an Okinawan friend who he was. It turned out that he was a master who only practiced sanchin ... no other kata. He was in his late fifties and had been practicing sanchin eight times in the morning and eight times at night for 35 years!

In my opinion, sanchin is of the utmost importance for a karate-ka trying to master goju-ryu karate. If a person neglects sanchin, it will affect his entire goju-ryu karate training. The teachings of goju-ryu are founded on the sanchin principles of proper inhalation and exhalation and the expansion and contraction of the lower abdomen. At Grandmaster Kanryo Higaonna's dojo, the students performed nothing but sanchin and basic techniques for the first three to four years of training. This kata is normally practiced with three steps forward and three steps back and then one step forward and one back. At Grandmaster Kanryo Higaonna's dojo, it was sometimes performed with 15, 20 or 25 steps forward and the same back. This karate training based on sanchin was very intensive and demanding.

"Both of Grandmaster Yagi's sons were students at the dojo when I was there. The younger son, Meitetsu Yagi, was about 9 or 10 years of age in those days, but he was already a highly spirited student."

Q: Do you think a practitioner can damage himself through improper practice of sanchin?
A: Yes. If a student doesn't practice sanchin properly, he could hurt himself. A practitioner must have good sound instruction.

Karate Masters

"The karate-ka who practices sanchin for many years will develop a strong physique and tremendous power through enhanced flow of Ki, the immaterial substance of life and energy. Sanchin will calm a student, develop composure and enhance self-control."

Q: You saw many grandmasters perform and teach sanchin. Have you ever seen it performed silently, with no audible breathing?
A: No, never. The level of breathing varied from school to school, but I've never known it to be performed silently.

Q: Was there more than one version of sanchin practiced at Grandmaster Yagi's dojo?
A: Yes, there were two versions. Originally, the sanchin that Grandmaster Kanryo Higaonna brought back from the Fukien province in China was done open-handed. On various occasions, Grandmaster Meitoku Yagi would have us perform this version. But the sanchin we practiced most was the closed-hand version Grandmaster Yagi learned from Grandmaster Chojun Miyagi.

Q: Was the sanchin testing similar at the respective dojo of Grandmasters Seikichi Toguchi and Meitoku Yagi?
A: No. Sanchin testing at Grandmaster Toguchi's dojo was harder and more dynamic. There was a lot of pounding on the shoulders to keep them down. Also, the testing of the legs was more intense. On the other hand, the testing at Grandmaster Yagi's dojo was slightly softer and more natural. There was more emphasis on posture and the proper positioning of the arms relative to the body. The hitting of the shoulders and legs was a little lighter. Great emphasis was also placed on proper breathing control, as well as tensing of the whole body.

Q: From your description, there seems to have been a powerful, unspoken etiquette in these Okinawan dojo. Did your masters discuss this?
A: Yes. My second goju-ryu karate master, Ryuritsu Arakaki, told me that if we take the morality, the ethics and the meditative aspects out of karate, we're left with only animal skills. In karate, he said, we learn to fight like

lions, tigers, monkeys, cranes, bears, dragons and the other animals from which we have adopted our fighting techniques. What balances this knowledge is the moral training imparted with the fighting skills. If you take the morality away from karate training, then you're left with something dangerously close to brutality. This is why dojo-kun is so important. No unseemly behavior, no rudeness, no harshness and no brutality was allowed in any of the Okinawan dojo I visited. The true philosophical concept of Okinawan goju-ryu karate is to seek the way of virtue. In karate, through training the body and mind, we strive to cultivate the ideal human nature of physical, mental and spiritual unity. The Okinawan masters felt that students should strive to be virtuous and pursue the ultimate goal, which is to win any situation with any skills but fighting. Grandmaster Kanryo Higaonna was the leading Confucian scholar on Okinawa. In the Confucian Analects, there is tremendous emphasis on filial piety. Grandmaster Kanryo Higaonna stressed that his students should have respect for themselves, their fellow students, families and life in general. Dojo kun reflects this aspect of karate training.

"The teachings of goju-ryu are founded on the sanchin principles of proper inhalation and exhalation and the expansion and contraction of the lower abdomen."

Q: You mentioned that the atmosphere in Grandmaster Meitoku Yagi's dojo was peaceful and relaxed. This sounds quite different from many modern karate schools, where the training is held in a stressful, almost militaristic environment.

A: Yes. We trained with a very relaxed but alert state of mind. The master conducted the training with a soft, subtle hand. There was no militaristic atmosphere, no rudeness, no harsh commands. You were expected to train with the attitude of a hawk that was ready to pounce on its prey. You needed a heightened concentration stemming from a relaxed state of mind. The most important aspect in karate training is the student's mental attitude. If the student entertains fear, apprehension and rancor, his movements are likely to become stiff, rigid and slow. Nervousness and a disturbed emotional state will cloud judgment and perception of an

Karate Masters

"My second goju-ryu karate master, Ryuritsu Arakaki, told me that if we take the morality, the ethics and the meditative aspects out of karate, we're left with only animal skills."

opponent. The training at the Meibukan dojo cultivated a calm, tranquil, alert state of mind.

There is a story about Yatsusune Azato, the famous Shuri-te master who lived in Okinawa in the late 19th and early 20th centuries. Some say his skills in karate and swordsmanship were unsurpassed. He once fought a duel against the most famous swordsman in the Ryukyu Islands, a tremendously powerful man named Yorin Kanna. He chose to fight unarmed, even though Kanna was armed with a long sword. Azato surprised Kanna by parrying his initial attack with a turn of the hand and then—with a lightning-fast karate technique—drove Kanna to his knees and ended the duel without killing him. He later told his students that Kanna was a swordsman of great skill who, because of his fearsome reputation, was able to terrify his opponents at the very beginning of duels. In every match, he immediately would go for the kill. Azato explained to his students that victory is possible if a practitioner refuses to be terrified and remains calm. It is not easy to remain calm and unperturbed in stressful situations. To develop a calm, undisturbed mind requires many years of training.

Q: Did you have a chance to view non-Okinawan martial arts during your years in Okinawa?
A: Yes. I traveled extensively in Japan, Taiwan, Korea and Hong Kong. I have an avid interest in the history of the martial arts. I visited many martial arts schools, observed a variety of styles and met prominent masters. I still keep in touch with many of them today. For instance, I met the eminent Hung Master and famous Chinese actor Dr. Kwan Tak Hing in Hong Kong in 1968. I still keep in touch with him today and value his friendship greatly. He visited and demonstrated his *Hung* style of Chinese martial arts in my dojo. His demonstration was so impressive that my students still recall his outstanding techniques and forms. He demonstrated all of the Shaolin Monastery animal movements.

Q: **Detractors of Okinawan karate maintain that Okinawa was a cultural backwater and that it was the Japanese who breathed life into Okinawan karate. How would you respond to this?**

A: I would say that this is not true. These claims are based on a limited knowledge of Okinawan karate. Sure, there is merit in what the Japanese and other outsiders have done for Okinawan karate. They have helped make karate popular, and it is now practiced all over the world. And yes, there have been some external changes in Okinawan karate attributable to outside influences. But the essence of Okinawan karate has not been changed. It was and is extremely rich and powerful. Karate is a pure Okinawan traditional art. It is part of the Okinawan culture. Throughout the world, Japan is called the "Home of karate." But in Japan, Okinawa is called the "Home of karate." In Okinawa, karate has been practiced for more than 1,000 years. Outside of Okinawa, karate has been practiced since 1923. Now where do you think the vast store of knowledge would be?

"The most important aspect in karate training is the student's mental attitude. If the student entertains fear, apprehension and rancor, his movements are likely to become stiff, rigid and slow."

The Okinawans are the true masters of the art and they have a deep knowledge and repertoire. Okinawans are humble, peace-loving people. Like the Chinese, they refrain from ostentatious display, wild claims and ego trips. They do not brag about their knowledge or skills. These traits are assets in most cases. But they can also be liabilities, in that the Okinawan karate masters often don't bother to refute the excessive claims of others. There are many karate masters making great claims for themselves who have far less skill than the great Okinawan karate masters such as Juhatsu Kiyoda, Seiko Higa, Meitoku Yagi and Shinken Taira. These masters were not interested in promoting themselves. As for those who would say that 19th-century Okinawan martial arts were not of a particularly high standard, this is based on hearsay from the reports of travelers and old photographs. Did these people ever stand in front of Ankoh Itosu, Kanryo Higaonna or Yatsusune Azato in combat? Nineteenth century

Karate Masters

"I traveled extensively in Japan, Taiwan, Korea and Hong Kong. I have an avid interest in the history of the martial arts. I visited many martial arts schools, observed a variety of styles and met prominent masters."

Okinawan karate masters were extremely powerful. Their skills were highly sophisticated and deadly. But until 1902, the art was taught in complete secrecy, and it was taught only to a select few. Outsiders traveling to Okinawa obviously wouldn't be shown these secret arts. And you can't judge the skills of masters by photographs. The only way to find out about the history of Okinawan karate-do is by going to Okinawa and studying with the masters. The history of Okinawan karate-do is not in books. I was fortunate to be in Okinawa during the golden era of karate, when karate was slowly being presented to the outside world. I lived there in an era when Okinawan karate masters were beginning to selectively teach their unique art of karate-do.

Many outsiders went to Okinawa to study karate. But many of them studied Okinawa karate for a relatively brief period, sometimes for as little as a few months. They might have learned a small part of the art and then gone back home. Many of them, because of their limited knowledge, eventually came to a stumbling block and could progress no further. This does not mean that the art is not sophisticated but that many practitioners have incomplete and limited knowledge of it.

Q: You met many great Okinawan karate masters. How do these masters compare to modern karate practitioners?
A: There is no comparison whatsoever. These great Okinawan karate masters are in a class by themselves because they trained intensively their entire lives—day in and day out—year after year. They were highly motivated to perfect and master their art. For modern practitioners, there are many distractions and less time is spent training.

Q: **What philosophical and ethical concepts did the masters pass down to Okinawan karate practitioners?**
A: The Okinawan masters taught that the karate practitioner should refrain from pettiness and trivialities. Ankoh Itosu, the great Okinawan Shuri-te grandmaster, said: "The more a karate-ka practices, the more modest he should be."

The great Okinawan naha-te Grandmaster Kanryo Higaonna left an important philosophical saying for future generations: "Those who train in the great Okinawan art of karate should help others. Never seek trouble and refrain from arguments and senseless fights." The founder of goju-ryu karate, Grandmaster Chojun Miyagi, taught his students the ethical philosophy of avoiding any serious incidents or confrontations that could lead to a fight. He also said: "Do not hit anybody and do not let anybody hit you." The karate-ka should strive to have a very calm and unperturbed nature and avoid situations in which it might be necessary to resort to physical confrontation. The greatest form of self-defense is to avoid situations in which self-defense will be necessary. Discretion is the better part of valor.

"The Okinawans are the true masters of the art and they have a deep knowledge and repertoire. Okinawans are humble, peace-loving people. Like the Chinese, they refrain from ostentatious display, wild claims and ego trips. They do not brag about their knowledge or skills."

Q: **Could you explain the meaning of the practice of karate-do?**
A: Traditionally on Okinawa, goju-ryu karate is taught as karate-do or as a "way of life." "Do" is the Japanese pronunciation of the Chinese ideograph tao. Tao, or "the way," is the dominant idea of all Chinese philosophy, the foundation of the ancient Chinese world concept. All things are indissolubly interrelated and influenced by each other. In karate-do, the training will influence the practitioner, and the practitioner will influence the training. The balance between the karate-ka and his art is influenced by the manner and presentation of the training. Karate-do seeks to attain that most harmonious stage so the karate-ka will follow the true philosophical concept of karate as a way of life. The practice of karate-do is training with the awareness of *jingi* (humanity, morality and an ethical

Karate Masters

"These great Okinawan karate masters are in a class by themselves because they trained intensively their entire lives—day in and day out—year after year."

code of conduct). It is very dangerous to teach karate without teaching the *Do*. Do is the true philosophical concept of karate, as it teaches the importance of moderation.

Following is an Okinawan saying, "If the heart is right, then the hand will be right." The karate masters of Okinawa emphasize setting the heart of the student right from the beginning. In the traditional long, slow, patient approach, the true essence of karate is not distorted.

Q: Did you study kobudo under the eminent Grandmaster Shinken Taira?
A: Yes. Grandmaster Meitoku Yagi invited his good friend Grandmaster Shinken Taira to his dojo to instruct the students in kobudo. He was a famous kobudo master, a man of very high reputation. He was in his 60s when I studied with him, but he still moved quickly and adroitly. He was graceful and strong, and his techniques were flawless. He was a great master. We studied mostly the sai, tonfa and bo. Grandmaster Shinken Taira was a traditional Okinawan master, firm and strict, but also a jovial and friendly man. It was enjoyable studying under him. He took a liking to me and was very gracious. He asked me to teach his kobudo kata in the United States when I returned.

Q: Most Okinawan kobudo masters have a background in karate. Was Grandmaster Shinken Taira associated with a particular karate style?
A: Yes. He had studied *shorin-ryu* going back to Grandmaster Funakoshi's time. He was a student of Kentsu Yabu, but he didn't elaborate about his karate training. He did mention that he used to work out with Grandmaster Funakoshi in his youth. He taught me some shorin kata on the side. I learned *kusanhu* kata and *chinto* kata from him.

Q: Hard and soft are among the most difficult concepts for martial artists to understand. These are frequently discussed in goju-ryu karate. What is your interpretation of these terms?

A: When a karate-ka starts talking about hard and soft, he starts falling into dualistic thinking. The hard and the soft are not separated in true goju-ryu karate. The hard and the soft are harmoniously interwoven. It is very difficult to tell when one leaves off and the other takes over. There is hardness in softness and softness in hardness. They complement each other. Many masters in Okinawa spoke to me about the hard and soft aspects of goju-ryu karate. The hard external side of karate is easy to understand and practice. The soft side is deceptive and more difficult to develop. When karate students who have developed the soft internal side of their art go through kata, you can notice something different about their performance ... something mysterious that is difficult to put a finger on and something unique that denotes a superior mastery. There is a different emotional state in the practitioner. There is something that is not sheer physical strength. Something not based solely on muscular contraction and expansion but based on inner force, the circulation of chi, which has an explosive, devastating power. Hard and soft can only be understood through long practice. In goju-ryu, the practice of sanchin and tensho enhance the development of soft internal powers. When I was training in goju-ryu karate at the Meibukan dojo, I witnessed Grandmaster Meitoku Yagi's mastery of the hard and soft aspects of goju-ryu karate when he taught and demonstrated the various kata. His mastery, especially of the soft inner aspect, was superb. His top student, Master Yushun Tamaki, also showed great inner strength when performing kata and techniques.

"The Okinawan masters taught that the karate practitioner should refrain from pettiness and trivialities. Ankoh Itosu, the great Okinawan Shuri-te grandmaster, said: 'The more a karate-ka practices, the more modest he should be.'"

Karate Masters

"The practice of karate-do is training with the awareness of jingi *(humanity, morality and an ethical code of conduct). It is very dangerous to teach karate without teaching the* Do. *Do is the true philosophical concept of karate, as it teaches the importance of moderation."*

Q: Is it true that some techniques do not require power or physical force?
A: No. I do not believe that such a thing exists. I had the honor of meeting the great Tai Chi Chuan master Dr. Cheng Man-ch'ing. The famous Chinese Grandmaster, Yang Cheng-fu, who was in Shanghai, taught Dr. Cheng Man-ch'ing. Dr. Cheng Man-ch'ing told me that he once asked Yang Cheng Fu to practice pushing hands with him. While they were practicing, he said that Yang Cheng Fu put his hand on Dr. Cheng Man-ch'ing's throat. He said the hand felt like soft velvet. Suddenly, Dr. Cheng Man-ch'ing was propelled more than 10 feet backwards against the wall, hitting with so much force that he was knocked out for half an hour. He said that was the first and last time he asked to perform pushing hands with his master. So, there is even strength in soft techniques. There is no such thing as magic. Although the internal energy (Ki) looks like magic to the untrained eye, it has great power and physical force when the internal energy is brought forth.

Q: Do you think karate training can increase extrasensory perception?
A: Yes, it might. Master Ryuritsu Arakaki told me that some karate masters do possess extrasensory perception. He said that one day when he and Mr. Meitoku Yagi were training with Grandmaster Chojun Miyagi during the late 1930s in a Naha park, he and Mr. Yagi were walking together. Mr. Meitoku Yagi was a few feet in front of him, so Mr. Arakaki began thinking, "What could Mr. Yagi do if I suddenly hit him from behind? There is nothing he could do because he is walking in front of me." At that precise moment, Mr. Yagi turned around, looked at Mr. Arakaki straight in the eye and said: "What do you have in mind? You want to punch me, don't you?"

Mr. Yagi's younger son, Meitetsu, described to me another incident. He said that when his father was a police officer around 1938, Mr. Yagi arrested an Okinawan for disturbing the peace and causing trouble in a business district in Naha. When he took him to the police station, the man threatened to kill Mr. Yagi. Six months later, Mr. Yagi was walking home late at night on a dirt road. It was pitch dark and the road was lined with heavy bushes on both sides. The Okinawan, whose name was Mr. N, was waiting behind a bush with a knife. When Mr. Yagi was about 20 feet away, he stopped and shouted: "Mr. N. You are hiding there with a knife, and you want to kill me, don't you?" The man ran away because he was so unnerved by the fact that Mr. Yagi could sense the danger without even seeing him. When I was training in Mr. Yagi's dojo, I repeatedly had the feeling that Mr. Yagi could sense my innermost thoughts. He has extrasensory powers developed by his karate training.

"When karate students who have developed the soft internal side of their art go through kata, you can notice something different about their performance ... something mysterious that is difficult to put a finger on and something unique that denotes a superior mastery."

Q: In the 1950s, what did the Okinawans think of foreign students?
A: The Okinawans were skeptical and with good reason. The karate masters wanted to know the true intentions and characters of all their students. The masters were very observant, and I felt I was watched very closely at first. Eventually, after I proved that I could handle the physical and mental rigors of the training, I felt accepted. I had to show that I was sincerely and honestly interested in learning the art of goju-ryu karate-do. In 1958, I represented the Meibukan at a large martial arts demonstration in Ginoza, which is in Central Okinawa. There were more than 2,000 people in attendance. I was the only Westerner participating. When I got up to perform *shisochin* kata, the crowd began booing and whistling. When they saw me performing and recognized that I was a serious student, they calmed down. When I finished, they gave me one of the biggest ovations of the day. After the demonstration, some of the Okinawan karate masters commended me on my performance. Okinawans were very gracious and friendly once they saw that you had a respectful and sincere attitude towards their national art of karate.

Karate Masters

"I witnessed Grandmaster Meitoku Yagi's mastery of the hard and soft aspects of goju-ryu karate when he taught and demonstrated the various kata. His mastery, especially of the soft inner aspect, was superb."

Q: What differences do you find in the way Okinawans and Westerners approach karate?
A: In Okinawa, and in Asia in general, one of the goals of karate training is to minimize the ego. In the West, unfortunately, the emphasis in much of martial art training is in building the ego, which is quite the opposite of the training in Okinawa. There's a saying in Okinawa that comes to mind. "When the rice grain is plentiful, the stalk bows. When empty, it stands tall." This saying is analogous to the Westerner saying, "An empty barrel is apt to make the most noise." The Okinawans are generally more disciplined, patient and motivated than Westerners in their approach to karate training. Also, the Okinawans have an initial advantage as karate is their national art. Therefore, the Okinawans have a better awareness of the goals of karate training than Westerners. In the beginning, self-imposed discipline will make the karate-ka feel uncomfortable and restricted. Okinawans understand and accept this, while most Western karate practitioners are unwilling to endure this initial hardship. After a while, of course, the self-imposed discipline brings the practitioner tremendous inner freedom and harmony.

Q: What were the major styles of karate practiced in Okinawa when you lived there?
A: The major, official styles of Okinawan karate, as recognized by the Zen Okinawa Karate-do Remmei, were goju-ryu, uechi-ryu, matsubayashi shorin-ryu and kobayashi shorin-ryu. These were the four preeminent styles. This is still true today.

Q: Were relations between the major styles friendly?
A: Yes. I frequently attended the meetings of the Zen Okinawa Karate-do Remmei in Naha City. This is where the leading masters and their top students would come together and discuss matters of mutual concern,

including how best to enhance the development of Okinawan karate, how best to present it, standards of etiquette and standards of promotion. I attended these meetings with my second karate master, Ryuritsu Arakaki, and also occasionally with Grandmaster Meitoku Yagi. These were very polite, dignified gatherings. The masters were courteous to each other and presented their views in a dignified, respectful manner.

Q: How did you happen to visit Grandmaster Nagamine's dojo?
A: Goju-ryu karate Master Ryuritsu Arakaki invited me to attend one of the meetings. At that time, Master Arakaki introduced me to Grandmaster Nagamine, and I also met many of his students.

Q: What were the workouts like at his dojo?
A: The practice at his dojo included a lot of weight lifting. They had a full range of barbells, dumbbells and other free weights, and they practiced many different weight-lifting techniques. Grandmaster Nagamine told me that he encouraged his students to engage in

"The Okinawans were skeptical and with good reason. The karate masters wanted to know the true intentions and characters of all their students."

strength building as well as karate training. Even though the students were muscular, I noticed they had excellent speed and reflexes. They were powerful karate-ka. I still remember seeing one of Grandmaster Nagamine's top students, Omine, throwing sequences of punching techniques. I could hear the sound of his punches breaking the air all the way across the dojo.

Q: How was the training at Grandmaster Kanei Uechi's dojo?
A: I visited Grandmaster Kanei Uechi's dojo in Futenma City many times. He is a highly respected and very powerful grandmaster. Uechi-ryu and goju-ryu karate systems have a natural affinity. They both were influenced

Karate Masters

"The Okinawans are generally more disciplined, patient and motivated than Westerners in their approach to karate training."

by the martial arts of Fukien Province in China and have a common geographical background. The uechi-ryu karate training was very intense, and the students were superb karate-ka. They had a controlled form of free-fighting that featured classical uechi techniques. They exercised enough control that they stopped their techniques short of full contact.

Q: I've seen films of their *sanchin* testing. Perhaps it was only because of the camera, but it looked extremely hard. Were the students really being tested that hard?

A: Yes, it was hard. I remember seeing 2-inch-by-4-inch boards broken over the students' arms, legs and abdomens. I saw Grandmaster Kanei Uechi, in a horse stance, testing the sanchin by hitting the students in the abdomen with hard punches. The students looked rugged and highly conditioned, and it appeared as if their entire bodies had been hardened through sanchin training and testing.

Q: Grandmaster Kanryo Higaonna's most famous students were Chojun Miyagi and Juhatsu Kiyoda. Did you ever meet Grandmaster Kiyoda?

A: Yes. I had the great honor of meeting him in 1958 at his home in the city of Beppu, Kyushu, in Japan. He was in his early 70s when I met him, and he was an extremely powerful man. His posture was erect. He had a strong voice, and his eyes were very sharp and penetrating. He was a large man. I saw a photograph of him in his younger years, and he was six feet tall or more and perhaps 180 to 190 pounds. He had a very muscular build. Grandmaster Kiyoda told me that the study of kata should be supreme. He said: "The true karate is in the practice of the kata, and the practice of kata is true karate." I will never forget those words. I also met his son, who was more than 6 feet tall and around 200 pounds. They showed me their photo album that went back many years. They had a variety of group photographs with Grandmaster Kanryo Higaonna that included Juhatsu Kiyoda, Chojun Miyagi, Kenwa Mabuni, Higa Seiko and many other great Okinawan karate masters. There was one particular photograph of Juhatsu Kiyoda wearing the traditional black uniform used in Okinawan festivals. He was holding a thick wooden pole about six feet long. I asked his son what Grandmaster Juhatsu Kiyoda was doing. When practicing karate in Okinawa around 1920, two advanced students would sometimes be paired in a controlled version of free-fighting, he said. This fighting was designed to practice the techniques of a specific style. When the students engaged in kumite, two masters would stand on either side of them. If the action got too fierce and there was the possibility of severe injury or even death, the masters would cross the poles in front of the students and end the fight. He said that this was a very fierce form of kumite that was practiced only by highly trained karate-ka.

"I frequently attended the meetings of the Zen Okinawa Karate-do Remmei in Naha City. This is where the leading masters and their top students would come together and discuss matters of mutual concern, including how best to enhance the development of Okinawan karate."

Q: Grandmaster Miyagi's teacher, Grandmaster Higaonna, who trained in China for more than 20 years, laid the foundation of goju-ryu karate. Is there one particular Chinese style to which goju-ryu is related?
A: Yes. Okinawan goju-ryu karate is related to Chinese chuan-fa. Kanryo Higaonna sailed to Foochow in the Fukien Province, China, when he was 15. There he met the famous Chinese chuan-fa Grandmaster, Liu Liu Ko with whom he studied for more than 20 years. Kanryo Higaonna became Grandmaster Liu Liu Ko's top student. Little is known about the actual style that Liu Liu Ko taught. Some karate masters say it was the *hung* style; others say it was another style that had been indigenous to Fukien Province for more than 1,000 years.

Q: Who was Grandmaster Liu Liu Ko?
A: There isn't much written information on Grandmaster Liu Liu Ko. I was told that he was of the Chinese nobility and had been tested to become the equivalent of a knight three different times. He failed the imperial test

Karate Masters

"Grandmaster Nagamine told me that he encouraged his students to engage in strength building as well as karate training. Even though the students were muscular, I noticed they had excellent speed and reflexes."

at age 37 and again at age 50. On his 73rd birthday he was tested again, before the Emperor of China, after walking hundreds of feet carrying a rock weighing 180 kilos strapped to his back. When Grandmaster Liu Liu Ko arrived in front of the Emperor, he performed sanchin kata and passed the test. The Emperor then knighted him. Grandmaster Liu Liu Ko's training was said to have been very arduous. Anyone who aspires to practice karate must keep in mind the Chinese character "Nin," which means "to endure." There is no easy way of attaining mastery. It was through this long and difficult kind of training that Grandmaster Kanryo Higaonna was able to develop his exceptional skills. In 1890, he returned to Okinawa and began teaching in Naha. His skill, knowledge and dedication soon became legendary.

Q: When he returned to Okinawa from China, did Grandmaster Higaonna make changes to the Chinese martial art that he learned from Grandmaster Liu Liu Ko?
A: Yes. Grandmaster Higaonna did make changes to the Chinese martial art that he learned in the Fukien Province, China. Even though the style that he mastered in China was superb, he felt the need to revise and adapt some of the techniques to make his art suitable to the Okinawan lifestyle and culture. Also, Grandmaster Higaonna, for some unknown reason, changed the name of the highest kata from the Chinese pronunciation *yepatlinpa* (meaning 108) to *suparimpei*.

Q: Was Grandmaster Higaonna a strict karate master?
A: Yes, a very strict teacher. He would not allow or teach any student with a violent nature. He was very selective as to whom he accepted. His training was very strenuous. The sanchin kata was practiced for three to four hours during each session. A new student was taught only the sanchin kata and this went on for as long as three to four years before going into

another kata. While practicing the sanchin, some of the students would collapse from sheer exhaustion. That's how intense Grandmaster Kanryo Higaonna's training was. The sanchin kata taught at that time by Grandmaster Higaonna was performed open-handed. When Grandmaster Higaonna demonstrated his sanchin breathing kata, he would occasionally allow four Okinawans to try and dislodge him from his standing position. They could not move him. When he finished the sanchin kata, the floor where he stood would be hot from the friction of his toes gripping the floor.

Q: Who were Grandmaster Higaonna's top students?
A: Juhatsu Kiyoda, Chojun Miyagi and Kenwa Mabuni. Miyagi founded goju-ryu karate from Nahate; Kiyoda founded *toon-ryu*, a karate system named after the first character in Grandmaster Higaonna's name; and Mabuni founded shito-ryu karate.

Q: Did Grandmaster Miyagi make any changes in the naha-te system that he inherited from Grandmaster Higaonna?
A: Yes, Grandmaster Miyagi studied with Grandmaster Kanryo Higaonna for 13 years. Upon his master's death, Miyagi went to China for two years to conduct further research into the martial arts. While he was in China, he met and befriended the Chinese *White Crane* Master, Go Ken Kin. Miyagi then traveled around with him to several provinces, studying with a number of great Chinese masters. When Chojun Miyagi returned to Okinawa, he decided to take the art of naha-te and expose it to scientific scrutiny. His approach was very critical, and he discarded the techniques that did not meet strict scientific standards. Chojun Miyagi incorporated many Chinese martial arts techniques that he had learned while in China to the naha-te system of Okinawan karate. He refined the existing kata and developed his own kata, *gekissai* I and II and tensho. Chojun Miyagi designed the auxiliary exercises, kata-bunkai-kumite, and other forms of kumite that are performed in traditional

"I saw Grandmaster Kanei Uechi, in a horse stance, testing the sanchin by hitting the students in the abdomen with hard punches. The students looked rugged and highly conditioned, and it appeared as if their entire bodies had been hardened through sanchin training and testing."

Karate Masters

"When the students engaged in kumite, two masters would stand on either side of them. If the action got too fierce and there was the possibility of severe injury or even death, the masters would cross the poles in front of the students and end the fight."

goju-ryu karate training dojo. He modernized the training and developed the structures that we still follow. He also changed the practice of open-hand sanchin to closed-hand sanchin.

Q: What is known of Master Go Ken Kin?
A: He was a Chinese white crane master whom Master Miyagi met in Fukien Province, China, in 1915. They traveled together for two years, visiting and training with Chinese masters of various systems of chuan-fa. Master Go Ken Kin introduced Master Miyagi to many great masters. In 1936, Grandmaster Miyagi visited China again and studied Chinese martial arts at the *Seibu Dai Iku Kai* (Great Gymnastic Association, Pure Martial Arts Spirit) in Shanghai. Years later, Master Go Ken Kin moved to Japan and lived there under the name Yoshikawa. He passed away in 1940 in Japan at the age of 55.

Q: There are many versions of the origin of the name goju-ryu. Where did the name come from?
A: From the old Chinese book *Wu Pei Chih* (Army Account of Military Arts and Science) by Yuan-i Mao. It was published in 1636. Grandmaster Miyagi named the system of karate goju-ryu (hard/soft style) from the term "goju," which appears in the sentence: "The successful method requires both give and take (go-ju)." When Grandmaster Miyagi was asked why he gave this specific name to his style of karate, he replied that goju defines the hard and soft nature of his style. Grandmaster Miyagi named his style of karate goju-ryu around 1932. He was teaching and promoting goju-ryu karate-do up to the time of his death on October 8, 1953 at the age of 65. He was called the last great samurai warrior of Okinawa because of his legendary strength and skill, as well as his intense dedication to the martial arts.

Q: On what principles did Grandmaster Miyagi base the foundation of goju-ryu karate-do?
A: Grandmaster Miyagi subjected the art of naha-te, as received from Grandmaster Kanryo Higaonna, to strict scientific examination. Originally, a martial arts expert was trained for killing an enemy with one blow. Karate, as such, was unsuitable for the contemporary world. Miyagi studied the basic "go" of sanchin and the six rules and formed the *ju* or tensho form, thus combining soft and hard movements. He also organized the auxiliary movements designed to help develop karate techniques by strengthening the body through calisthenics. He organized these exercises in preparation for practicing the *kaishu* kata. Thus, he determined the theory for the practice of karate and organized it as a martial arts educational subject, an art of self-defense and as a spiritual exercise. Grandmaster Miyagi spent his entire life contributing to the improvement and proliferation of karate-do. Before his intervention, karate had been considered a very mysterious practice. By using a scientific approach, Miyagi created, through his goju-ryu karate-do, a clearly defined and universal platform for the art, and that gave it a basis for mass acceptance.

"There is no easy way of attaining mastery. It was through this long and difficult kind of training that Grandmaster Kanryo Higaonna was able to develop his exceptional skills."

Q: What is the origin of the term karate?
A: Originally, this Okinawan fighting art was simply called "Te." Then, the Okinawans made a strict distinction between their native art "Te" and "Tode," which meant "Chinese hand" (for the Chinese art of Ch'uan Fa or *kempo*). The Chinese ideogram "To" of "Tode" means "Chinese" or "Tang" (The Tang dynasty ruled China from 618 to 906 AD). A tremendous cultural revival occurred during the Tang Dynasty that was symbolic of the finest Chinese culture and enlightenment. Because Chinese culture was highly respected in Okinawa, anything labeled "Chinese" was regarded as superior. The word "To" is very elegant and raises the value of everything it is applied to. There is a certain snob appeal in calling any-

Karate Masters

"The sanchin kata taught at that time by Grandmaster Higaonna was performed open-handed. When Grandmaster Higaonna demonstrated his sanchin breathing kata, he would occasionally allow four Okinawans to try and dislodge him from his standing position."

thing "To." Gradually, the Okinawans came to apply the term "To" to all "te," especially those of Chinese influence. According to Grandmaster Miyagi, karate, written in this way, is the special word used only in the Ryukyu and it came from the Chinese ch'uan-fa (kempo).

Q: When was *tode* changed officially to karate?
A: On October 25, 1936, a karate symposium sponsored by Mr. Choju Ota, chief editor of the *Ryukyu Shimpo* newspaper, was held in the Showa Kaikan, at Naha City, Okinawa. Among the Okinawan karate grandmasters present were Kentsu Yabu, Chotoku Kyan, Chomo Hanashiro, Chokei Motobu, Chojun Miyagi, Juhatsu Kiyoda, Chosen Chibana, Mashige Shimma, Asatada Koyoshi and Eijo Shin. At this conference, it was agreed that the Okinawan martial art, which previously was called "Te" or "Tode," be called karate or "empty hands." From 1936 on, the practitioners of this Okinawan martial art began referring to it as karate, using the ideogram meaning empty hands. In this way, the emphasis shifted from technique alone to spiritual values as well.

Q: At what age did Meitoku Yagi start his training with Grandmaster Miyagi?
A: Meitoku Yagi was 13 years old when his paternal grandfather took him to Grandmaster Miyagi, who was 37 at the time. His grandfather told Grandmaster Miyagi that Meitoku Yagi was a descendant of the leading samurai of Okinawa and the first minister of the three ministers of Okinawa ... Jana Oyakata. His grandfather also said: "Meitoku Yagi has Okinawan samurai blood in him, and I think he will be able to take over your place some day in the future, so please teach him your karate." That

is how Meitoku Yagi was able to start training under Grandmaster Miyagi in 1925.

Q: Jana Oyakata was one of his ancestors. Who was he?
A: He was a very important official in Okinawan history. He was so influential that he escorted the king of Okinawa when the king had to go to the peace talks after the Shimazu clan of Satsuma Province, Japan, defeated the Okinawans during the conflict of Keicho in 1609.

"Sensei Meitatsu Yagi invited me to participate in a special celebration in honor of his father's (Grandmaster Meitoku Yagi) 73rd birthday. That was on February 10, 1985. As the United States representative of Meibukan Goju-ryu karate-do, I attended this event and gave a congratulatory address and performed the seienchin *kata on that day."*

Q: You studied with Grandmaster Miyagi's senior student and met many of his other students. How did they describe the Grandmaster as a person and a teacher?
A: Grandmaster Miyagi's nickname in Okinawan dialect was "Busamagunku" or "samurai" Miyagi. He was a very demanding and strict teacher. Meitoku Yagi began studying with him at age 13, after undergoing an eight-month probationary period during which he had to perform chores around Chojun Miyagi's house and backyard. Grandmaster Meitoku Yagi said that Grandmaster Chojun Miyagi had fierce eyes. "When you saw them," he said, "you wouldn't be able to say a word. You would never dream of telling him something that wasn't true." Grandmaster Miyagi was hard on his students. While doing *zazen*, he would not allow his students to relax as some of the other karate teachers would; instead, he would make the students sit and meditate for one to two hours without moving. Sanchin was taught one step at a time. Sometimes a single movement would be practiced over and over again for several months ... nothing but one movement for hours a day. When Meitoku Yagi would go to the communal bathhouse, people would see the bruises and welts on his shoulders from Sanchin testing and say: "Aha, you have been training with

Karate Masters

"The Meibukan goju-ryu kata of Grandmaster Yagi are unique. They have a flair, elegance and fluidity."

Chojun Miyagi." Grandmaster Chojun Miyagi placed great emphasis on developing the character of his karate students. He only kept those students who had high moral ethics. He was a strict disciplinarian. One day one of the students arrived for karate training with a towel wrapped around his neck, singing a popular song. Grandmaster Miyagi expelled him from the school. The student tried to apologize for his careless behavior but Grandmaster Chojun Miyagi felt that if a student behaved in front of him in such a careless and disrespectful way, then he would do even worse things away from the master's presence. Grandmaster Meitoku Yagi said that an average person could not have tolerated Grandmaster Miyagi's very intense karate training. You had to be highly motivated. Grandmaster Miyagi would often tell his karate students, "Lions push their cubs over a cliff and they raise only the cubs that are able to struggle back up the cliff. That's how I teach here in my dojo." Grandmaster Miyagi taught only those students who could withstand the rigors of the training. If a student dropped out, he made no effort to draw him back.

Q: What were Grandmaster Miyagi's favorite kata and techniques?
A: I was told in Okinawa that Grandmaster Chojun Miyagi's favorite kata was *shisochin*. He had exceptionally powerful open-hand techniques, especially *nuki-te*. Open-hand techniques take much longer to master than closed-hand techniques. His other favorite kata were sanchin and tensho. Grandmaster Miyagi had very strong punching and kicking techniques. His punches and kicks had explosive power. He was said to have superhuman strength. Grandmaster Miyagi was renowned for having a vice-like grip. It was said that he could put his hand on a four- or five-pound piece of raw meat and squeeze it into hamburger. When he was in China, I was told that he dropped his wallet in a rickshaw. When he went back to get it, the rickshaw driver refused to hand it over and tried to strike him. Grandmaster Miyagi instantly grabbed the driver's forearm

and squeezed so hard that it paralyzed his arm, forcing the driver to give the wallet back.

Q: Did Grandmaster Miyagi teach different versions of the kata to students according to their level of development?
A: Yes. As Grandmaster Chojun Miyagi kept teaching, he kept refining the kata. Also, he taught beginners simplified versions of the kata. Later, as they practiced longer and learned more, they were taught more refined, advanced versions. Therefore, in evaluating the level of any goju-ryu kata, you have to know how long the master studied with Grandmaster Chojun Miyagi. He taught slowly and patiently. Clearly, someone who studied with him for a few years would not have kata and techniques as sophisticated and advanced as someone who studied and practiced with him for decades.

Q: Who was Grandmaster Chojun Miyagi's top student and successor?
A: Grandmaster Meitoku Yagi was the top student and successor to Grandmaster Miyagi. He studied with him from 1925 to 1953. He learned the most advanced and sophisticated versions of goju-ryu kata and techniques. The Meibukan goju-ryu kata of Grandmaster Yagi are unique. They have a flair, elegance and fluidity. Grandmaster Miyagi passed away on October 8, 1953. Ten years later his widow and family gave the Grandmaster's karate uniform and his black belt to Mr. Yagi. According to a speech given on the 25th anniversary of Grandmaster Miyagi's death, his daughter Suruki said that her family had decided to give her father's karate uniform and black belt to Mr. Yagi because he contributed the most and trained the longest with Grandmaster Miyagi. She said: "Mr. Meitoku Yagi was with my father for the longest time practicing karate. I think my father would be glad to see Mr. Yagi getting his uniform."

"Originally, this Okinawan fighting art was simply called "Te." Then, the Okinawans made a strict distinction between their native art "Te" and "Tode," which meant "Chinese hand" (for the Chinese art of Ch'uan Fa or kempo)."

Karate Masters

"From 1936 on, the practitioners of this Okinawan martial art began referring to it as karate, using the ideogram meaning empty hands. In this way, the emphasis shifted from technique alone to spiritual values as well."

Q: Who promoted you to black belt?
A: Grandmaster Yagi promoted me to black belt. Before I left Okinawa, he promoted me to *san-dan* [3rd dan]. In 1985 while we were in Okinawa, Grandmaster Yagi promoted me to *hachi-dan*, kyoshi [8th dan].

Q: What was the occasion for your visit to Okinawa in 1985?
A: Sensei Meitatsu Yagi invited me to participate in a special celebration in honor of his father's (Grandmaster Meitoku Yagi) 73rd birthday. That was on February 10, 1985. As the United States representative of Meibukan Goju-ryu karate-do, I attended this event and gave a congratulatory address and performed the *seienchin* kata on that day. My wife, Helen, and my daughter, Doreen, presented Grandmaster Yagi with flowers during the ceremony. Representatives from the United States, Japan, Brazil and India were present for this birthday celebration, as well as many prominent Okinawan masters. Grandmasters Kanei Uechi, Shugoro Nakazato, Shoshin Nagamine and Shinho Matayoshi all attended. The son of the late Grandmaster Chojun Miyagi, Ken Miyagi, was there, as was the son of the late Grandmaster Seiko Higa, Seikichi Higa. Hundreds of practitioners demonstrated kata and kumite in front of thousands of spectators. Afterwards a gala reception was held for special guests. This was a major cultural event in Okinawa that featured radio, television and press coverage.

Q: Are you the first person to receive the high rank of 9th dan (hanshi) from Grandmaster Yagi?
A: Yes. Outside of Okinawa, I am the first and only one who has received the 9th degree from Grandmaster Yagi, who is the chairman of the Meibukan Goju-ryu Karate-do Association.

Q: Your dojo in Watertown, Massachusetts, is known as the most traditional Okinawan karate school in North America. Have you made many changes over the years in the way you teach karate?
A: No. I haven't made any changes. Basically, I am teaching the same way I was taught at the Meibukan Honbu Dojo in Okinawa. I also keep the same attitude that permeated Grandmaster Yagi's dojo, and that means there is respect, cooperation, discipline and hard work.

Q: Could you describe the benefits of traditional Okinawan goju-ryu karate training?
A: Traditional Okinawan goju-ryu training is very strenuous and disciplined. It develops a very strong foundation of fighting skills in the karate student. Traditional Okinawan goju-ryu karate training emphasizes the repetitious practice of basic karate techniques, kata and sanchin training. Because of these intense and demanding training requirements, it develops and produces the best long-term results in the karate practitioner. Traditional day-to-day, continuous karate training strengthens the body, improves the health, cultivates the mind and develops an indomitable human spirit that can be applied to any activity in life. Grandmaster Chojun Miyagi used to say that winning and losing are part of each other. "Don't be afraid to fail one day," he said, "because the next day you might win." Life is a constant struggle, and traditional Okinawan goju-ryu karate training will prepare a person to face that struggle and deal with life's ups and downs in a very confident way. O

"Traditional Okinawan goju-ryu training is very strenuous and disciplined. It develops a very strong foundation of fighting skills in the karate student. Life is a constant struggle, and traditional Okinawan goju-ryu karate training will prepare a person to face that struggle and deal with life's ups and downs in a very confident way."

Seinosuke Mitsuya

The Distant Dream

HE IS ONE OF THE MOST EXPERIENCED KARATE MASTERS IN THE WORLD, AND HIS KNOWLEDGE OF SHITO-RYU IS ABOVE AND BEYOND WHAT MOST OF THE CURRENT INSTRUCTORS OF THE ART KNOW. STUDENT OF THE LEGENDARY HAYASHI TERUO, MITSUYA SENSEI ADHERES TO THE TEACHING OF HIS INSTRUCTORS AS MUCH AS POSSIBLE AND INSISTS THAT TECHNIQUES HAVE NOT CHANGED MUCH. "KARATE TECHNIQUES HAVE NOT CHANGED FROM WHEN I STARTED. DEVELOPED? YES. BUT NOT CHANGED. SOMETIMES THEY ARE TAUGHT INCORRECTLY OR ADAPTED BECAUSE SOME INSTRUCTORS ARE UNABLE TO CORRECT TECHNIQUE, BUT THIS IS NOT BECAUSE THE TECHNIQUE IS LACKING."

IN DEFENSE OF YOUR LIFE, SENSEI MITSUYA BELIEVES THAT YOU MUST BE CAPABLE OF KILLING YOUR ENEMY WITH ONE BLOW. THAT IS WHY HIS TEACHING EMPHASIZES THE TRUE ELEMENTS AND PHILOSOPHY OF JAPANESE BUDO. LESSONS WITH HIM ARE MORE THAN A PHYSICAL WORKOUT. THEY ARE ALSO A KARATE HISTORY LESSON. "THE PHILOSOPHICAL ASPECTS OF KARATE-DO MUST BE LEARNED FROM THE KARATE-KA'S VERY FIRST VISIT TO THE DOJO, SO THAT, FROM THE OUTSET, HE WILL PROGRESS BOTH PHYSICALLY AND MENTALLY. IN THIS WAY, AS THE COMPLEXITY AND POWER OF THE PHYSICAL TECHNIQUES INCREASES, THE KARATE-KA'S DISCIPLINE AND CONTROL EVOLVES TO COMPLEMENT IT."

MITSUYA SENSEI HAS REACHED A LEVEL OF KARATE THAT—FOR THE MAJORITY—IS NOTHING BUT A DISTANT DREAM. HE REPRESENTS THE TOTAL KARATE EXPERIENCE.

Q: How long have you been practicing the martial arts?
A: I have been practicing for more than 45 years and that includes both karate and kobudo simultaneously. I also practiced sumo between the ages of 6 and 12 and judo between 12 and 18. I started in karate (hayashi-ha shito-ryu) at the age of 14. My first teachers were my elder brother, Jinichi, and Soke Teruo Hayashi.

Q: Tell us some interesting stories of your early days in karate under the guidance of Grandmaster Soke Hayashi Teruo.
A: Soke Hayashi used to give very little explanation about the technique. He just gave his commands to perform the techniques and the kiai. That's all. It was up to us to watch carefully when he was moving and notice the

Karate Masters

"Western people are generally very interested in those aspects [traditional Japanese training that] they like, especially [things like] ethics and morality. They also wanted to learn about the traditional art and today's Japanese culture."

details of the techniques. Our ability to do this was directly related to our level of knowledge and maturity in the art. But I also was very lucky. Somehow, when Soke wanted to study, analyze, and practice techniques and actions he would call me aside and make me attack him. He would tell me which *atemi* to perform, and I was unaware of what would happen next. I couldn't really see much, but I surely felt it. I was very lucky that he chose me. At that time, no one else but me was used for that purpose. I learned very much from those intense training sessions. Not only were they were very satisfying, but they stimulated me to continue karate with more passion and dedication than before. At night, the only thing I could do was rest so I would have the energy to train the next day. It was very intense training, and my body literally dropped after the last workout. Today, virtually nobody is willing to undergo such training, and that may be simply because this is a different time.

Q: When you began teaching outside of Japan, how did you find that the Westerners responded to traditional Japanese training when they visited your dojo?
A: Western people are generally very interested in those aspects [traditional Japanese training that] they like, especially [things like] ethics and morality. They also wanted to learn about the traditional art and today's Japanese culture. The Japanese culture of yesterday, as well as the one of today, is very much interconnected with the spirit and technique of budo.

Q: Were you a natural at karate? Did the movements come easily to you?
A: Yes, for me it came quite easy. I felt it inside myself from the beginning.

However, even if it is easy and natural [for anyone], it is important to always improve. There is no end to that. It is necessary to coordinate your thoughts and actions, and you need to continuously practice hard every day and never give up your personal training. Obviously, I always try to improve, and I continue learning, studying and practicing. I realize how the maturity of the physical techniques develops through time, especially when I trained with Soke Hayashi.

Q: What are the most important points of your teaching philosophy?
A: Harmony among mind, spirit and body. Also, I make sure that I teach the right strategy (mental and spiritual) and tactic (action). There should be coordination in the body and in the mind, too. To get the maximum benefits from the art, it is very important to learn how to put together and coordinate all the mental and physical elements of karate.

"Masters transfer the "purity" of the styles to the students who are strong spiritually and technically, because these students have the "strength" to continue the tradition."

Q: With all the technical changes during the last decades, do you think there still are "pure" styles of karate?
A: Masters transfer the "purity" of the styles to the students who are strong spiritually and technically, because these students have the "strength" to continue the tradition. That's why they are "real" masters; they are the ones who have a serious school and a real grandmaster. Each style represents a different flavor in the big landscape of the art of karate.

A *ryu* (a style or system) is a method, and it is tradition, manners, philosophy, culture, science, technology, et cetera. Styles are different methods of training and represent different answers to the same problems. All of these aspects are like a sort of genetic identity or a DNA. The more talented old masters studied for many years ... even the smallest details. Some of the characteristics of hayashi-ha shito-ryu include the trust and credibility that Soke Teruo Hayashi gained through [many] great sacri-

Karate Masters

"Master Teruo Hayashi traveled often to search for the most traditional masters so he could study their techniques, their kata, and their methods both in karate-do and kobudo."

fices. Every style reflects the method, the correctness and the rectitude of the master who created it. Some great masters have practiced for many years under their teachers and then created their own style and unique method. After years of study, they implemented the most effective and functional techniques. Master Teruo Hayashi traveled often to search for the most traditional masters so he could study their techniques, their kata, and their methods both in karate-do and kobudo. Through these experiences, he founded the hayashi-ha shito-ryu of karate-do and the kenshin-ryu of kobudo. Soke Hayashi was a man of great temper and charisma, as well as a great fighter. He gained respect from the most relevant masters in budo—and became one of them—due to the great depth of his knowledge in martial arts. He demonstrated this knowledge on a number of occasions, and many considered him No. 1 among the current masters of karate and kobudo. He not only prepared technicians and fighters on a very high level, he successfully asserted his school all around the world.

Q: How would you describe the life and dedication of Soke Hayashi to the arts of budo?
A: Soke Hayashi practiced karate-do and kobudo with the spirit of the Japanese budo [Yamato Damashii] for all of his life. For decades, he demonstrated the art in world championships and events in front of the most respected martial artists and politicians around the world, and the public always anticipated his presentations the most. And this is how people from all cultures and styles were able to recognize the art and the value of these arts. Because of his enormous knowledge, he was president of the referee council of the WKF (previously known as WUKO) for more than 10 years, and he greatly contributed to the revisions and improve-

ments of the competitions and rules. A change in kumite is one example of that. In earlier times, there was the *ippon shobu*, which was the traditional Japanese form. To make the competitions more sport-oriented, Soke Hayashi created the system of *sanbon-shobu*. While this made it more accessible to the rest of the world, it kept the traditional elements. Certainly, he was the person who has contributed the most to the development of traditional karate-do and kobudo.

Q: Do you think that karate in the West is at the same level with Japanese karate?
A: If we talk about sport competitions, then the West and Japan are at the same level. Philosophically and culturally, however, the differences are obvious and this affects the way karate is not only practiced in the dojo but also how the practitioner understands the art. Generally, karate is a serious matter for Japanese; it is not simply a sport. Unfortunately, due to the differences in culture with the Western world, I often notice a certain lack of seriousness from the Westerners who are involved in the arts of budo.

"If we talk about sport competitions, then the West and Japan are at the same level. Philosophically and culturally, however, the differences are obvious and this affects the way karate is not only practiced in the dojo but also how the practitioner understands the art."

Q: Do you feel that there are any fundamental differences in approach or in the physical capabilities between Japanese karate-ka and European or American karate-ka?
A: There should not be any difference in the sport competitions. The referees, however, make a difference through their interpretation of the rules, their ability and knowledge.

Q: Karate is nowadays often referred to as a sport. Would you agree with this definition or do you think it is only budo?
A: Sport is governed by rules for athletic reasons. Karate-do is fundamentally a study for the body, mind and spirit. Therefore, it requires physical and mental discipline. Due to these reasons, karate-do can be considered as budo and can be practiced for life. Karate as sport is only a small part of karate-do and can only be practiced as such for a few years. A true practitioner of budo must study and practice his entire life. The study of

Karate Masters

"Every weapon has its peculiarities, and the body has to adapt and become stronger when using the weapon. All this preparation helps a student improve the mechanics behind the physical movements of karate."

the martial arts is similar to the research of modern technology; you never stop learning and studying. Soke Hayashi was a perfect example of an individual who studies, practices and lives the art of budo.

Q: At the present time, how do you see karate in general and hayashi-ha shito-ryu in Europe and the rest of the world?
A: In these last decades, karate has transformed a lot. It is following a sportive path more and more, and it is losing the effectiveness of its actions. In sport competitions, nowadays, what really matters is the spectacle. This is probably due to the big influence of the movies, but what you see in the movies has nothing to do with real fighting or real self-defense. Many referees, often influenced by the public, don't know how to be objective and thus lose credibility in front of competitors and spectators. The hayashi-ha system, in my opinion, not only has excellent technique, but it's very efficient and functional, and it is rich in beauty, elegance and refinements. And this is how karate should be.

Q: Does it help empty-hand karate physically to train with weapons?
A: Yes. Every weapon has its peculiarities, and the body has to adapt and become stronger when using the weapon. All this preparation helps a student improve the mechanics behind the physical movements of karate.

Q: What's your opinion of makiwara training?
A: Makiwara training is not indispensable, but it can be useful if it is practiced properly. Young people and teenagers—especially—should not practice this before they have reached a certain physical maturity, as there is risk of serious deformations in the hands. The makiwara is necessary to develop precision of technique and resistance at the moment of impact against an object. However, practicing with the makiwara properly is very difficult, so a teacher must not only have thorough knowledge of this

training but also a lot of common sense. He must make sure that a student's hands do not become deformed or bleed because that can lead to serious problems, including HIV and infections.

Q: To progress in the arts, how should a sensei prepare his personal training? Once he reaches a high technical level, what elements should be emphasized?
A: He must dedicate special attention to the weakest parts of his body, acknowledge them and strengthen them, and continue to develop his strengths. When a sensei arrives at a high technical level, he must emphasize the coordination between the mental and physical because this is an important aspect of the whole picture. It is also important to search for a great master or teacher who can help him go forward and improve, assisting him in reaching the higher levels of the art.

"When a student is young, it is easier to practice kumite, but this should be done with discipline and proper manners. However, after a student reaches the age of 30, maybe he will naturally feel more [inclined] to do kata."

Q: When teaching the art of karate, is self-defense, sport or tradition the most important?
A: Self-defense, tradition and sport. That is the order of importance, but each one is individually important because they all support each other to create a strong unit. Thus, you should not focus on only one or two of the elements. Instead, you should try to balance your practice. Of course, when you get older, the emphasis switches to tradition and self-defense because the sport aspect is gone.

Q: In training, what's the proper ratio between kata and kumite?
A: It is difficult to answer because it depends on the age, physical capabilities and character of the person, and all of these elements [combined] generally make the "perfect" proportion for an individual. When a student is young, it is easier to practice kumite, but this should be done with discipline and proper manners. However, after a student reaches the age of 30, maybe he will naturally feel more [inclined] to do kata.

Karate Masters

"My advice is to always train with dedication and attention and, in addition to getting the proper education, you should incorporate the following values into your life: discipline, seriousness and respect."

Q: Sensei, do you have any general advice you would care to pass on to the karate-ka?
A: To the karate-ka of today, my advice is to always train with dedication and attention and, in addition to getting the proper education, you should incorporate the following values into your life: discipline, seriousness and respect. In other words, focus on technique, intelligence and spirit. For the art of karate-do, these are the most important values, and they are much more important than punching, kicking and muscle power.

Q: Some people think it is necessary to train in Japan. Do you agree with this point of view?
A: Sometimes it may be useful if you don't have a good master, but it is not necessary because the best masters often travel outside of Japan [and thus are accessible] and many of them are already living outside of that country.

Q: What would you say to someone who is interested in learning karate-do?
A: First, I'd say that it is a great idea! Learning this discipline brings much serenity to a practitioner's life and one should stick to the art and have a strong will to succeed. If the practitioner puts in the time and effort, everything is possible. For every age and everybody, there is a better way to practice karate. It is not necessary to use the same method or approach for every single student. Each practitioner must take care of the details. This is the essence of traditional Japanese karate-do. Personally, I try to follow this principle. Thanks to my passion and thanks to the teaching of Soke Hayashi, I have always been among the best ones [instructors], and I intend to continue being among the top instructors in the world. I have always wanted to do better than others.

Q: What is your opinion about mixing karate styles? Does the practice of one nullify the effectiveness of the other or can it be beneficial to the student?

A: The mixing of styles often may cause mediocrity if [they are] studied superficially, because every style has its particular characteristics. The only way to attain time-lasting results is to carefully study the particulars of each style. Personally, I don't think that it is a good idea to study and mix styles, because it requires time and ability and a very high level of technical understanding that many people don't have. Thus, a serious karate-ka should dedicate more [time] to in-depth study of his style instead of jumping from one style to another without any logic behind [that decision].

"Kata is essential to karate. Kata organizes the technical foundation of the style from the base (kihon) to very high levels of technical expertise. Due to this, the ratio between form and action is often hard to understand. Sometimes it is simply the student's lack of study or capability."

Q: Modern karate is moving away from the bunkai in kata practice. In general, how important is bunkai in the understanding of kata and karate-do?

A: Kata is essential to karate. Kata organizes the technical foundation of the style from the base (*kihon*) to very high levels of technical expertise. Due to this, the ratio between form and action is often hard to understand. Sometimes it is simply the student's lack of study or capability. That is also why the bunkai is sometimes very difficult to understand and tiring from a psychological point of view. I think that the best way to learn is to have a good and competent master who can truly teach you the essence of the form, its meaning and its applications, many of which are hidden, both for self-defense and for the health of the person.

Q: What is the philosophical basis for your karate training?

A: Harmony among mind, spirit and body. This has always been the key factor for me. Also, I always wanted to study, learn and exercise to keep my body and mind in perfect shape.

Karate Masters

"With correct training and the guidance of a good teacher, you can learn the right attitude, modesty, self-control and courage, and every black belt must maintain these principles."

Q: After all these years of training and experience, could you explain the meaning of the practice of karate-do?
A: Self-control or *seigyo*, which is what we call it in Japanese. To apply this in your life, you have to completely understand it. It can be interpreted as seriousness and dignity, and as I said, it can be applied to every aspect of life. The practice of karate-do begins at black belt level—not at white belt. Prior to this phase [black belt], students are only going through a period of study and refection to try to understand their own tendencies. With correct training and the guidance of a good teacher, you can learn the right attitude, modesty, self-control and courage, and every black belt must maintain these principles. At that level, black belts must become examples for their kohai. The only way to understand every aspect of karate-do is through constant practice and dedication. As in any other activity, it is necessary to have professionalism and dignity.

Q: Compared with those who were being taught in your early days, is there anything lacking in the way karate is taught today?
A: Generally, teachers today provide plenty of explanations, but they do it with more talking and less action [or demonstrations]. In the early times, there were few explanations, and it was necessary to pay strong attention. [In those days], there was more action and less talking.

Q: Why is it, in your opinion, that a lot of students quit after two to three years of training?
A: The reasons vary from person to person, but the majority of students. After two or three years of practice, many believe that they are already good, and they don't think that they need to train anymore. They think that they are "there" because they have developed an evident skill [compared to when they started]. This is the wrong approach, and the only

way to prevent that is to teach the student he is still a beginner, regardless of how far how he thinks he has progressed ... even if he has been training for two or three years. This is the reason why it is so important to teach the philosophy of budo. It simply keeps the mind at the right place and prevents the ego from getting too big.

Q: There is very little written about you in magazines. You obviously do not thrive on the publicity. Why?
A: I am not an exhibitionist. I have had chances to appear in magazines all over the world, but that is not my goal. I am well known in the karate world because I have always demonstrated my qualities and the authenticity of my teacher's art with actions and not just with words. The little publicity I have received from magazines may result from the fact that I never wanted to compromise my goals to anyone, and I have always kept my professional dignity untouched. I am Japanese deep to my core, and I have the spirit of the samurai. We all know what conditions of servility you need to undergo to be considered by the politicians of the sport, and I can't accept that. Now it should be easy to understand why I don't pursue publicity.

"I am Japanese deep to my core, and I have the spirit of the samurai. We all know what conditions of servility you need to undergo to be considered by the politicians of the sport, and I can't accept that."

Q: Is there anything else you would to add for the readers?
A: Seek and strive to be the best. Do not let yourself get dragged [down] by anyone's words or by what only appears to be good. This can be very deceiving. O

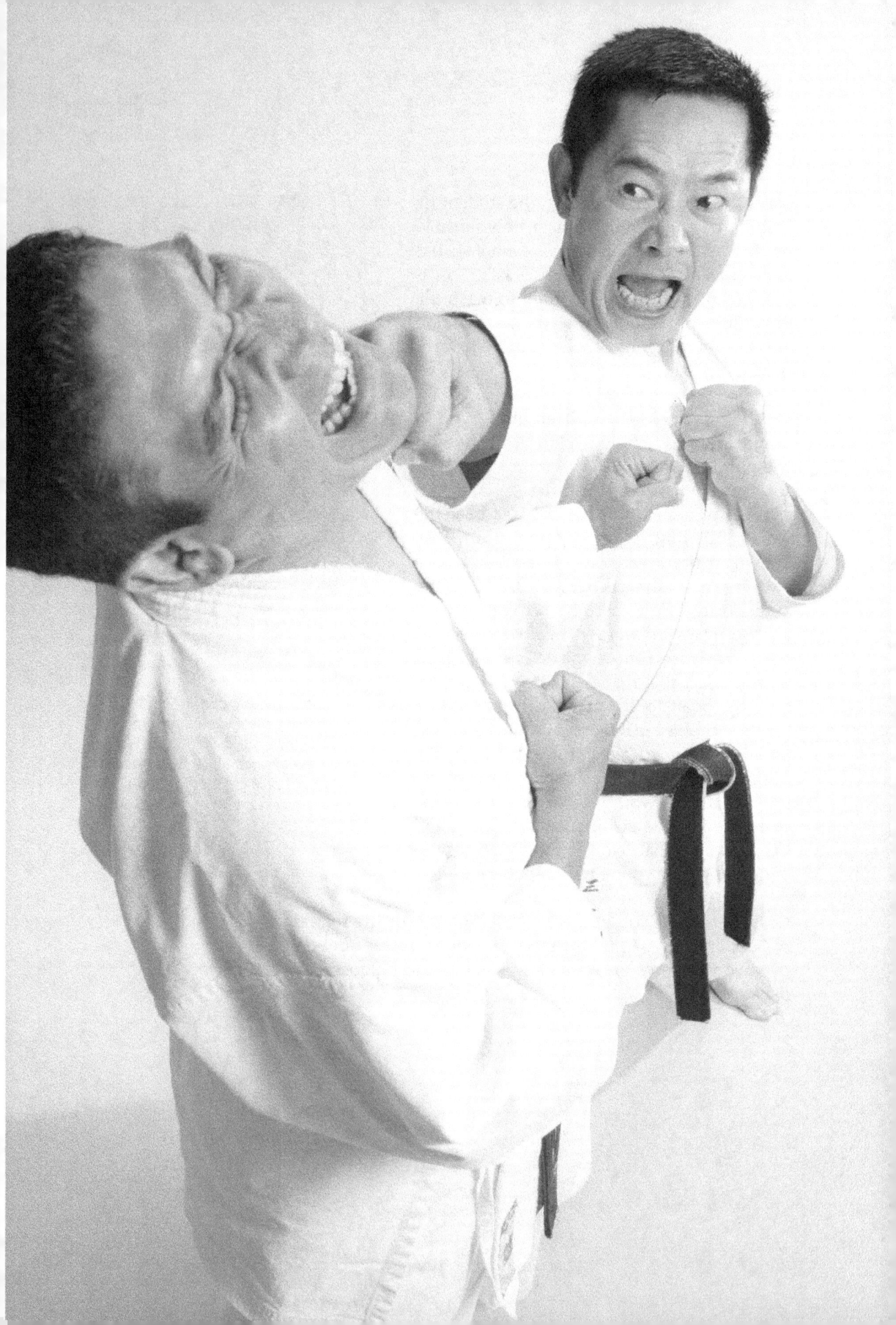

Kunio Miyake

The Power of Will

Born in 1946, Miyake Sensei began teaching the martial arts in Japan. At the same time, he was teaching modern Japanese language and literature at the high school level. He moved to the United States in 1985 and—with permission from Shuko-Kai Tani-ha Shito-Ryu and Soke Chojiro Tani—quickly established Shuko-Kai U.S.A. in Southern California. Founder of Shuko-Kai International, Miyake Sensei currently holds an official U.S.A. National Karate-Do Federation 8th degree in karate-do and a 6th degree in Shorinji Aiki Jiu-Jitsu. The All-Japan Karate-do Federation and the World Shorinji Kempo Federation issued his instructor's licenses. Both associations require the highest caliber of karate and jujitsu knowledge. In 1982, he was the All-Japan champion in Shito-Ryu Shuko-Kai and the 1988 U.S.A. Karate Federation National Champion. He was also selected as the representative at the All-Japan Martial Arts Demonstration (Budosai) — a distinctive honor because representatives are chosen throughout Japan based on their superior skills in their respective arts. With many years of experience in the arts of budo, Miyake Sensei is considered one of the most knowledgeable instructors in the art of karate. Miyake Sensei has earned a high level of respect by sharing karate-do with love, empathy and dedication. He strives for a life of tranquility and contentment, refreshed by the satisfaction derived from pursuing the way of martial arts with discipline and commitment.

Q: How long have you been practicing the martial arts and in how many styles have you trained?
A: I began practicing the martial arts when I was about eight. I started with kendo, and then I moved on to judo, shorinji-kempo, karate and iaido. Sensei Doshin So, the founder of shorinji kempo, was my first teacher. I had other sensei in kendo and judo, and they were extremely important in my training. Of course, in karate, it was Tani Sensei.

Karate Masters

"Traditional Japanese training means students have to do kihon drills everyday, and they have to be done with manners and patience. The sensei never explains anything, nor does he smile."

Q: Tell us some interesting stories about your early days in karate training.
A: My early days in karate were based on simple and pure *kihon* training. Only a few people stayed because there wasn't anything very interesting [going on]; repeating the same techniques thousands of times is not amusing to most practitioners. In my shorinji kempo dojo, my *senpai* always came to me and told me that we [*kohai*] had to fight a yakuza for our black belt test. I didn't want to go to the test for a long time because of this, and it never happened anyway. The main reason [I didn't go] was because I was still a kid, and I was afraid. From the physical point of view, I was a natural at karate. The kumite movements came more easily to me than kata movements. I believe that fighting is more natural for a human than learning a kata. In order to do a kata well, you have to "mold" your body so it "shows" the karate movement with precision and proper technique. Kumite seems to be a more natural approach, although it requires mastering other important elements that make fighting a different thing all together.

Q: When you started teaching, how did the Westerners respond to traditional Japanese training?
A: In 1985, I started teaching in California, and most of my students were juniors. They never stayed quiet when I was explaining [techniques] in class. In Japan, the students are afraid of the sensei, so they don't move around ... let alone when the teacher is explaining a technique or a principle! In my dojo, it was impossible for me to give them traditional Japanese training because of the Western mentality. Traditional Japanese training means students have to do kihon drills everyday, and they have to be done with manners and patience. The sensei never explains anything, nor does he smile. Now, I teach traditional karate with manners but not like before when I was in Japan. I always explain why they need to do certain techniques, and they [seem to] enjoy traditional Japanese karate

more. By providing explanations of why they have to behave in a certain way, it seems to help them truly appreciate the culture of budo.

Q: How has your personal karate developed over the years?
A: One way is my general approach to the art. In the very beginning, I always thought only about kumite. During my first years of training, I was not interested in kata at all. I only practiced kata for my rank testing because it was a requirement—not because I enjoyed it. As I grew up and gained maturity in the art, kata became more interesting to me, and I started to look at it from a very different perspective. Nowadays, when I conduct seminars, instructors and students ask me to do kata. They think that I specialize in kata instruction, which I don't, but it's very interesting to me because I enjoy instructing both kata and kumite. Life changes in very interesting ways!

"Nowadays, when I conduct seminars, instructors and students ask me to do kata. They think that I specialize in kata instruction, which I don't, but it's very interesting to me because I enjoy instructing both kata and kumite. Life changes in very interesting ways!"

Q: With all the technical changes during the last 30 years, do you think there is still pure shotokan, shito-ryu, goju-ryu, et cetera?
A: When you compare current WKF rules with old tournament rules, you can tell the differences right away. In kumite, we were looking for one punch, one kill techniques, but now we stress speed to win. In kata, more variations are acceptable for *tokuigata* and competitors, to impress the judges, adopt fancier versions of the same kata. I noticed that Japanese kata champions are performing their kata differently in WKF championships than when they compete in Japan because the judges from the WKF have a different viewpoint on how the kata should be performed.

After karate became an international sport, every country brought its own flavor. As a matter of fact, the Europeans made the WKF rules. Anyway, to question whether things are pure is hard to say. First of all, we need to

Karate Masters

"Sometimes fighters focus more on the efficiency of the technique and don't necessarily devote the proper attention to the development of the technical skill."

define what pure means because all the legendary masters learned from their teachers and then modified the teaching when they taught to the next generation of practitioners. We know, anyway, that karate has been changing rapidly for the last several decades, and it is very difficult to say that this or that style is pure.

Q: Do you think different ryu are important?
A: Yes, because each ryu has its own characteristics. Depending on the style, kata has different sets of the principles that help you to develop the "flavor" in the art of karate. Unfortunately, modern kumite does not show the characteristics of each ryu anymore because everything is extremely unified in movement and approach. This is the result of sport competition. Back then, shotokan used *zenkutsu-dachi* and goju-ryu used *nekoashi-dachi* in kumite so you could tell the practitioner's style by just looking at the way he fought. Because karate now has a sport aspect, it has been losing a little bit of its own character. Nowadays, we have only two styles for kumite: Japanese and rest of the world. And even the Japanese are changing to better accommodate the sportive approach.

Q: What is your opinion of full-contact karate and kickboxing?
A: I respect full-contact karate and kickboxing because those combat sports are extremely demanding and require a lot of dedication from the practitioners. For some, it isn't always easy to pursue good techniques. Sometimes fighters focus more on the efficiency of the technique and don't necessarily devote the proper attention to the development of the technical skill. Depending on what the individual person wants from karate or other martial arts, he should choose a style and try to do his best. I happened to choose traditional karate-do for myself because I wanted to practice the art my whole life. Combat sports are good when you are young and strong, but when you start to get older ... you simply can't perform them well.

Q: In regards to karate, how would you describe the life and dedication of Tani Sensei?

A: Tani Sensei dedicated his life to karate more than any other karate-ka that I have ever known. Sensei used to think of karate all the time, and he had thought up new, unique ideas for the art, including the double-twist or kick-shock, which increases the power in the techniques.

Before Tani Sensei passed away, he insisted that the name *tani-ha shito-ryu* should be changed to *tani-ha karate-do*. Some senior students didn't like the idea of changing the name. I think he changed his karate's name because he was open-minded and wanted to make the style deeper by incorporating other styles. Eventually, it was not pure shito-ryu as he learned from Grandmaster Mabuni. After I studied goju-ryu kata, I understood naha-te more thoroughly than before. This is a good example of why Tani Sensei took the title shito-ryu out and simply called it tani-ha karate-do. It was shito-ryu, but it wasn't shito-ryu as everybody understood it.

"After I studied goju-ryu kata, I understood naha-te more thoroughly than before. This is a good example of why Tani Sensei took the title shito-ryu out and simply called it tani-ha karate-do. It was shito-ryu, but it wasn't shito-ryu as everybody understood it."

Q: In regards to approach or physical capabilities, are there are any fundamental differences between Japanese karate-ka and Western karate-ka?

A: When describing physical capabilities, there aren't many differences. Nowadays in the U.S., many children start practicing karate at an early age ... just as they do in Japan. Fundamentally, I feel that there are more differences, and I think that is because karate in Japan is taken more seriously than here. In the Western world, in some cases, karate is used as a way for parents to keep their children occupied or to teach them discipline. In Japan, from an early age, the discipline is already there and doesn't need to be taught. When the art of karate is taken seriously, karate-ka are able to learn much more easily.

Karate Masters

"Budo is more important as the driving force of my training. Karate and budo are life experiences that never end. There is always another level of achievement to obtain, a higher plateau to be reached."

If you compare karate in the United States today to 25 years ago, the art has improved tremendously. But still Japan generally performs at a higher level. Hopefully, the Western world will soon reach the level at which Japan performs.

Q: Karate is often referred to as a sport. Would you agree with this or do you think it is only budo?
A: As a younger man, I felt that I was seeing the sport aspect. Competition was exciting to me, and it was more of the driving force. Now, as an older person, budo is more important as the driving force of my training. Karate and budo are life experiences that never end. There is always another level of achievement to obtain, a higher plateau to be reached. The technical aspects are mastered earlier in life while the spiritual aspects become more apparent and are of more importance as you become older. I truly believe that age is an important factor in this matter.

Q: In general, how do you presently see karate and shuko-kai around the world?
A: Because of the sport aspect of karate, the popularity has increased dramatically. The interest around the world is increasing; therefore, the exposure of Shuko-kai International has become increasingly more visible to practitioners. The increase in the availability of worldwide communication has brought my organization to the forefront of karate-do.

Q: Do you think kobudo helps karate-ka to improve their empty-hand skills?
A: Weapons training is not an important aspect in my way of training. Karate and kobudo are separate and don't assist each other in the physical aspect. You can be a great karate-ka without training in kobudo, but it is very difficult to be an expert in kobudo without having previous knowledge of karate-do.

Q: How should a teacher prepare and schedule his personal training to progress in the arts?
A: As a younger sensei, I did daily repetition training similar to that of my students, and I truly thought it was important. However, I now feel that my personal training should revolve around the concept of quality. Of course, I spend time away from my students to prepare for my own training, but I also spend time exercising to stay in my best physical condition and to perfect my technique. The teacher should allocate time for personal training. According to his age, he needs to develop and maintain other physical elements such as agility, limberness, endurance and good health. These elements require specific training sessions separate from karate training.

"The teacher should allocate time for personal training. According to his age, he needs to develop and maintain other physical elements such as agility, limberness, endurance and good health."

Q: When teaching the art of karate, what is the most important element: self-defense, sport or tradition?
A: My techniques are a balance of all three. As my students progress and obtain more knowledge, their techniques can be used for whatever avenue they want to follow. Many enjoy the sporting aspect; however, others report to me how many of their experiences in life are enriched by the physical training, focus, and spiritual teachings they have learned. For the sporting aspect, we focus on strength and physical abilities. For tradition, we focus our attention on knowledge and spirituality.

From the technical point of view and specificically for beginning students, we focus more on kumite to build coordination, speed and flexibility. As students progress, we introduce more complex techniques for kata to improve their form. Once they have obtained a higher level of achievement, I try to balance the training so their abilities increase for both aspects at the same rate.

Karate Masters

"My motivation has always been to make myself stronger, both mentally and physically. As a young person, I was shy and the martial arts helped to build my confidence. As the years passed, the philosophies helped to motivate me in many directions and to achieve my goals."

Q: Some people think that it's critical to go to Japan to train. Do you agree?
A: Not for everybody and not all the time. Right now many good karate-ka from Japan live overseas. Therefore, the level of karate all over the world is much higher than it was in the past. So, if you are going to go to Japan to learn karate, you should know what you want to learn, where you want to train and from whom you want to learn it. Otherwise, you will be disappointed. About 30 years ago, when karate was exported from Japan to other countries, any instructor in Japan could teach someone at the beginner's level better than a foreign or non-Japanese instructor. That's why if you want to go to Japan today to learn karate you must make a plan to determine where you are going to go, with whom you are going to train and determine, to the best of your ability, if you are going to learn what you set out to learn.

Q: Whom would you like to have trained with that you have not?
A: The people I would have most wanted to train with would have been the founders of each style. It would be important to me to learn their philosophies, along with their techniques, to further enhance my own techniques.

Q: What keeps you motivated after all these years?
A: My motivation has always been to make myself stronger, both mentally and physically. As a young person, I was shy and the martial arts helped to build my confidence. As the years passed, the philosophies helped to motivate me in many directions and to achieve my goals.

When I began training, karate was known as an art form for people who wanted to learn aggressive techniques. At the time, there weren't that many people who wanted to learn, so there were not many dojo available. Now karate has evolved into a sport, and this has made it more attractive to everyone. As a result, the karate community has grown rapidly.

Q: Do you think it is necessary to engage in free fighting to achieve good self-defense skills for a real situation?
A: I do not believe that it is necessary to free fight in order to defend yourself. If you prepare physically and mentally for tournament-style fighting, you should easily be able to adapt to the street … in most situations. But definitely, you need to understand that a sport competition is not real self-defense.

Q: What is your opinion about mixing karate styles? Does the practice of one nullify the effectiveness of the other? Can it be beneficial to a student?
A: In kata, each style has its own character and flavor that shows the roots of the style. Therefore, mixing styles creates difficulty with mastering a true technique. However, in kumite, it is more acceptable because the object is to dominate your opponent, so having more techniques in your arsenal can enhance your ability to overcome the ever-changing situation.

"In kata, each style has its own character and flavor that shows the roots of the style. Therefore, mixing styles creates difficulty with mastering a true technique."

Q: How important is "bunkai" in the understanding of kata?
A: Contrary to what others may feel, my opinion is that bunkai is of great importance for the true understanding of kata. Different styles have different references, so if the bunkai of a style is not practiced properly, then there can be no true understanding of what the movements represent.

Q: Do you have a particularly memorable karate experience that has remained as an inspiration for your training?
A: When I was in my twenties, I trained in shorinji-kempo and karate and did not have time to compete. But when I was in my early thirties, I began to compete. I enjoyed the competition, and it enhanced my experience and motivated me to train harder to be the best that I could. I concentrated on my kumite techniques and enjoyed the spirit of the competitions. It was an exciting time of my life, and it gave me the drive to better myself to this day.

Karate Masters

"Karate-do is a life-long experience that has many levels of achievement. As you experience the mental and physical aspects at different stages in your life, you seem to grasp the higher levels of knowledge and use these tools in all life experiences."

Q: How can practitioners increase their understanding of the spiritual aspect of karate?
A: Before you can increase your spiritual awareness, you must learn patience and realize that the karate experience takes many years of training. With this understanding, you realize—as in all spiritual journeys—that the more you know and realize, the deeper the spiritual experience. The first thing new students should learn is to enjoy all the basic aspects of karate-do. If they enjoy what they are doing, they will be more receptive to the disciplines that follow and be able to endure the rigorous training. Karate-do is a life-long experience that has many levels of achievement. As you experience the mental and physical aspects at different stages in your life, you seem to grasp the higher levels of knowledge and use these tools in all life experiences.

Q: How much training should a senior karate-ka be doing to improve?
A: As a senior, you must learn to use your time and energy efficiently. A younger person can afford the luxury of longer and more repetitious training because the body can easily absorb the physical activity. When you are older, you do not have the same luxury. Thus, you have to train as intensely [as a younger student], but you cannot waste any energy that you need in the other aspects of your life.

Q: Compared to the "early" days, is there anything lacking in the way karate is taught today?
A: These days karate has more of a sport aspect. Many people think the goal of training is to be a kata or a kumite champion. Some of these competitors think they are already the best because they have won championships. Many become champions by using only a few techniques or a few kata. However, these techniques or kata are only the tip of the iceberg. While some competitors focus [solely] on training to win competitions, they

lose out on more important aspects of karate. Things like the right attitude, manners and respect. A karateka needs to remember to be humble, even after winning many championships. In my early days, the spiritual side of karate was emphasized. In the early days, there were competitions, but they were very different from now. If you were punched in the face, you did not show weakness. Instead, you would wait for an opportunity to hit your opponent back. After the tournament, the fighters became friends because there was respect for each other. They would also compliment one another and humble themselves. This spiritual side of karate would also be shown in our dojo as well.

"The makiwara is an important aspect of training, and it should be used for achieving perfect form by practicing striking and relaxation techniques."

Q: What advice on supplementary training can you give to students?
A: When I was competing, I used to jog about three miles four or five days a week, and I would lift weights three days a week to build speed and strength. You need to think about speed and power together—not separate. If you use too much strength, you will decrease the speed of your technique. For instance, the makiwara is an important aspect of training, and it should be used for achieving perfect form by practicing striking and relaxation techniques.

Q: Why, after two or three years of training, do a lot of students quit training?
A: I think it's because there are a lot of very young students. Many of them seek other avenues of knowledge ... may it be intellectual or sport. Our world has become a wealth of diversity, and it is difficult to concentrate on our subjects long enough to begin to understand the actual complexities and depth [of those subjects]. Children have a tendency to want to know about everything that goes on around them, and it is difficult for them to focus on one subject. Thus, we need parental guidance to help children focus on what is necessary ... in lieu of what is available.

Karate Masters

"Fame is not what I seek. My quest is for the betterment of karate-do. I train and teach to be an example to my community. I must be in the best physical condition I can be and communicate my philosophy to my students."

Character is one of the most important qualities of a successful karate-ka. If a student has good character, he will build a good relationship with the sensei. With a good relationship comes a good attitude and mutual respect. After this, the student's techniques will improve naturally because the technique is simply a result of the student's attitude. That's what Funakoshi Sensei meant when he said you should develop character through karate training. The more character the student has ... the better and more mature the technique is.

Q: There is very little written about you in magazines. You obviously do not thrive on the publicity like some martial artists. Why?
A: Fame is not what I seek. My quest is for the betterment of karate-do. I train and teach to be an example to my community. I must be in the best physical condition I can be and communicate my philosophy to my students. This is more important than being in the spotlight of the martial arts. My karate training has always been for the evaluation of my fears, and my philosophy is to always conquer myself. Fear is an emotion that is always tested in all aspects of life, and my training—both physical and mental—is focused on the release of fear.

Q: What are your thoughts on the future of karate-do, and what's your opinion about karate entering in the Olympic games?
A: Although the Olympic Games may represent only one aspect of karate-do, I feel that it is important. The exposure to the world will increase the involvement of all nations and will help participants get funding through their national Olympic committee. This involvement will increase the amount of younger students who participate and encourage them to stay

with the sport because they will want to achieve Olympic honor. In the process, they will obtain the deeper knowledge of karate-do with the additional years of training it will take to get to the Olympics.

Q: Is there anything else you'd like to add?
A: When we are advanced in age, we need to continue being strict on ourselves. When people get older, they often tend to become lazy. As a matter of fact, we often don't train enough as a karate-ka. Of course, it's natural to slow down and lose some physical strength when we get older. But if we become strict in our training, we can become mentally stronger and train with quality. Then, our advanced teaching will compensate for any loss of speed or physical strength. Karate-do is not only a method of fighting, but it's also a way of strengthening relationships between yourself and society. In the future, I hope that all practitioners and teachers continue to focus on the traditions of karate-do without allowing business or personal gain reasons to overtake them. Failing to concentrate on tradition and knowledge seems to be a new trend in the martial arts. People new to karate-do need to realize the difference when beginning their new experience. If a practitioner finds a teacher who has trained hard and has followed the traditional way, he will become a better martial artist—and person—in general. O

"Karate-do is not only a method of fighting, but it's also a way of strengthening relationships between yourself and society. In the future, I hope that all practitioners and teachers continue to focus on the traditions of karate-do without allowing business or personal gain reasons to overtake them."

Tom Muzila

Conquering Fear

SENSEI TOM MUZILA STANDS IN THE WORLD TODAY AS ONE OF A HANDFUL OF PRIVILEGED STUDENTS OF THE GREAT KARATE MASTER TSUTOMU OHSHIMA—A DIRECT DISCIPLE OF GICHIN FUNAKOSHI AND ONE OF THOSE TALENTED FEW WHO HAVE BECOME LIVING LEGENDS. MUZILA STANDS APART FROM THE REST BECAUSE HIS UNIQUE CHARACTER, INTELLECT AND PERSONALITY. FROM HIS EARLY DAYS HE HAS BEEN A MAN OF CONVICTION AND DISCIPLINE. KNOWN AMONG HIS PEERS FOR BEING AN INNOVATOR AND A WELL-RESPECTED WRITER, TOM MUZILA HAD THE OPPORTUNITY OF TESTING HIS BUSHIDO SPIRIT AS A FORMER GREEN BERET, SKYDIVER, FIREWALKER AND MOUNTAIN CLIMBER—BESIDES ALL THE HIGH-INTENSITY MARATHON TRAINING SESSIONS WHICH EXEMPLIFY THE MENTAL DISCIPLINE AND SELF-EFFACEMENT NECESSARY IN THE SAMURAI CULTURE OF FEUDAL JAPAN.

THIS PHILOSOPHICAL APPROACH STILL HOLDS TRUE FOR MUZILA SENSEI, WHO MAKES IT THE BASIS NOT ONLY OF HIS MARTIAL ARTS TEACHINGS BUT ALSO HIS OWN LIFE AND WORK. FORTUNATE ENOUGH TO WORK WITH SOME OF THE MOST RECOGNIZED ACTION MOVIE STARS IN HOLLYWOOD, HE HAS ALWAYS USED HIS KARATE-DO TRAINING TO KEEP HIMSELF MENTALLY AND SPIRITUALLY GROUNDED. AS AN ARTIST OF LIFE WHO STRIVES TO ADHERE TO TRADITIONAL VALUES, THE PHILOSOPHY OF BUDO IS AN INTEGRAL PART OF MUZILA'S LIFE. HE HAS FIRM BELIEFS AND APPLIES THEM TO CONTEMPORARY MATTERS IN AN ENDLESS JOURNEY OF CONQUERING AND CONFRONTING FEAR AND PAIN—NOT ONLY AS A KARATE-KA BUT AS A HUMAN BEING AS WELL.

Q: When did you get started in the martial arts?
A: As a teenager I became curious about the martial arts. When I was 16 years old, I walked into a downtown Long Beach dojo that Caylor Adkins was sharing with John Ogden, a premier judo player. This dojo was right next to a bar. As I walked into the dojo, it was like one big street fight. I had to step back to realize that I hadn't gone into the bar. It was so impressive that it didn't register that I was in a martial arts establishment. Caylor was one of Mr. Ohshima's six original students—they consisted of Caylor, Jordan Roth and four Japanese students in the 1955 era. My impression that first night was that this was an example of a true warrior's spirit and the practice resembled that of a real fight. The tidal wave of

Karate Masters

"After I began learning the principles Mr. Ohshima was teaching, I began to learn about life—about the roots as opposed to the leaves. He taught with real style and class and showed how karate could be tempered with courage and humility. He always emphasized that our worse opponent was ourselves and we had to face ourselves very strictly, if we truly wanted to be mentally strong."

energy I felt from that practice made the hair on the back of my neck stand up. They were fighting standing, against the wall and on the ground grappling. I knew right there that this was the type of spirit and training I wanted.

Q: How was the training at that time?
A: A basic practice in those days was almost like, life and death survival. I would have to get so psyched up mentally to just survive a practice, without getting busted up and hit too much. It felt like getting ready to go into live combat and not knowing if you were going to make it. Then I attended my first special training in Long Beach led by Caylor Adkins. Mr. Ono came over from Japan to this event. After the first workout I was facing Mr. Ono and I attacked him and he knocked me down. I wondered who was attacking whom? Then it was his time to attack me and again he knocked me down again. It was like he was playing with a little kid. I was using all my abilities and he was just toying with me. The next morning we stood in *kiba-dachi* stance for 1 1/2 hours. The first evening, we had already run nine miles, right after executing over one-thousand basics. Then the following day, we had a practice which was about three-hours long. Another practice, we did 100 repetitions of the same kata one right after another. There were 30-40 people there and they were going crazy. Caylor pushed us to 110 percent on everything we did. And he participated in every thing we did as opposed to standing around. Caylor's ability was incredible. I never saw anyone cover distance so fast. If you were six feet away from him, facing him as an opponent, the next moment his face would be right in front of yours and you had no idea how he got there so fast. It was like he skipped or jumped through time and space. Ken Osborne was another senior who also made an incredible impression on me, from training with him. Ken was originally Chuck Norris's first black belt and his top tournament competitor. In 1966, Chuck and Ken came to one of Mr. Ohshima's Special Trainings and later, Ken ended up joining our group, Shotokan Karate of

America. I trained with Ken once a week in those days and he moved like a machine. I couldn't believe his phenomenal foot sweeping ability. There was hardly anyone who could escape from his foot sweep. Don Depree was another senior, who I trained directly with, which had a major influence upon me. He was the toughest and strongest karate fighter I have ever seen and still is today. In any kind of a real fight, I would categorize him as not just one of the toughest fighters of our time, but in a life-and-death situation, I would label him as one of the toughest fighters in history. Even though he is incredibly tough, I was amazed at how humble he is too. This is an example of some of the seniors, fighters and the realism in which we trained in those early days.

"A basic practice in those days was almost like, life and death survival. I would have to get so psyched up mentally to just survive a practice, without getting busted up and hit too much. It felt like getting ready to go into live combat and not knowing if you were going to make it."

Q: When did you meet Sensei Ohshima?
A: Caylor Adkins would ask Mr. Ohshima to come down once a week to lead the workout. The first time I saw him, I was dismayed that he was so nice and polite before practice—very tranquil and serene. The first time I shook his hand, it felt like a tidal wave of energy went into me. Then when he started teaching, it was like Dr. Jekyl and Mr. Hyde. He was unrelenting. His techniques were unbelievable. He would move like a ballet dancer and with the finesse of a cat. He would face anyone in the training hall. There were many people that I feared in the class, but when they went up against Mr. Ohshima he would demolish them. He would also tap into the deep portion of your mind and motivate you to do more. Everything he did was positive. He gave you a bigger capacity. At this time, shotokan karate became my life. After I began learning the principles Mr. Ohshima was teaching, I began to learn about life—about the roots as opposed to the leaves. He taught with real style and class and showed how karate could be tempered with courage and humility. He always emphasized that our worse opponent was ourselves and we had to face ourselves very strictly, if we truly wanted to be mentally strong. I was amazed how knowledgeable and wise he was about so very many different topics. When he focused his eyes were piercing. He would look right through you and that gaze would penetrate right to your soul. You felt like he was

Karate Masters

"Karate aligned the very being of physical existence to face, harmonize and extinguish weaknesses. This allowed me to look at myself with "severe eyes." The only thing that can cut a diamond is another diamond and the only thing that can cut our consciousness is our own consciousness."

hypnotizing you and he could make you do or not do anything he wanted with you in a fight.

Q: How were the testing sessions back then?
A: The testing sessions were so long and grueling that everyone was totally exhausted afterwards. The tests were conducted first on the brown belts and then downward. We had to wait at the side until our turn. I remember that Caylor said that while waiting for your test, you had to keep focused. I was impressed with this strictness. It was like an ancient atmosphere. Everyone was so serious. During kumite, the most important part was hitting the other guy and also how you took getting hit. Everyone got hit. All these impressions presented a challenge and standard that drove me to work out harder. I have never failed a shotokan test, but I appreciated passing this first test more than any other. The whole atmosphere was out of an ancient time period in Japan.

Q: What was Sensei Ohshima like?
A: Mr. Ohshima would face a student and when they attacked, he would avoid them and go through them without leaving the line. This concept is called *irimi*. It means "entering mentality or technique." When an opponent attacks, you mentally catch the moment and go in with your attack, actually beating and destroying him before he realizes it. Mr. Ohshima had practiced this concept for many years, but applied it to many types of attacks. He eventually was able to expand on it to a very interesting application. Mr. Ohshima said he discovered this unique technique by accident. He was sparring with Mr. Honda (one of Mr. Ohshima's top students in Japan) and saw a kick coming in. It was supposed to be a round kick, but Mr. Honda instead executed a straight front kick. Mr. Ohshima continued to go straight into the kick, slipped under the leg and went behind him. He then worked on it and perfected this capability. In SKA, one of the requirements for a brown belt is to display this mentality. This is tough since it's not the Westerner's mentality to go under and avoid a kick that is coming straight at you! Sensei Ohshima is only 145 pounds,

but he could not be lifted by two larger guys. He would get two guys to lift him up by his armpits, which they easily did. He would then imagine he was a large steel liberty bell, very heavy, and they couldn't lift him! He also had an unbendable arm. Three people would try unsuccessfully to bend it. Also, he would touch his thumb and first finger and two people couldn't pull these fingers apart. He would image that his fingers were fused together. Mr. Ohshima's punch was phenomenally penetrating. He once stood three guys together, stomach to back, all facing the same direction, with a pillow in between them. He would already have his arm extended and put his fist right on the guys stomach in front of him, while he was in a front stance. He would connect his back foot to the ground extend his hips, Ki (energy), and mind in and the power of the punch would penetrate all three guys. The last guy would feel the penetration as strong as the first guy in line. It would knock the wind out of all of them.

"Mr. Ohshima would face a student and when they attacked, he would avoid them and go through them without leaving the line. This concept is called irimi. It means "entering mentality or technique." When an opponent attacks, you mentally catch the moment and go in with your attack, actually beating and destroying him before he realizes it."

Q: What approach did he use to teach the philosophical aspects of the art?
A: Early in our training with Mr. Ohshima, we were taught to defeat our strongest opponent—ourselves—and our fears and weaknesses. Karate aligned the very being of physical existence to face, harmonize and extinguish weaknesses. This allowed me to look at myself with "severe eyes." The only thing that can cut a diamond is another diamond and the only thing that can cut our consciousness is our own consciousness. Mr. Ohshima popularized many old sayings, such as, "If you don't want to get wet, jump in the lake!" I made *sho-dan* right before I went into the service where I signed up with the Special Forces. This was my first test of Mr. Ohshima's philosophy. It allowed me to stay alive. I went on several covert operations in the early 70's in South America. You had to have high academic skills in the Special Forces or Green Berets, while you were learning survival skills. The biggest thing I noticed is that if I faced these situations head on, I could throw out

Karate Masters

"When I faced life and death situations against revolutionaries, I would always hear Mr. Ohshima's words echoing in the back of my mind and I would not get attached to the fear involved with life-threatening situations. Negative mind talk will put you on a downhill spiral toward defeat."

my fears and therefore had a better chance of surviving. When I faced life and death situations against revolutionaries, I would always hear Mr. Ohshima's words echoing in the back of my mind and I would not get attached to the fear involved with life-threatening situations. Negative mind talk will put you on a downhill spiral toward defeat. A real turnaround happened when my friend and I, with six indigenous personnel went on a longer jungle mission. We thought we were ready to go but when we got there, we started worrying about trip wires, mines and booby traps, and we were totally exhausted after the first few days. I heard Mr. Ohshima's words in my mind again, saying, "face yourself courageously." I then said to my friend, "We have to stop this type of thinking and quite worrying about getting killed. If were going to get killed, it is heavens will and there is nothing we can do about it. We had to be positive, thinking positively how we were going to get through it. If we got taken out, we would go out in style." I noticed when we got that mentality we became liberated and it started to protect us. This type of thinking got us through several situations of firearm encounters at 20-to-30 feet. In one situation, we had to burrow into the undergrowth and become one with the jungle while the enemy was searching for us and coming as close as a few feet. We had to disappear mentally, become one with the jungle and think that they couldn't detect us. At one time, I saw this one-inch long ant and I just became that ant, since it was right after a ferocious firefight. All this related to the martial arts training. I never forgot it.

Q: Did you do any karate during your military service?
A: While I went through all my training, I continually tried to apply karate concepts and Mr. Ohshima's philosophy to everything I did. When I would come back in town on a leave and face the same black belts I did before, I was surprised that I didn't lose anything, in fact, I felt that I had gotten better from applying those concepts to life in realistic situations.

During the last 10 months, I was transferred to the 101st Airborne. I started boxing for the post and had eight fights. I was on 24-hour duty and boxed three times a day. This was opportunistic to be able to work out that much as we didn't have anything to do until there was an emergency. Then I got 10 guys together and we trained twice a day and went to open tournaments and won lots of trophies. We had all different styles, so we did a lot of eclectic stuff. I met Bill "Superfoot" Wallace in the early seventies, when his fighting career was just starting. I was amazed at his incredible fighting ability, especially, when I found out later he was primarily self-taught. I went back to Cal State Long Beach and got my degree in Asian Religions to study the Asian mind behind this whole martial arts thing. I then got connected to the *kundalini* yoga organization. They wanted to learn karate via Mr. Ohshima. He started teaching them and it was then handed down to Caylor and then it came to me. I went to special yoga training, which was 12-hours per day. There was no talking for 9 days. You really got to feel people behind you without seeing them. I taught the world's largest karate class at that time. There were over 1,000 yoga people, which I taught at one time in Taos, New Mexico at 7,500 feet. This was a real challenge, but worked out fine. Getting into marathon karate training was one of the greatest experiences of my life. At special training, we were doing 1,000 front punches and one day I started wondering how long it would take to do 10,000. I had to acquire a "no limit" mentality. I found if I could execute 10,000 techniques at one time, then I knew I could do 100,000. It was similar to climbing mountains. If you climb the Colorado peaks, maybe Everest would be OK. Also, I would hear from Mr. Ohshima that old warriors in Japan would train for phenomenal durations. In the 1600s they would

"I had to acquire a "no limit" mentality. I found if I could execute 10,000 techniques at one time, then I knew I could do 100,000. It was similar to climbing mountains. If you climb the Colorado peaks, maybe Everest would be OK. Also, I would hear from Mr. Ohshima that old warriors in Japan would train for phenomenal durations."

Karate Masters

"You must have a burning desire to discover what exists behind this long-distance training. You are talking about doing 10,000 punches with each hand in the morning session and another 10,000 kicks in the next training session, repeating a kata 1,000 times without stopping, hitting the makiwara 1,000 times, et cetera. Not everybody has the spirit and mental disciple necessary to experience this kind of training."

train 8-to-10 hours per day. These guys could do phenomenal things. This thought pushed me onward. I wanted to attempt to scratch the surface and experience a small essence of how these super ancient warriors trained.

Q: What drew your attention to marathon karate training?
A: Prior to my training experience I was doing a lot of short-span explosive training activities and I didn't pay any attention to the long-distance training approach. It was my Green Beret Special Forces experience that changed the way I looked at things. I was also inspired when Tsutomu Ohshima told me stories about the old samurai monks training 12 hours a day for 50 days in a row. That really caught my attention and I became interested in the mental approach to this kind of elite training. This type of training is such that you are challenged in every aspect of your existence from physical to mental. What is important is that you, as a student, must be inquisitive about it. You must have a burning desire to discover what exists behind this long-distance training. You are talking about doing 10,000 punches with each hand in the morning session and another 10,000 kicks in the next training session, repeating a kata 1,000 times without stopping, hitting the makiwara 1,000 times, et cetera. Not everybody has the spirit and mental disciple necessary to experience this kind of training. I stayed on this long endurance karate training for many years. It was very hard to stop or slow down. I felt as though I was achieving a bigger capacity after every karate feat I had accomplished. I felt as though I had no limits, mentally or physically. If someone asked me, "Tom, Why don't you swim across the Pacific ocean?" My mind would immediately start contemplating how I could achieve that? A friend was joking around and actually asked me this. My mind immediately said: "Ok!" I really started to want to do it, but was able to distract myself and dream up something a little less challenging, that took less time.

Q: What is the most basic aspect a student needs in order to undergo this extreme training?

A: Of course, you first have to believe that you can do it. You also need the inner self-confidence and be able to visualize yourself accomplishing it. The most important and basic element is concentration. It is not simply a matter of going through the movements physically. You must control your mind so it is behind each and every single technique you perform. You can't let the physical or external stimulus be in control of what you are doing. Focus and concentrate, then fight internally to avoid the body signs of exhaustion and to keep that mental concentration. The real goal of this training is not the physical part—it is concentration—concentration in every single technique. It is a vehicle to improve your mental concentration, not just grunt endurance. The more experienced the practitioner is, the deeper his concentration is.

Q: What do you mean by "deeper?"

A: Deeper means less influenced by external stimuli and operating from the deepest part of your subconscious mind. In martial arts, to acquire anything, you must practice, and the same thing happens with concentration. In order to acquire and build it, you have to practice it. And it is difficult to focus on your mind when the physical training is so demanding and painful. Your subconscious mind has to be programmed with total confidence and it will make your body find a positive successful way to achieve it. If your conscious mind say, "yes," I want to do this and for some inner fear or phobia your subconscious mind says, "no I can't," or it doesn't want too, its going to be very hard to accomplish the feat successfully.

"When you put yourself near the fire, you have to be prepared for the possibility that you may get burned. In most cases, your opponents are mentally prepared for this situation. You must be mentally ready and not hesitate when the time is appropriate. Even traumatic professions become routine for people after a while."

Q: When you face this kind of training, fear seems to be something natural, right?
A: It's very natural. Fear is not a bad thing if you understand it. My favorite definition of fear is: false, evidence, appearing, real. We fear, worry or are too concerned about 50% of thoughts in our minds, that never really happen to us. Maybe we should just be concerned about 10 or 15% of our thoughts? Then about 50% of the time we are more focused on the past or the future and not on this present moment.

Q: What do you mean?
A: We have to teach ourselves to be totally aware and mindful of every moment in life, if we what to live most advantageously? In other words, what is the best thing we can do with this moment? How can we use this moment wisely? What is the best mentality or attitude to have for this moment? Fear is a human sensation. You have to recognize you do have fear, identify where it comes from, and where you acquired that fear. Then you analyze the benefits of getting rid of it and how things are going to change if you do. If you follow this process, you have a very good chance of getting out from under that fear. I know that many people deal with fear by running away from it, but this is not a very constructive way. You have to see you fear and get close to it. Simply don't let it go to your emotions. The main idea is that you must be in control, and this only happens when you face fear with your conscious mind. The best way, like I said, is to face your fear—but you also need the help of a good teacher or instructor who can pull you along. He has to be an example for you, someone you know had fears like yourself and did overcome them. Someone who is an example that it is humanly possible to do that.

Q: What physical training would recommend to aid fear elimination?
A: The first thing is breathing. You have just got to use your breathing, collect yourself and don't let your breathing get carried away. When you face a situation of fear, you should try to shut down the inner turmoil of your thoughts—and here is when meditation comes into play. You need to calm that inner garble and relax if you are knowledgeable in meditation techniques. If you are not, just calm your mind and thoughts down, through your breathing. It is very easy and effective.

Q: What about the pain in this kind of training?
A: It is definitely a factor. Your body has to go through a great deal of pain but your ability to deal with it and overcome it has to be gradually

increased under the supervision of a qualified sensei. This is not a joke. You don't want simply to "push through it." You have to develop an understanding of what it is and when you are going to injure yourself. Facing pain has to be done and learned in a progressive way. Pain is also very relative to each individual. Everyone's capacity is different. Punching a makiwara 1,000 times with your knuckles bleeding is something that requires more than a simple ability to overcome pain. It is a mental ability, something that you have to develop throughout the years under the supervision of an authentic sensei. You can't let your mind become imprisoned with the idea of fear or pain. You should first analyze the feat to make sure it isn't too dangerous or stupid to do.

Q: What is the story behind the use of different colors in uniforms and in belts?
A: There are an incredible amount of different uniforms today, and most did originate for a specific reason. Uniform styles have changed many times throughout history, and it is very hard to pinpoint the exact time the colors of these uniforms originated. To study this, we should look at the three main countries from which the martial arts originated: China, Okinawa and Japan. In China, the martial arts uniforms came from the monasteries and Shaolin Temple monks. They utilized a few basic-colored robes, depending on which religion they were a part of. They also used various shades of black. Okinawa was starting to develop a gi-type uniform before the 18th century, but it was a darker, earthy color. Japan had various colored kimonos and *hakamas* for centuries. Kendo practitioners traditionally used a blue uniform, and still do. When Gichin Funakoshi started teaching karate in Japan around 1922, he adopted a white uniform. As you know, the two colors of the yin and yang symbol are black and white with a dot of each within both halves of the design. All colors combined together at one end of the scale make black, while at the other end, they make up white. The colors have always stood for the two polarities of the universe—positive and negative. The yin/yang symbol emphasizes living in harmony with both. The white gi under Funakoshi was used to represent the purity

"Your body has to go through a great deal of pain but your ability to deal with it and overcome it has to be gradually increased under the supervision of a qualified sensei. This is not a joke. You don't want simply to 'push through it.'"

Karate Masters

"Circular strikes are more emphasized in Chinese styles. Straight line strikes are more emphasized in Japanese styles, but eventually they both come together at the higher levels of practice."

of mind and spirit. A white gi is also a mental reminder for an individual to shed and extinguish their mental blocks. It represents non-attachment to the physical world. The black gi represents similar aspects, depending where it originated and why. The Japanese karate black belt also has an interesting origin. Before karate was founded by Gichin Funakoshi, kendo already had a very sophisticated ranking system developed by the samurai warriors. Funakoshi's ranking system was similar to the kendo system. When Funakoshi first started teaching, he didn't have a ranking system. He had many serious and loyal individuals who had trained under him for years. At the beginning stages in Japan, there was only the white belt. Eventually, Funakoshi wanted to give a gift back to his dedicated students for training so hard. When certain individuals acquired a specific mental, technical and physical level, he gave them a black belt. This was first done very personally and informally. It was a reflection of the individual's mentality and recognized this person as possessing a specific skill level. A few years later, Funakoshi's seniors implemented the stages of brown belt, helping to harmonize the contrast in levels from white to black.

Q: It is said that for a perfect punch the heel of your back leg has to be fully planted on the floor, but some other instructors claim that hip rotation is more important than keeping the heel flat on the ground. Which is it?

A: Both concepts are actually right. The back heel and outside blade edge of the foot should have a good connection with the floor when executing a specific straight line technique. The hip must also be aligned properly to acquire the connection and benefit of the heel being down on the ground. If the hip is in and heel is up, power will generally be lost from the technique. Ideally, a technique is much more effective if the hip is in and heel down. There are always exceptions to the rule, however. If the body and hip are traveling with a lot of momentum and speed at the moment of connection, the heel does not have to be directly down. The majority of pivoting and turning should be executed on the heel, but there are instances when the back or front foot can be pivoted on the ball or outside blade edge. Circular strikes are more emphasized in Chinese styles. Straight line strikes are more emphasized in Japanese styles, but eventually they both come together at the higher levels of practice. There are also different types of power, which I like to refer to them, as: thrusting, snapping and swinging. Each are related to various types of specific techniques and are governed by specific principles.

Q: Do you think any style is better than all others?
A: There are hundreds of styles in the martial arts today. Every country has many systems of its own. China, for example, has hundreds of kung-fu styles. The majority of martial arts are broken down into many different organizations. Each association has its own interpretation of that style, which all depends on the head instructor's interpretation. Junior members will always copy the senior instructor's positive and negative qualities. In the United States, there are at least 20 or 25 major shotokan karate associations. Each group has its own interpretation of shotokan. Some emphasize high-level elements, some stress low-level points, while yet others never seem to get past a certain level in technical practice. Shotokan karate can either be practiced hard or soft—like any other style or it can also be practiced with both elements. In a single punch, there are both soft and hard qualities. It all depends on the practitioner's level. The usual route is to go from hard to soft levels, but each person must discover the path that is best suited to their needs. Styles do not make the person; the person makes the style. The first thing to keep in mind is that there is no best martial art. There are many illegitimate schools and martial artists. You have to be aware of them, but there are also many authentic styles and instructors. A student is usually attracted to the style and school they can personally identify with. There are many independent organizations existing for the same style, but they all have various interpretations and group levels. It all depends on what their major emphasis is. When studying with an authentic instructor and system, the student has to practice the techniques diligently to find out how to make it work for them. This may take years and thousands of repetitions, all with the right mentality. Traditional martial arts are geared for the whole life, not for a short span of time. You must be patient for the benefit of the martial arts to sink in. Don't be too eager to judge the style. Rather, examine yourself first. It

takes time to learn and develop a skill in anything that's worthwhile. You must criticize yourself first before you earn the right to criticize others. There are many martial artists from the styles you mentioned making the techniques work. The original lineage of these authentic arts came from actual combat. Those who stayed alive in combat proved which techniques worked with rigorous practice, then they passed on the concepts. It is up to us to keep those original, realistic techniques alive, but it will only occur through diligent practice.

Q: What is your advice on supplementary training for karate?
A: If you diligently practice karate (or any martial art) in all of its facets, you should acquire a sound foundation. But it is hard to develop your cardiovascular system just by practicing the basics. It all depends on the pace of your training. You can acquire cardiovascular conditioning in many ways: kata (forms) practice, a regular regimen of free sparring, or aerobic activities such as running, swimming, or bicycling. A karate practitioner will naturally condition all of their muscles, but with an emphasis on a few in particular. Practitioners must have correct alignment and a strong connection from their technique, through their hips, to the ground. Upper body and shoulder strength are not especially important. The outside back muscles must be strong to transfer the connection through the hips and down to the back leg. It is very important to have strong legs, hips, underarm and back muscles. Any kind of weight training for the legs will assist your foundation. The back muscles can also be worked through any type of pulling exercise. Remember, in martial arts your center of gravity is just below your navel. You do not want to be top heavy and acquire a lot of shoulder power. Asians usually have a long torso and shorter legs. This naturally helps root their center of gravity in the middle of the hips.

Q: How important is mental attitude in karate training?
A: A certain mental attitude and spirit must supplement technical skill before you can persevere in realistic combat. It is sometimes very hard to acquire this combat instinct, unless you were naturally born with it, but it's not impossible. You must train intensely until your mind becomes much stronger than your body. Your mind must be tempered—do not give in to pain or discomfort. You must face your fears, weaknesses, inhibitions and insecurities so they won't get in the way of a confrontation. Your technical training must emphasize what is realistic and effective in combat. This will help give you technical confidence. The practice of concentrating and focusing your mind in every activity you participate in will

greatly enhance your mental attitude in the martial arts. Remember, attitude is the one thing we always are in control of. No one can take it away from us, unless we decide to give it away. If we change our attitude, we did it. You can always blame or make excuses why you changed your attitude, but when it comes down to it, you made the choice and did it.

"You must train intensely until your mind becomes much stronger than your body. Your mind must be tempered—do not give in to pain or discomfort. You must face your fears, weaknesses, inhibitions and insecurities so they won't get in the way of a confrontation. Remember, attitude is the one thing we always are in control of. No one can take it away from us, unless we decide to give it away."

Q: Can karate training sometimes give individuals too much self-confidence?
A: There are many benefits of the martial arts and a primary one is to develop self-confidence and a strong mind. When this is achieved a student can utilize that development to help others do the same. A martial artist must first set a good example for others to follow. Many times, we must sacrifice unselfishly for others. Accordingly, the stronger you mentally become, the greater the potential to help those around you. For ones own practice, the stronger you are, the more humble you must practice to be. This keeps a good balance in our mentality. Sometimes it can sound, as though you still have the attitude that you must prove yourself. But you first need to prove yourself to you, not to others. Don't take advantage of someone, even if they are wrong and you have the ability to dominate them. Only do what is absolutely necessary to handle the situation. Don't seek situations where you have an advantage simply to prove yourself. Rather, look for situations where you can assist others with your new self-confidence.

Q: Why is the meditation ritual before and after a training session so important?
A: There are many groups which practice the *rei* and *mokuso* meditation before and after practice. Most, however, do not know what these rituals and practices are for. The primary purpose of mokuso meditation before practice is to prepare the mind and clear it for disciplined, rigorous martial

Karate Masters

"The bow is also an expression trust and humility. We not only bow to our seniors, training hall, and martial arts' heritage, we also bow to our higher selves. In yoga, certain body forms and positions create a specific mentality. Bowing creates a humble mind. It naturally balances our egos."

arts practice. An individual should throw everything out of their mind before training or practice may be drastically impaired. First, one concentrates on breathing in the lower abdomen. Later, one practices as if the mind has stopped. One must empty the mind and keep it totally clear. The mind does not think—a condition called "no mind" or *mushin*. This is an ideal state of mind in which to face your opponent. So in mokuso meditation, you are preparing your mind for practice, for opponents, and for life. Of course, there are many different levels of mushin, and it takes years of practice to use effectively. At the end of practice an individual is usually very tired. Therefore, they should clear the mind once more. Although tired, they will then feel very clean and mentally clear. The karate-ka should try to integrate this mentality and keep it in their daily life. One eventually learns how to instantly develop this mentality and use it such as in a combat situation. After a good strong practice, you should try to hold this mentality and apply it to life's situations, the rest of the day.

Q: How important is bowing to the Japanese culture?
A: Many different states of mind are integrated into bowing. It goes deeply into the culture and heritage of the Eastern world. A bow can be a simple greeting, or it can be a very perfected as an art form in itself. Martial artists stick more to the definition of bowing taught within the training hall. The junior/senior relationship is very important there. We bow to our seniors in respect for what they have learned and for what they are going to teach us. The senior is supposed to be an example whom we follow mentally, technically, physically and spiritually. The bow is also an expression trust and humility. We not only bow to our seniors, training hall, and martial arts heritage, we also bow to our higher selves. In yoga, certain body forms and positions create a specific mentality. Bowing creates a humble mind. It naturally balances our egos. Even if an individual does not understand humility, by practicing the bow with the right state of mind, the will eventually become humble to a certain degree. There are many levels of the bow. An true sensei can

watch ten different martial artists bow and immediately know what kind of mental and technical level each person has. He can see all of this in their form, breathing, eyes, state of mind and mannerisms.

Q: Describe *kime*.
A: One word in Japanese often takes an entire English paragraph to explain. These words generally represent a specific mental state, experience, or feeling. In English, no specific words exist to describe some of these one-word meanings. Americans would have to compile a number of closely related words and descriptions to get a true meaning of certain words. Kime is one of these words and it means more than just "focus." There are four major elements which are a part of kime. The first is size, which is the fundamental element that makes a technique work against a smaller person. The second element is strength void—a karate-ka's strength will fill-in where another person's void is created. The third element is to attack an individual's vital point. The fourth kime element is a big category that basically includes asignments, connection, focus, spirit and penetration. Any one of these categories can make your technique effective. If you can effectively apply one of the elements against your opponent, it will make your technique work reasonably well. If you can apply two elements, your technique will definitely work. If you can activate three or all four elements, it will probably be overkill. There are many other elements which can contribute to creating a kime-type technique. They include timing, distance, rhythm, and strategy. The more elements you can integrate within one technique, the more effective it will be.

Q: What is your opinion on awarding black belts to children and teenagers?
A: Children have many advantages and disadvantages in the martial arts, just as with any other sport. Some of their advantages are flexibility, stamina, energy and youth. They naturally have clearer, uninhibited minds. Some of their disadvantages are immaturity, small size, lack of concentration and attention, and emotional sensitivity. Every child is different and needs to be taught in a specific way to bring out his or her potential and capacity. Children training in the martial arts can build a strong foundation in many elements of their life. One example of this is Tsutomu Ohshima, Head Instructor of Shotokan Karate of America (SKA). Mr. Ohshima started practicing judo, kendo and sumo when he was 5 years old and trained in these arts until he was 16. It was not until then that he started practicing karate and eventually received his black belt. Can you imagine the incredible foundation

he had already built up in all aspects of his life by starting martial arts training at such an early age? The worst disadvantage a child black belt faces is mental immaturity. A young practitioner needs to digest his mental training experiences and let them develop and evolve naturally. This is why Mr. Ohshima has a rule in the SKA that no matter how technically skilled a child is, they had to be at east 16 years of age to receive a black belt.

Q: What are the mental and physical levels a person goes through in regards to fighting ability?
A: This is a very broad topic. There are so many facets that can make a difference in one's fighting ability. Many people get stuck at one level and tend to rely on their favorite technique. There are numerous ways you can beat your opponent. The two most important elements are your mental and technical level, and your opponent's. At this point we can start to activate some of the other elements which can contribute to beating an opponent. You must keep in mind that one level is not necessarily higher than another. You may simply decide that one concept would be best used against a specific opponent, while another concept is best against another type of opponent. The first level is to beat and overwhelm your opponent with continuous attacks and combinations. The second level is to catch or attack your opponent the moment they move or attack. A third level is to be so powerful in spirit and mind that your opponent cannot move. The last level is to be so highly trained that you do not reveal anything mental or technical to your adversary. In this instance, you draw your opponent in with 100 percent commitment and use their strength against them.

Q: What are the most important elements a good teacher should provide?
A: A good karate teacher has an excellent balance in their personality and their mentality. They first, actually live what they are teaching and preaching is very important. A good teacher must be able to jump in the fire during practice and show the students they it can be done and be a good positive example for the students. The teacher must know how to inspire and motivate every student in the class to their fullest capacity. He or she must know how to get the best out of everyone. It is similar to that of a great film director, getting the most out of his actors. Then if he or she sacrifices him or herself appropriately for the students and the school, the students will be more apt to do the same, not just for themselves, but also for the teacher and the school. You need theIr consistent mental and financial support. If you truly have that, you can move to the next issue, to analyze

the town or city you live in by looking at its population and potential for growth. If you need to have 30 active, practicing and paying members to financially support a dojo, a city must have enough people interested in attending. Various styles attract different types of individuals, depending on what concepts are stressed in the training. Promotion of the dojo is very important, too. What colleges, high schools and elementary schools are near you? Will the dojo have a children's class? A children's class can be very successful and supportive for the dojo. Some of the most successful dojos are promoted only by word of mouth. A dojo can be compared to fish. Depending upon location, size of building and type of facilities, the dojo can only grow so big, like a fish in a small aquarium. You must strive to acquire a certain mix of elements if you want to create a successful dojo.

Q: What is the best way to train to cope with a life-threatening situation?
A: You must prepare for this possibility or your hesitation could cost you your life or that of an innocent companion. You have chosen a profession, which is very honorable, with the appropriate

"Always wear the belt low on the hips and abdomen. If a martial artist wears his belt tight around the waist, he likely does not understand correct breathing."

mentality. When you put yourself near the fire, you have to be prepared for the possibility that you may get burned. In most cases, your opponents are mentally prepared for this situation. You must be mentally ready and not hesitate when the time is appropriate. Even traumatic professions become routine for people after a while. In an emergency ward, doctors get used to working on people who have been mangled in car accidents. They become very objective and learn to keep their emotions separate from their work. You must train yourself to act instinctively. Remember, the true samurai would never draw his sword until he was ready to take a life for honor and justice. In Japanese, there is a word referred to, as *kokoro.* It is one of those words that would take a whole paragraph in English to explain properly. Basically, it is sounds like to contradictory elements, but they are very integrated together. The first is to not except or give in to surrender in real combat, under any circumstances. The other is to be able to completely throw your life away and not be concerned

Karate Masters

"A good karate teacher has an excellent balance in their personality and their mentality. He or she must know how to get the best out of everyone. It is similar to that of a great film director, getting the most out of his actors. Then if he or she sacrifices him or herself appropriately for the students and the school, the students will be more apt to do the same, not just for themselves, but also for the teacher and the school."

about living or dying. Then you can really express yourself in battle from the deepest levels.

Q: Which is more efficient, Japanese karate straight-line attacks or Chinese circular motions?
A: Circular and straight-line styles evolved in different ways but eventually achieved similar results. Each has its advantages and disadvantages. The ultimate technical level is to integrate the concepts. Circular attacks are more fluid, efficient, and economical in many situations, but generally the straight approach is more direct and strong if aligned properly. The straight-line attack can be rigid, but so too can the circular. If an individual trains diligently, a straight-line puncher will integrate more circular attacks and become more fluid. And a circular stylist will adopt more straight-line attacks when appropriate to generate more power.

Q: What are the main benefits a person gets from martial arts training?
A: One major goal of the martial artist is to be mentally strong and therefore live as an independent human being. In our world there are followers and leaders. However, martial artists should train themselves to be strong leaders in all facets of life. Of course, first you have to learn to be a humble follower. Yet martial artists should not immediately buckle to the criticism of the masses or even small groups. While you must be open to productive and positive criticism, many times you must go deep within your consciousness in order to make the most appropriate decisions. What is really the best thing to do? Many times you may not like the obvious answer to any dilemma and others may not either. Your mind may find every excuse to discredit the best solution, but you shouldn't let that be an influence. Thus, instead of looking for support from others, you should look for support from the deeper self. You may have to face many mental blocks

to achieve this, but that is part of the process. If a strong-minded person finds his decision within and feels it is the right thing to do, nothing will change his mind— not embarrassment, criticism, nor even the possibility of death. In this state of mind, problems only belong to the criticizers. Of course, if a person is practicing a bogus style with a phony instructor, and the criticism comes from a knowledgeable source, then it should be heeded. Additionally, under certain circumstances, no one including friends really needs to know that you're practicing a martial art. It's something personal for your own fulfillment. Later, you can reflect developments to others as a mentally strong human being.

"A talented instructor should be well-versed in many areas, from biomechanics and anatomy, to nutrition and diet. There are many karate schools that practice the basics in an extremely mono-rhythmic manner. Thus, the student ends up resting more than they should between repetitions and doesn't achieve a heart rate equal to an aerobics workout."

Ultimately, you want to be able to train to connect your mind, body and spirit with also your technical level. Where everything is working in accordance to one unit. If you apply the karate philosophy of facing yourself as your worse opponent, you will make yourself a better and more positive individual for others to learn from and follow. This doesn't only have to be at the dojo, it can be at your job, position, related to any business or organization and what those responsibilities are? Again, you must continually look at yourself with very strict eyes. Judge and criticize yourself first, before your judge others. If any individuals cheat others, they are only really cheating themselves in the long run. A strong individual will not look for excuses, but focus on ways something can be accomplished, when he or she has a goal or has to solve a problem. A weak mentality individuals will always look for excuses and never take responsibility for themselves. It is an endless cycle for them. Once you take responsibility for something, you then have the power to change it. As Mr. Ohshima says, "You should eventually be able to look at yourself and your life and see no shame." O

Hironori Ohtsuka II

A Heart of Peace

HIS FATHER WAS ONE OF THE MOST INFLUENTIAL KARATE MASTERS IN THE WORLD. HIS EFFORTS TO BRING THE EAST AND WEST TOGETHER WERE VITAL TO THE DEVELOPMENT OF THE JAPANESE ARTS IN THE WESTERN WORLD. A TRUE ENCYCLOPEDIA OF THE ARTS OF BUDO, JIRO OHTSUKA WAS BORN IN 1934 IN TOKYO AND STARTED HIS TRAINING IN KENDO UNDER THE GUIDANCE OF THE LEGENDARY MIYATA SENSEI. IT WASN'T UNTIL 1949 THAT HE BEGAN THE PRACTICE OF KARATE UNDER THE DIRECT SUPERVISION OF HIS FATHER, THE GREAT HIRONORI OHTSUKA SENSEI, THE FOUNDER OF WADO-RYU. SINCE THE DEATH OF HIS FATHER IN 1982, HE WAS APPOINTED AS OFFICIAL SUCCESSOR AND BECAME THE HEAD OF THE WADO STYLE OF KARATE-DO. THE SAME YEAR—TO HONOR HIS FATHER—HE CHANGED HIS NAME FROM JIRO TO HINORI, AND HE BECAME GRANDMASTER ON AUGUST 5, 1983. THROUGH HARD WORK AND DEDICATION, THE WADO-RYU STYLE HAS SPREAD ALL OVER THE WORLD WITH THOUSAND OF SCHOOLS.

OHTSUKA SENSEI'S STRONG MIND AND SPIRIT HAVE BEEN THE MAIN CHARACTERISTICS OF A MAN WHO ALWAYS USED THE BUDO PRINCIPLES TO BRING PRACTITIONERS TOGETHER FROM DIFFERENT CULTURES AND BACKGROUNDS.

Q: Sensei, when you started training in karate, who were your teachers?
A: I began my martial arts training when I was very young. My karate teacher was my father, Hironori Ohtsuka, the founder of wado-ryu. I also trained in other martial arts styles such as judo, kendo, ju-jitsu, et cetera.

Q: Your father was a student of the great Funakoshi Gichin, but he decided to break away and start his own school of karate. Did he mention why he did that?
A: To begin with, the shotokan Funakoshi Sensei was practicing and teaching at that time was not the shotokan we know today. It was more Okinawan in nature. My father took that and incorporated other principles more [along the lines of the] Japanese [into it]. He also added certain exercises for combat. My father always considered wado-ryu as a school of Japanese arts and that included jiu-jitsu, karate, and certain concepts

Karate Masters

"My father was very traditional, and the knowledge he was sharing was a true treasure. The idea of going to a school after work, paying the teacher, exercising a little and having fun before going home to rest simply wasn't there."

and principles of the weaponry schools of Yagyu and Toda. He never saw karate as a sport; instead, he saw it as true budo.

Q: How was the training in your early days?
A: It was very different than the way the martial arts are taught nowadays. To begin with, society and people's values were different so everything else was impregnated by it. My father was very traditional, and the knowledge he was sharing was a true treasure. The idea of going to a school after work, paying the teacher, exercising a little and having fun before going home to rest simply wasn't there. The sensei was like a father or a member of the family. Respect and courtesy were in every single thing we did. This is the true spirit of the martial arts, and this is how a relationship between a student and a teacher should be. The principles of budo are the guidelines for a successful experience in the martial arts.

Q: Speaking of budo, the education in budo is based on the concept of self-activity. How do these principles apply to the evolution and growth of a martial artist?
A: First and foremost, a student should be ready for training. This readiness is not [only] physical but mental and spiritual. He needs to be sure that his training is going to be an important part of his life and act accordingly. He must embrace the idea of complete respect for his teacher, his chosen art and accept the fact that training will be demanding and disciplined. In short, he must subordinate all other things in his life to the way of budo. In order to reach the high levels of budo, he needs to understand that he needs to find a master ... not an expert technician. An expert technician is not a master of budo. In the ways of budo, there is no substitute for a true master.

The high level is Do, but there are four stages the student must go through before reaching this point. The first is called *gyo*, and it involves

Ohtsuka II

"The student simply follows the master. Not asking but simply doing. The hard training in the gyo stage will make or break the student."

the initial phases of physical training. He enters a dojo, and this must fulfill the classical elements of austerity, cleanness, purity and rusticity. A dojo should display the qualities of a place where the trainee disciplines himself. In the phase of gyo, the student learns and experiences the techniques. He must be humble. In this phase, he still is outside of what true training is. He needs to let the master guide him at all times. The student simply follows the master. Not asking but simply doing. The hard training in the gyo stage will make or break the student.

If he endures the hard training of the initial phase, he will get into what is called *shugyo* or austere training. Spirituality is a very important element here. The student will be asked to solve technical dilemmas during training without realizing that the only way out of these dilemmas is to rely on his own intuition and copy the master's technique. A certain amount of confusion will occur because of the high number of movements that the student may know at this moment. His over reliance on his physical eyes is the key to the problem. At this point, the student can become discouraged, but the master does not smooth the training and relieve any pressure from him. The master allows the student to reach a certain state of hopelessness before giving him any advice or technical

Karate Masters

"When the student realizes that all technical mistakes can be corrected through diligent training, he is entering into the next phase, and that is called jutsu. *He has enough skill to start believing he can come close to his master's level and only training will fill this gap."*

help. The student who passes this stage will learn that intuition and spiritual energy are the spine of the training. Through this phase of shugyo, his mental and spiritual energy will increase and improve.

He now begins to realize what the truth is, but he can't attain it yet. He is still very far from it, but he knows it is there and it is moving toward it. A necessary immersion of his self will occur and this will bring understanding and enlightenment to his own life. He will start to see life from a different perspective. He is getting a glimpse of the knowledge and experience of the ancestors. Physically, all the techniques fall into place. In both gyo and shugyo, the endless and tedious repetition of each technique is the core training method.

When the student realizes that all technical mistakes can be corrected through diligent training, he is entering into the next phase, and that is called *jutsu*. He has enough skill to start believing he can come close to his master's level and only training will fill this gap. He is immersed and concerned mostly with the combative meaning and value of what he is learning. Vanity is the most dangerous threat here. And the master can see it happening. This is the moment when the master personally trains the student (who thinks highly of his technical level), and the master begins to indicate all of the student's mistakes and limitations. The student desperately tries not to make mistakes, but his mind is too busy trying to perform correctly. He is thinking too much because he is trying to impress his master. The master simply advises more training and that causes the student [to experience] disappointment. This is important because many students will stop their training here. Not all that glitters is gold, as they say. The student's spiritual development is not enough yet to understand things. If the student passes this stage, the master won't allow more mistakes, and he [will require the student to pay] strict attention to details. No mediocrity is allowed at the phase. Not only will the student be happy with his high technical level, but he will learn that more arduous training is necessary to maintain what he has. At this moment, master and student understand each other without words. A true master at this point will show the student the way to achieve Do. The student will realize he must leave the master and start to travel on his own, trying to surpass his master's level. The student needs to evaluate all the training and effort that has brought him so far and increase his efforts. Once again, technical training must be the vehicle to improve. The student will be able to solve problems while adapting things to himself. His physical skill needs no thought. They are simply moves.

At this stage, the student has great control of the technique, but Do is not there yet. He still cannot control himself. He doesn't posses self-perfection. It is only when the student reaches the state of artless art that he has become a master himself. He has reached Do, which is nothing else that gyo, shugyo and jutsu brought together. He doesn't do anymore. His mind is pure or what is known as *makoto* in Japanese, and he has no awareness of the mechanical actions. They simply flow. Here, even Do is forgotten, because he is truth in action. People from outside can see this as supernatural power or something similar, but they can't realize it because this stage can only be experienced.

"The importance of timing and positioning are some of the main concepts involved in our system. This type of philosophy can overcome speed and brutal power."

Q: In a confrontation against another individual, what are the more important elements of which we need to be aware?
A: The importance of timing and positioning are some of the main concepts involved in our system. This type of philosophy can overcome speed and brutal power. A person's mind can always out think an aggressive fighter. Students should try to develop their fundamental skill rather than concentrate on developing aggressiveness and brute strength. It is not how much strength or speed you have but the knowledge and skill to accomplish what is necessary. Softness can be used against hardness and

Karate Masters

"When you compete, regardless at what, you must prepare well if you are really serious. This preparation is crucial for the final result. You must dedicate more time to practice and train diligently."

hardness against softness but never to over stress any one aspect. In wado-ryu, the principal concept is the distance between you and your opponent. This distance varies depending on your reach and height.

Q: How should a student mentally and physically prepare for competition? How can we adapt aspects of classical budo to a modern activity?
A: When you compete, regardless at what, you must prepare well if you are really serious. This preparation is crucial for the final result. You must dedicate more time to practice and train diligently. You must relax more and focus deeper within yourself. You must constantly ask yourself what is correct and incorrect in the type of training you are doing at that particular time.

Q: Who is a black belts most dangerous opponent?
A: Himself! On occasion, the most dangerous opponent in a martial art school is a beginner because he has no control or technique and no awareness or rhythm. When the student learns more, he becomes more predictable. He is more knowledgeable, but at the same time, he begins to move and react within the style's rhythm and limitations. In a way, he is being constricted within the parameters of the art. The idea is—after many years of training and experience—to gain what we can call sophisticated unpredictability. You become unpredictable but now you have knowledge and technique.

Q: Times have changed and the martial arts have evolved in many ways. Sometimes this is good and sometimes it is bad. What do you think about the evolution and changes that have occurred in the world of martial arts?
A: That's a very difficult question. From a technical point of view, the level of skill that the arts enjoy today is much better and higher than 15 or 20

years ago. No doubt about it. The problem lies in the educational and spiritual aspects. Due to an excessive emphasis [placed] on the physical and fighting aspects, many of the important elements have been lost and relegated to the back seat. People talk about courtesy, respect, etiquette and then you see them arguing and insulting each other about some irrelevant technical issue. You find them fighting for power and money within the different federations and organizations. They yell at the referees in a tournament if their students don't win a match. This tells us that all of the important philosophical and spiritual aspects intrinsic to the martial arts have been forgotten because the emphasis in the schools is not on developing the individual as a whole but on creating fighters and performers for competition. After the competitive career of these individuals is over, this is the main reason why these individuals move into something else and abandon the practice of martial arts completely. Sport certainly has its place in our society, and the modern sportive connotations of the martial arts are valuable too, if they are kept in perspective. If the martial arts continue to be valued as a sour world changes, it is the Do that will carry through the centuries. We should consider ourselves martial artists first and remember that sport cannot be the goal of a way of life.

"Sport certainly has its place in our society, and the modern sportive connotations of the martial arts are valuable too, if they are kept in perspective. If the martial arts continue to be valued as a sour world changes, it is the Do that will carry through the centuries."

Q: Are budo values outdated and obsolete for our society? If not, how we can apply them to our modern times?
A: Well, this is a very difficult question to answer. First, we must accept that the way budo and the traditional samurai approach to the arts developed were based on the time. Budo and its spirit had a purpose for the

Karate Masters

"Nowadays, the wars are fought in a very different way. There is no need for swords and punches. Therefore, we can't try to use the old budo elements in the same way they applied to our ancestors."

old Japanese society and culture. The necessity of a philosophy and a belief that helped the old warriors face death is what really pushed Zen and budo as a warrior's religion. During war times, the main idea was to survive. All the training was geared to protect your life and kill your enemy. The rituals during the training were pretty much discarded and efficiency was all what mattered then. The self-analysis and way of life approach was not important. They were in the middle of a war, and the battlefield was their training ground.

Once the war was over and they found themselves in times of peace, the fighting and violent aspects of the arts passed to the back seat. Then, the warriors focused more on maintaining the philosophical and spiritual aspects that helped them to keep their minds focused for fighting during war. The physical techniques weren't totally focused on efficiency but on developing training methods that allowed the warriors to be in shape for future battles. Specific training [methods] and attaining higher spiritual goals were the key elements they wanted to develop. Society and circumstances determined the aspects that were more emphasized at certain times. During times of war, efficiency and real combat are the main objectives in practice; during peace times, good health and spirituality should be our goals in training.

Nowadays, the wars are fought in a very different way. There is no need for swords and punches. Therefore, we can't try to use the old budo elements in the same way they applied to our ancestors. It would be silly. Society is different. Things aren't even done in Japan the same. We need to see how classical martial arts apply to our society today and how to integrate the important elements of courtesy, etiquette, respect, et cetera into our lives. They can't be applied totally the same, but we can use them a lot in our modern society.

Traditional martial arts masters are against sport competition because it doesn't reflect the old approach to combat. And it is true. The problem is that modern combat involves tanks, airplanes, bombs, et cetera. There are no katana! Sport is not a bad thing. My opinion is that sports can help modern practitioners because it represents a modern battlefield. The important point here is to create a sport environment that displays the qualities of budo. Competitors should show respect, etiquette, mental and physical control, et cetera. This way the sportive competitions will fall in line with our modern society. Of course, the connotations and elements of the old battlefield can't be duplicated today, but that's what life is all about ... change and evolution. The problem occurs when the sport is managed poorly and all the traditional values that should be kept during a modern, sportive competition are not enforced and therefore lost in the past.

Q: Sensei, allow me to be more specific. How can you apply the traditional elements of budo to a modern competition?
A: Keeping the right technique. For instance, in a karate competition, referees should never award a point to a sloppy technique. A clean movement—with power and control, with *zanchin* and the right fighting spirit—should be the only technique receiving recognition. All these sloppy, loose and uncontrolled punches and kicks that simply touch the opponent's body shouldn't score a point. Instead of awarding six or eight points for improper delivered techniques (*wazari*), reward only the clean and powerful techniques (*ippon*). Don't forget that *wazari* were created because of the impossibility of competitors scoring full points or ippon. Well, what the student should do is to train hard to score a decisive technique. That's budo. And that's how we can duplicate the old battlefield. Sport events should keep the idea of living or dying. If we are capable of keeping this spirit, the student will be more careful with what kind of techniques he uses.

Q: And in kata?
A: Kata should be rewarded based on focus, spirit and body control—not on how high the competitor jumps or how loud he breathes. Kata should be displayed as a martial form, not like a gymnastic routine. Unfortunately, those who jump higher and breathe very loud are the ones winning the kata competitions these days. Kata shouldn't be flashy. It should be a representation of the practical fighting techniques and spirit of the past.

Karate Masters

Q: Sensei, nowadays practitioners tend to study several systems and create their own. Do you think it is correct to do that? And how far will the student get using this approach?
A: It depends on what he is looking for. Studying different approaches to combat is not something new. Old samurai studied several arts ... from *iaido* to *jiu-jutsu* to *kyudo*. All of these had elements in warrior's training. That's why they did it. Nowadays it is a little bit different. The student should ask himself where he is going and what he wants to get from training in the martial arts. For any expert in karate, it is good to learn some judo because this will enable him to throw an opponent and [learn] how to deal with a situation on the ground. He may not need to learn three different styles of karate, but learning some aikido will help him to understand how to use wristlocks and *tai-sabaki* more effectively. I truly don't see a reason why anyone should not expand his knowledge and perspective of fighting by learning another art. I don't recommend this in the beginning of the training because the student will become extremely confused and never understand one system that should be his base or foundation.

You also asked about using this approach to create a new style of martial art. Well, if you combine karate, judo and aikido, what do you call that? There is no reason to give it a new name. I understand that giving a [style] a new name is based on the idea of having lots of followers who pay fees and then it becomes a business. But sincerely, you won't receive credit from any true master of the martial arts if you take pieces of different styles and come up with a "new" style, because what you are doing is rearranging things—not creating anything original. When they justify what they have done, these individuals usually say that they are "trying to find the most effective system by putting together the best of each style." Excuse me if I say so bluntly, but that is ridiculous! It is a waste of time and a nonsensical, childish journey. Today, with all the knowledge and fighting methods existing, there is no reason to create a "new" style. Do you truly think any of these people will "discover" a new way of punching or kicking?

Q: When should a student break away from his teacher and become more independent?
A: In budo and traditional karate, a good student never *breaks away* from his teacher. There is no reason to do this ... just as there is no reason for a son to break away from his father or mother. He may move out of his parent's house, but it doesn't mean he is *breaking away*. He is becoming independent, and that's logical. It is the same in karate. The sensei stays there, although he will get older and his techniques will be slower and

weaker as time passes by. However, a good student will always be with him and listen to what he has to say. It is when a teacher is not truly a teacher by budo standards that—after a few years—a talented student needs to move on. At that stage, the teacher has nothing to teach him anymore ... not technique nor how to become a better human being. Usually every karate practitioner reaches a point in which it is no longer feasible to accept his instructor's words based on faith alone. Maybe the student is at a level in which he is exhibiting his martial arts skills as they come into conflict with the very essence of the art of karate-do, which, depending on the age, may simply be for self-defense. Any karate-ka who finds himself at this point should abandon any notions of what he still cherishes regarding his physical abilities. He will have to evaluate the techniques he knows and those he really likes, because some of those techniques he really likes may be of almost no intrinsic value on the street, especially if he has always trained under an instructor who uses a sport approach to karate.

"Usually every karate practitioner reaches a point in which it is no longer feasible to accept his instructor's words based on faith alone. Any karate-ka who finds himself at this point should abandon any notions of what he still cherishes regarding his physical abilities."

Once he re-evaluates this, he may find that he needs to work on areas that don't really thrill him. It is then up to him to see how much he is willing to move into a higher level of practice, but it is important to always stay with his sensei. The teachings of the past are seeds for growth. Appreciate the sensei's teachings. Treat them like seeds and cultivate them to be the truths of the future.

Q: Is sport karate sparring a valid method to develop self-defense skills?
A: First of all, let's not forget that sport karate fighting is conducted under an artificial environment. Everything is under controlled regulations, and the circumstances are far from a real life dangerous situation. In a real self-defense situation, the attacker is not looking for a sparring partner to test his skills. Instead, he's looking for a victim. Rules, referees, ring size, illegal techniques and the realization that losing the match will only entail going

Karate Masters

"In a competition, the main objective is to deal with the opponent and win the match; in the street, the goal is not to be defeated and beaten."

home without a medal pretty much invalidate sport competition as a testing ground for real self-defense skills.

The approach to fighting is totally different. In a competition, the main objective is to deal with the opponent and win the match; in the street, the goal is not to be defeated and beaten.

On the other hand, traditional kumite is more relevant for the street because of the format. True self-defense techniques can be delivered, provided they are controlled and do not land. When someone attacks you on the street, he is your enemy—not another competitor. You are not engaged in a friendly match of skills. It is important to work hard to simulate an actual self-defense scenario and practice ruthless and effective responses to it. A real self-defense situation is not a duel or face off in which you deal with your attacker in a romantically stereotypical manner. In short, sport competition probably is not the best method for developing self-defense expertise.

Q: What about kata? How useful is it?
A: Let me tell you this. For my entire life, I have been hearing how useless kata training is for real self-defense. However, I haven't heard more than a few people talking about the distinction between the *concept* of any particular kata and the physical form. The fighting concept behind any kata is completely valid for self-protection, but very few people understand this. Every single kata, regardless of the style, has a concept and principle behind it. This is what is relevant. It is here where the true meaning of kata training lies. When you know and understand this, then—and only then—can you really see the utility of the form you are practicing. If you are training in traditional karate, don't assume that the forms you are practicing are worthless. They are quite practical in nature.

Q: You are talking about the concept that lies in the form, but what about the actual movements? Are they obsolete?
A: In some cases, but you have to keep an open mind to really under-

stand kata and its meaning. Traditional kata are like "technique reservoirs" in that an old master added additional movements so he could practice them in a sequential order. Once [that is] said, the true application of the movements found in kata is not the simple bunkai. That is pretty much a no-brainer once you have an understanding of the technique. The real application is usually hidden. You can't decipher this on your own. You need to learn from a master how to use certain keys that "open" the logic of reading the true self-defense [moves] behind the movements. Due to the way the old master formatted the kata, it is true that we can find some inconsistencies in certain forms, but you also have to keep in mind that these forms were put together a long time ago and the methods used by attackers at the time have very little to do with the modern times. It is important that you understand kata for what it is and evaluate his relevancy as a great traditional training method that supplies a lot of efficient information for all karate-ka.

Q: We have talked about the physical and technical aspects of self-defense, but what about the mental element of a confrontation?
A: By far, it is the most important. If you are not mentally ready to act and protect yourself, the best technique and training in the world won't do much for you. Karate is a martial art. As such, it is limited by the structure used by the art to deliver the physical techniques we learn. Self-defense is an important concept that cannot be limited at all by esoteric considerations. It is about self-preservation. That's what old traditional karate has always been about.

Q: If a student learns a large number of kata, will he have more knowledge?
A: We must differentiate between *quantitative* knowledge and *practical* knowledge. Obviously, from a quantitative perspective, the more kata a practitioner knows the more knowledge he has. From a practical point of view ... not necessarily. It depends on how deep he has studied, analyzed and researched the forms he knows. That will determine the real amount of knowledge he has. On the top of that, you have to consider if he is able to apply the techniques under pressure. It is not how much he has accumulated but how much he can really do when it counts.

If you take a kata and train in its whole dimension, you'll find out that it takes years to master the mold of the basic format. Then, you have to go into the bunkai and master that, which takes more years. Later, you have to go deeper into the hidden aspects of each movement, which is not so obvious and easy. Only then you can put [together] all aspects of the form, study the concepts behind them and how they apply to fighting and life itself. This process takes many years for a single kata, so how are you going to go deep into 40 different kata in a lifetime? You have to choose and prioritize your training. Even if you know 20 forms, you need to select and choose those you want to study deeply and those that fit into your own structure, both physical and mentally.

Q: Are you against sport karate?
A: No, sport is good as long as the true essence of the art is not lost because of the sportive practice. Sport competition helped to promote karate, but I believe that since the 1990s the right perspective of the art has been modified and lost in many cases. People are not so dedicated and willing to go through the hard training anymore. A new generation of student came along ... a generation that couldn't be pushed in the old way. I honestly think that we should go back to the old values and ethics. Budo develops the spirit ... sports only the body.

Q: How should karate training change when the practitioner ages?
A: We all would like to stay young and strong, but the universe doesn't work that way. That's why knowing how to breathe properly and using Ki are extremely important when you get old. Movements in training, when you are young, come from the muscles, tendons and ligaments. When you get old, these three elements weaken drastically and you need to have another source for your physical activity. Internal training is very important—not to win tournaments—but for a healthy life. A good karate-ka should know how to change and adapt the art to his own current capabilities. Karate is a way of life for your whole lifetime ... not only for when you are young. There is no end in karate training. Once you think that there is an end, you walk in that direction. If it happens you accomplish and reach it, then it is over. You'll be satisfied and that's the end of budo. You must train all your life; never think you had enough training because physical training is parallel to self-improvement and you never stop improving the self.

Q: Any thought you'd like to leave with the readers?
A: Karate and all the budo arts should help a student develop positive attitudes about life. It is a path for self-discovery and personal analysis of who we are. The true art of karate is a way of thinking, a way of life. In a way, it can be described as an art of winning. We win when we get what we

"The true art of karate is a way of thinking, a way of life. In a way, it can be described as an art of winning. We win when we get what we want to make this world better. But there are many ways of winning, and the higher level is not physical. You don't have to be physical to defeat obstacles to get what you want in life. This is the true main idea of karate."

want to make this world better. But there are many ways of winning, and the higher level is not physical. You don't have to be physical to defeat obstacles to get what you want in life. This is the true main idea of karate. Today, there are many who do not have an understanding of the art, and with only two or three years of practice, go out and teach it to others. This is the main reason why so many today don't know the real meaning and history behind the techniques they are teaching. They never studied enough to learn. All the widespread misconceptions about karate are from the people who have not yet acquired enough years of practice and wisdom teaching their limited knowledge to the public. The true spirit and essence of karate-do lives on through those who were dedicated enough and chosen by the ancestors to preserve the heritage for future generations. O

Edmond Otis

The Art and the Way

EDMOND OTIS IS CHAIRMAN OF THE AMERICAN JKA KARATE ASSOCIATION AND HAS BEEN TRAINING SINCE 1967. HE BEGAN HIS TRAINING AT THE AGE OF 12 UNDER THE LEADERSHIP OF HIDETAKA NISHIYAMA OF LOS ANGELES. AT THE AGE OF 17, HE MOVED TO RIVERSIDE, CALIFORNIA, TO BECOME A FULL-TIME STUDENT OF FORMER AJKA CHIEF INSTRUCTOR, SENSEI RAY DALKE, AN 8TH DAN AND THEN ONE OF ONLY THREE NON-JAPANESE GRADUATES OF THE PRESTIGIOUS (USA) JKA INSTRUCTOR'S PROGRAM. IN ADDITION TO HIS DUTIES AT UNIVERSITY CALIFORNIA RIVERSIDE, SENSEI OTIS TRAVELS EXTENSIVELY THROUGHOUT NORTH AMERICA AND EUROPE CONDUCTING SEMINARS AND CLINICS ON ALL ASPECTS OF SHOTOKAN KARATE. SENSEI OTIS TEACHES KARATE AS A SAFE AND HIGHLY EFFECTIVE MEANS OF SELF-DEFENSE, A RIGOROUS FORM OF EXERCISE, A PHILOSOPHY OF LIFE, AND AN EXCITING COMPETITIVE SPORT. HE IS INTERNATIONALLY KNOWN AS A REFEREE, INSTRUCTOR AND JUDGE AND HAS COACHED NUMEROUS YOUTH AND ADULT COMPETITORS TO NATIONAL AND INTERNATIONAL CHAMPIONSHIPS. ALONG WITH RANDALL G. HASSELL, WROTE *THE COMPLETE IDIOT'S GUIDE TO KARATE*. MACMILLAN USA PUBLISHED THIS IN 2000. EDMOND OTIS IS ALSO FEATURED IN THE OUTSTANDING VIDEO SERIES, *ESSENTIAL SHOTOKAN*. HE IS ONE OF THOSE TALENTED PEOPLE WHO FOUND HIS WAY THROUGH THE ART AND HAS BECOME ONE OF THE MOST SOUGHT-AFTER KARATE EXPERTS IN THE WORLD.

Q: After all the technical changes in the last decades, do you think there is a "pure" shotokan, a "pure" shito-ryu, goju-ryu, et cetera?
A: Yes. I think pure styles still exist, are still practiced and still have value.
I tend to think of karate in the same way that I think of language or music mastery. In both, we want to be fluent … express ourselves spontaneously and completely, depending on the need at the time. The more disciplined and well-studied we are in a language, and the more deeply we understand it's structure and rules and vocabulary, the better prepared we are to use the language powerfully—not superficially—in a wide range of situations.

That is not to say, however, that languages (verbal, musical, physical) do not change and evolve over time and from individual to individual. For example, *"Moby Dick"* is a very different book from *"The Great Gatsby,"*

Karate Masters

"Although we use throwing and restraints, karate is fundamentally a percussive or impact art. First and last, we strike our opponent. But the art isn't simply about hitting things ... any more than playing a drum is just about using sticks to make a lot of noise."

which is very different from *"Catch-22."* But they are all "pure" American English. Or, for another example, Scott Joplin's jazz is very different from Benny Goodwin's, which again, is very different from Winston Marcellus's ... yet all are masters of a clearly defined genre of "language."

With karate, and particularly shotokan, which I am most familiar with, you could say that Nishiyama's karate is very different from Asai's karate, which is different then Yahara's karate, and so on. Yet, all are "pure" shotokan.

Q: Sensei Otis, you always say, "There is nothing better than good shotokan karate and nothing worse than bad shotokan karate." Could you explain that statement?

A: All of the traditional martial arts approach both the "Do" and "jutsu" of their art from a specific, philosophical and physical perspective. As we progress, we develop more depth, greater skills, greater fluidity, and greater fluency in our ability to understand and use the art. But the essential principles that are unique to that art remain the same. Sometimes I think karate-ka, and especially shotokan stylists, lack an appreciation for what is special about our art. For example, most judo practitioners can tell you that the underlying maxim of judo is "minimum effort, maximum results." In the same way, most aikido practitioners know that their art is about harmonizing with, and redirecting their opponent's force. What's shocking to me is that many, many, karate-ka lack an essential understanding of what karate's underlying principle, or goal, is.

Q: And that is?
A: Although we use throwing and restraints, karate is fundamentally a percussive or impact art. First and last, we strike our opponent. But the art isn't simply about hitting things ... any more than playing a drum is just about using sticks to make a lot of noise. Karate is always about timing and distance. It is always about our relationship to our opponent. My view is that ultimately karate is about striving to be at our best, our most

focused, our most balanced, our most dynamic ... precisely at the moment our opponent is at his weakest. We seek to find and attack the momentary lapses in the opponent's physical and mental attention. Of all karate styles, JKA-style shotokan seems to focus on this principle almost to the exclusion of anything else. When one style of karate is compared to another, what you usually see is that the shotokan stylist is the least flamboyant stylist. Our kata are relatively simple, our strategies are fairly straightforward and our training depends heavily on the endless repetition of very basic techniques. In a sense, our style has no style. There's a great scene in the first *Indiana Jones* movie in which a huge warrior swinging a big sword in an elaborate pattern confronts the hero. Without missing a beat, Indiana Jones pulls out a 45, shoots the guy, puts his gun away and goes on with his business.

"Although it is stereotyped as a 'hard style,' the best shotokan stylists understand the fundamental principles of the system in a way that lets them be fluid and soft whenever they are not hitting their target."

I see that as a very shotokan moment. Basically, we [shotokan stylists] really seem to focus on just three things: The quality of our technique or our ability to focus and to make [or create] shock with our techniques; second, our sense of timing and our use of distance is third. That's it. The trouble is, if we don't do our homework and if we don't study the dynamics of our techniques and stances adequately, we really have nothing fancy to hide behind. Shotokan karate can then become very stiff and very awkward. In that case, it's and not very effective. Although it is stereotyped as a "hard style," the best shotokan stylists understand the fundamental principles of the system in a way that lets them be fluid and soft whenever they are not hitting their target.

Q: The AJKA was one of the first groups to break off from what was then a worldwide and centralized karate organization. How do you see the JKA shotokan world changing at the present?
A: In the last years, we have seen an increasingly rapid decentralization of JKA karate throughout the world. I think this is both positive and negative. On the positive side, we are seeing more openness and the greater exchange of techniques and training ideas from one shotokan group to another. As the boundaries break down, we are starting to see, in my

Karate Masters

"It often seems that without the late Nakayama Sensei traveling around, cracking the whip of correctness, many of the newer independent shotokan groups are less concerned about mastering the fundamentals of the art."

view, a return to what karate originally was supposed to be about. Separate shotokan families and dojo that develop their own skills have their own loyalties and affinities. Then they go out to compare and exchange techniques with other similar groups on an equal basis. However, on the other hand, there seems to be a negative side to the loss of centralization. Much of karate itself seems to be suffering. The fact that there is no central administrative standard seems to have translated into a loss of technical standard as well. It often seems that without the late Nakayama Sensei traveling around, cracking the whip of correctness, many of the newer independent shotokan groups are less concerned about mastering the fundamentals of the art. They seem to have thrown the baby out with the bath water.

Q: Someone who attended your seminars told us that at the beginning of your kata sessions you boasted about being the "antibunkai." What does that mean?

A: Actually, that was said half in jest … but only half. Obviously, understanding the application of a kata is crucial to the correct performance of our forms. It enhances our skills, our ability to defend ourselves and our appreciation of the art. However, my personal philosophy and, to a great extent, the official stated philosophy of the AJKA, is that bunkai really is not the main reason that we practice kata. First of all, while practicing bunkai is easy, practicing kata is difficult. As I said earlier, the JKA style of shotokan karate invests a lot of energy in understanding, practicing, and improving the dynamics of the individual and combined techniques. Ultimately, the goal of karate training is a marriage of physical mastery, emotional stability and intellectual focus. Kata develops all three of those in a synchronized and congruent fashion. Nothing is more personally challenging than that.

Kata teaches us to develop intense moment-by-moment focus, while at the same time, [it teaches us to] maintain an overall awareness of ourselves in relation to the world around us ... the whole. Kind of an ongoing, simultaneous, appreciation of both "the trees" and "the forest." On the other hand, bunkai is simply basic sparring. Nothing more, nothing less. Don't get me wrong ... I value basic sparring. I practice it, and I teach it. It's an important part of learning to use a variety of techniques in a controlled setting. It serves an important role, but it is not the heart of karate training. Here's my bunkai example for the year. My eight year-old son is studying music. He really loves it. Somewhere along the line he has picked up playing the first four notes to Beethoven's 5th symphony ... the really famous one: "Bom, bom, bom, booom!" So now he can sit down at the piano, with his back straight, his head up and he can knock out those four notes. When people hear it, they are surprised and stunned at how brilliant it sounds, and

"Kata teaches us to develop intense moment-by-moment focus, while at the same time, [it teaches us to] maintain an overall awareness of ourselves in relation to the world around us ... the whole. Kind of an ongoing, simultaneous, appreciation of both 'the trees' and 'the forest.'"

they expect him to continue the rest of the amazingly complex musical piece. Well, he can't. He is only eight. He has only been practicing the piano for about a year and a half. When he sits down and plays those four notes, he isn't playing Beethoven ... he is playing *Beethovenbunkai*.

Q: The WKF kumite rules are significantly different from the current sanbon and ippon rules. Any thoughts on how the changes will impact karate? Is the AJKA planning on going in that direction?
A: No, not really. We wish our friends in the WKF well, but we intend to continue practicing karate. My personal feeling is that many of us are selling our karate souls for Olympic recognition and Olympic affiliation. The new rules have nothing to do with what we think of as karate. Also, they

Karate Masters

"My personal feeling is that many of us are selling our karate souls for Olympic recognition and Olympic affiliation. The new rules have nothing to do with what we think of as karate. The truth is, or at least my understanding, is that if karate gets to the Olympics, it will no longer be karate."

aren't really very new. For the most part, they are versions of taekwondo Olympic rules. While there is nothing wrong with that, philosophically it's not karate. I appreciate sports. I appreciate the Olympics. But the two are not necessarily the same. My sense and information tell me that as the WKF goes further and further towards this goal and Olympic affiliation, they are going to go further and further away from karate. The truth is, or at least my understanding, is that if karate gets to the Olympics, it will no longer be karate. First of all, the Olympics already have a kick-punch sport, and that is taekwondo. It is very unlikely that the Olympics are going to host two very similar sports, especially now, when the rules are so close. So, what we are going to be seeing is one Olympic kick-punch sport. Perhaps it will be taekwan karate, karate kwan do or just Olympic kick-punch art. As far as increasing our popularity, I think that, unless we are careful, karate in the Olympics will do as much for karate's general popularity as it has done for judo. On the other hand, I am very pleased that the AJKA is actively moving in the opposite direction. We promote and participate in national and international ippon competition through a variety of shotokan groups and through the AJKA organization here and in Europe. It's interesting to me that this very intense and dynamic type of competition is once again greatly increasing in popularity. We, along with a large portion of traditional martial artists, are moving back to our traditions. Back towards recognizing the unique value and relevance of karate as a human art of personal development combat and self-defense. Additionally, we are very interested in seeing and promoting the individual arts as distinct and separate from each other. One of the things that surprised me when I was still involved the AAU and they made the intelligent decision to awarding national kata championships for different styles (for example the AAU has a national shotokan kata champion, a national goju champion, a national shito champion and so on) was how homogenized and similar the performances of the various kata had become over the last several years. Gradually, we have been moving away from the distinctive characteristics that make each style unique to a general standardized kata. While the WKF seems to think this is a good thing, I think it is an abomination.

"We, along with a large portion of traditional martial artists, are moving back to our traditions. Back towards recognizing the unique value and relevance of karate as a human art of personal development combat and self-defense."

Karate Masters

"Gradually, we have been moving away from the distinctive characteristics that make each style unique to a general standardized kata. While the WKF seems to think this is a good thing, I think it is an abomination."

Q: Can you talk a little bit about your current projects?

A: Sure, gladly. Several things have been happening in the last couple of years that involve the AJKA and myself. A while ago, karate instructor and writer Randall Hassell and I were contacted by Macmillan USA to write "*The Complete Idiot's Guide To Karate.*" This was part of their international series of instructional books. It's been on the market for a couple of years, and it is doing very well. I know from the mail and calls I have received that it is being used widely as a text for numerous traditional karate schools and programs. Second, I have also released a karate DVD series called *Essential Shotokan*. It's from Perfect Form, Inc. Basically, the production gives an in-depth overview of shotokan's techniques, principles, concepts and foundations. It then goes on to demonstrate key points, common errors, and provide beginning, intermediate, and advanced applications and training methods for each technique. The early response and reviews have been very, very good. I will say right here, right now, that to be very honest, the strength of this series is not the intricate and fancy graphics or effects, but rather the content and the clarity of the presentation. My hope is that it helps students of all levels to learn something new about basic shotokan techniques and basic methodology. I think it's very useful to instructors who want a little bit of added perspective and perhaps some different ideas on how to develop classes and training schedules.

Finally, and most exciting, because of our growth, and people's interest in our approach to traditional shotokan, combined with our view that a karate organization should help its members develop—not ignore, tax, or torment them, we are in the process of growing into the *American JKA Karate Association*—International (AJKA–I). The organization is growing dramatically in Europe, under the leadership of my instructor, Safar Sensei,

8th dan, and we are gaining members in Canada, and Central and South America. We quietly made the decision a while ago to actively help our members grow as well rounded karate-ka, and as successful dojos, and through word of mouth that approach is bringing clubs to us at a pretty good clip.

Q: Why do many shotokan groups frown on punches when they cause knockouts at tournaments?
A: I think this question can be answered in several ways. Here are three ways I might look at it. One answer might be that it is much easier to knock out someone who expects you to take control than it is [to fight] someone who is trying to stomp your head into the sidewalk and fully expects to take a few good shots from you while he is doing it. Another answer might be that I don't really think it is a matter of snapping techniques versus locking techniques. Instead, it's focused techniques versus non-focused [techniques]. The thing that sets shotokan apart from the rest of the world is its almost pathological,

"The thing that sets shotokan apart from the rest of the world is its almost pathological, philosophical and technical insistence that we always strive to create a fluid synergy between our breathing, our body actions and our techniques."

philosophical and technical insistence that we always strive to create a fluid synergy between our breathing, our body actions and our techniques. It is all supposed to work together. In these terms, I think of focus as the ability to transfer as much overall force as possible in the shortest amount of time and to the smallest impact area. We don't, however, apply this principle in the same way in different situations. For example, the sharp, backfist strike we deliver to someone's temple will not work in the same way to someone's torso. For that, we may change to a locking type of strike because different target density absorbs and disperses shock differently. In the same way, a punch to the jaw may require a different "type" of focus

Karate Masters

"In recent years, practitioners who have become more and more fascinated by the vulnerability of nerve centers and secret, or hidden techniques, are gradually finding that knowing where the nerve center is and effectively attacking it are two different things."

than one to the body. The other factor to consider is the ability of the individual. The advanced (trained) person can (hopefully) create this synergy in a shorter amount of time, and by virtue of that, create more shock—not less—in less time—not more.

I'd like to talk about something slightly off topic but relevant. In recent years, practitioners who have become more and more fascinated by the vulnerability of nerve centers and secret, or hidden techniques, are gradually finding that knowing where the nerve center is and effectively attacking it are two different things. "Nerve attacks" work by interrupting the nerve impulse to and from the brain for a prolonged and intense period of time. This requires a longer, deeper, contact time—not shorter. We can think of the round leg kick typically associated with Thai boxing. There the impact sticks, as opposed to snaps, because the contact needs to be longer to accomplish its goal of "killing" the nerve. Nerve attacks that work look an awful lot like the old "heavy" focus we see in the basic kata. If we just needed to lightly touch certain nerve centers to incapacitate our opponent, most of us wouldn't survive the accidental, random, physical contact of daily life. A ride in a crowded subway would be dangerous, a Saturday afternoon football game in the park would be crippling and no one would survive his honeymoon! A third answer might be to look at the "Do" aspect of our art. I imagine if you were to ask this same question of a student at a tea ceremony, or bonsai, you would have asked, "Hey, what's the fuss? Just pour the tea! Doesn't drinking from a Styrofoam cup in your car work as well?" Or, "Hmmm, cute tree, but why is it so small? Wouldn't you get more shade from a bigger one? What about firewood?"

What actual benefit does traditional karate practice bring to our daily life? Where do we as students, teachers and practitioners actually "walk the talk" about character and courage? Well, to be honest, I'm never sure about how all this character stuff shakes out in the real karate world. We all know that there are the full range of personalities involved in our art. Some you could trust in all circumstances and some not. Really, though I don't think that matters. Karate is an individual activity. However, there do seem to be certain characteristics or approaches to life that are shared, to greater or lesser degrees, by those who practice seriously. One seems to be the acceptance that if you want to get good at something, you need to work hard, because no one is going to do it for you. Another seems to be the ability to control our emotions and remain poised and focused at times of great danger or personal challenge. I think we develop this through our daily training focus of striving for the perfect technique, one that is totally finished, and creates a personal unity of our physical, mental and emotional energy, at the exact time that the stakes are the greatest.

Q: Keeping the tailbone tucked in is paramount in traditional shotokan. Why is this so important when other dynamic sports/arts don't do this?
A: I like this question, and to be honest, I totally disagree with its premise. All dynamic sports and arts do this and those that don't aren't very dynamic. Perhaps the confusion is in the translation of the word "tucked," which sounds awfully unnatural. Think of batting and throwing in baseball, the strength events in weight lifting, hitting a golf ball, bowling, judo, sumo, boxing (Western and Thai), or just chopping down a tree with an axe. Basically, to generate any force or movement, the hips and torso need to be engaged in the action. If we think just about our karate techniques (but this rule also applies to most of the other examples I gave), the body center (the hips) can only be engaged when it is between the driving point of the stance (far leg) and target or impact area. A simple way to say this is to tuck your hips. One of the gifts that the traditional martial arts provide us with is that they methodically teach us to move and use our bodies the way that natural athletes do. (Granted, for some of us this is a much longer and more arduous journey than for others). Basically, this means developing a natural relationship between the angle of the head and neck, the alignment of the shoulders, the natural curve of the spine and the position of the hips, along with the distribution of the weight in relation to knees and soles of the feet. Because the laws of physics and human physiology govern karate, we function best and our karate works best when we follow those principles.

Karate Masters

When a beginner starts karate, the most common mistake he makes is that he tenses his body inappropriately and compensates for a lack of power and coordination by overusing his shoulders and arms and underusing his legs and hips. In turn, this kicks the hip out and disrupts balance. Now, even though this is common, it is not natural. As I said previously, I think that much of the controversy about "hip tuck" is more of a problem of translation stemming from some instructors; it's a very abrupt and simplistic way of getting students to compensate for this initial tendency. However, to overcompensate by distorting the natural and efficient working of the body in some other way (the hip tucked to the point that the pelvis rolls up unnaturally, for example) is just as nonproductive and limiting.

Q: If you have to leave one single message for the future generations of practitioners, what that would be?
A: Man, messages for future generations sounds so ominous, but I do feel we are all, present and future generations alike, being weakened and numbed by how easy it is for us to get instant gratification in almost every aspect of our lives ... from instant food, to instant entertainment, to instant messaging. And the tragedy is that so much of that satisfaction is really an illusion. Technology changes quickly, human nature does not. It takes effort, an investment and commitment of energy and self—a risk—to experience and feel satisfaction and grow as a person.

I feel strongly that many of the true benefits of training come from the process, the struggles, and the lessons we learn in the day-to-day practice—not in the results. A main value of traditional karate practice is that it is anything but instant. Like real life, real karate training is actual; it is not virtual. It is interpersonal—not digital.

Aside from teaching us skills that make us healthy and potentially dangerous, the traditional arts teach us that by training to develop a combination of skill (technique, timing, distance, strategy, etc.) and spirit (the ability to create energy) with self-control (the ability to control that energy or to be brave when afraid or calm when angry, etc.), we learn to control of ourselves, which means that we have control of our lives. And means we can often determine the outcome of the challenges we face. When we can't, we have the resilience to get up when we've been knocked down and [the ability to] cope with disappointment.

Q: What is your opinion of makiwara training?

A: I like makiwara training for two main reasons. First, as has been written in several places, it is an outstanding training aid (which I actually don't feel I did enough of during the years that I was competing) and supplement to kata, kumite and kihon. It develops focus in a different way than other impact devices, such as shields, pads, bags, etc. Second, hitting the makiwara is a wonderful way to get a visceral appreciation for our traditions and the way that our art has developed and evolved, and it is different from the intellectual study of "the old days."

Q: And kobudo training?

A: I appreciate kobudo as a beautiful and effective category of martial art. But my feeling is that it is separate and different from karate, in the same way perhaps that judo and ju-jitsu are different. As karate-ka, we can learn judo and jiu-jitsu techniques and integrate them into our karate in a way that actually changes them into a part of our karate. But that is not the same as the learning the art specifically for what it has to teach us.

"The traditional martial arts are a type of 'emergency training' for life. They teach us a method for self-understanding that helps us to control our weaknesses and accentuate our strengths so that we are able to be at our best when we really need to be our best."

Q: Any final thoughts you would like to add?

A: The traditional martial arts are a type of "emergency training" for life. They teach us a method for self-understanding that helps us to control our weaknesses and accentuate our strengths so that we are able to be at our best when we really need to be our best. O

Ryusho Sakagami
The Gentle Master

RYUSHO SAKAGAMI EXEMPLIFIED ALL THE QUALITIES A MASTER OF BUDO SHOULD. BORN ON 1915 IN KAWANISHI CITY, WHICH IS IN THE HYUGO PREFECTURE, SAKAGAMI SENSEI BEGAN HIS MARTIAL ART TRAINING AT AGE 10. THE NIHON BUDO KYOGI-KAI GAVE HIM THE HIGHEST BUDO AWARD—THE BUDO KORO-SHO MEDAL. HIS EXTENSIVE TRAINING IN THE ART OF KARATE-DO UNDER GRANDMASTERS OF THE CALIBER OF CHOKI MOTOBU AND KENWA MABUNI, AMONG OTHERS, MADE HIM ONE OF THE TOP AND MORE KNOWLEDGEABLE MASTERS OF HIS GENERATION. WITH AN EXTENSIVE TRAINING IN JUDO, IAIDO, KENDO AND KOBUDO, SAKAGAMI SENSEI USED THE BUDO PRINCIPLES AND HIS EDUCATION TO LEAD AN HONORABLE LIFE. HE STAYED ACTIVE AT HIS DOJO IN TSURUMI WARD, BETWEEN YOKOHAMA AND KAWASAKI, UNTIL HIS VERY LAST DAYS OF LIFE. HIS TEACHER, SHITO-RYU FOUNDER KENWA MABUNI, ASKED RYUSHO SAKAGAMI TO SUCCEED HIM IN THE HERITAGE OF ITOSU ANKO'S ORTHODOX METHOD OF KARATE, APPOINTING HIM THE THIRD GENERATION LEADER OF THE *ITOSU-HA SEITO*.

IN 1980, THE FEDERATION OF ALL-JAPAN KARATE-DO ORGANIZATIONS AWARDED MASTER SAKAGAMI HIS 8TH DAN IN KARATE-DO, AND IN 1987 HE RECEIVED HIS 8TH DAN IN *MUSO JIKIDEN EISHIN RYU* IAIDO.

THE MOST IMPORTANT KARATE FEDERATIONS IN THE WORLD ACKNOWLEDGED GRANDMASTER SAKAGAMI TO BE A LIVING TREASURE AND A REPOSITORY OF THE HISTORY AND KNOWLEDGE OF BUDO. RYUSHO SAKAGAMI—A TRUE LEGEND OF THE ART OF KARATE, AN HONORABLE HUMAN BEING AND A GENTLE MASTER—DIED FROM HEART FAILURE ON DECEMBER 28, 1993.

Q: Master Sakagami, please tell us about your beginnings in the art.
A: My grandfather was a kendo master. I trained in *iaido* under Nakayama Hiromichi Sensei, who was a *meijin*, and in aikido under Hirai Minoru Sensei, who was a direct student of O'Sensei Ueshiba. I traveled often to Okinawa—though my parents didn't know it—to train in karate, because I was informed that there was an excellent master in Osaka. His name was Kenwa Mabuni, and I began my training under him around 1935. Training at that time was very different than today. I also trained under

Karate Masters

"Mabuni Sensei was the founder of Shito-ryu, which is a combination of naha-te, shuri-te *and* tomari-te. *In Japan, the son is always the heir to his father's throne."*

Choki Motobu. I have also trained in judo, jodo, *kobudo* and other classical arts of budo.

Q: Did you meet Funakoshi Gichin Sensei?
A: Yes I did. He visited Mabuni Sensei, and he had some of his students learn kata from Mabuni Sensei. Later on, they modified things to better fit the style Funakoshi Sensei was developing. Mabuni Sensei had a good relationship with Funakoshi Sensei.

Q: Why did you take over the Itosu-kai heritage after becoming one of the oldest students of Kenwa Mabuni Sensei?
A: Mabuni Sensei was the founder of Shito-ryu, which is a combination of *naha-te, shuri-te* and *tomari-te*. In Japan, the son is always the heir to his father's throne. Mabuni Kenei, although a junior to me, had to be the

leader of his father's heritage. Kenwa Mabuni Sensei, knowing that I was a senior, suggested that I carry on with the tradition of the Itosu-ha, which I honored and accepted. Mabuni Sensei learned from Master Itosu Ankho. Master Itosu was the teacher of other great masters like Chosin Chibana, Funakoshi Gichin, Choki Motobu, et cetera. For me, it was a privilege and an honor.

Q: Master Sakagami, how much influence of Zen is there in Bushido as a code of the samurai and budo?
A: The spirit underlying the arts practiced by the samurai was part Shinto and part Zen. This discipline was adapted from the Zen monastery and imposed on the martial arts elements and training. The most mundane act was to be performed with the utmost perfection. That ritual and tedious repetition in training provided not only technical expertise for the warriors but also a spiritual connection to the ancestors.

"The spirit underlying the arts practiced by the samurai was part Shinto and part Zen. This discipline was adapted from the Zen monastery and imposed on the martial arts elements and training."

Q: How do you feel after so many years of training?
A: I feel great about myself, but I'd probably be better if I had had more knowledge of the human body and proper nutrition. Knowing what I know today, I would have suffered fewer injuries and could have trained harder. To make their training and life more productive, new generations should study all of the information they have today. With that, they should be able to go farther than we old teachers did. In doing a martial art, the mind, spirit and technique should all be fully expressed. If your technique is correct and your mind and spirit fully expressed and arrived, you will progress very fast. In this case, you will get a different feeling everyday. Students should carefully realize this. If your technique, your

Karate Masters

"The main idea of budo is to remove all arrogance and pomposity and replace them with humbleness and the right spirit, and it's important to display those qualities that were established and sustained by generations of dedicated and devoted martial artists."

mind and your spirit do not arrive, you are wasting your time and will never succeed.

Q: What should be the main principles on which training is based?
A: All forms of martial arts start with courtesy and respect. The main idea of budo is to remove all arrogance and pomposity and replace them with humbleness and the right spirit, and it's important to display those qualities that were established and sustained by generations of dedicated and devoted martial artists. The true budo spirit is not something that you can put on and take off at will. It is something you become. It is in everything you do and permeates through all your acts. It puts us in accord with the flow of the universe. It is true that the value of a martial art depends on its application, but the goal is not always self-defense or self-protection. There are some other higher goals in budo training. In a true martial artist, all of the actions are geared [or designed] so that there is no dishonor or loss of face. The most important thing to keep in mind is that all forms of budo are not courses of study, but rather, a way of life.

Q: Sensei, what do you think is the most important thing a teacher should make sure the students learn, and what is the most relevant principle the student should keep in mind?
A: It is important that a martial art instructor foster a sense of self-responsibility in his students. For the students, the best way to learn is to practice, persevere and think about the intent behind the technique. It is too easy to look for magic while the real secret is sweat. There is no magic in the martial arts, just a good teacher and a lot of hard work. The key is to practice, and I have always been an advocate for teaching the students everything I know. Holding back just weakens the art. The old principle of saving a little,

which implies not teaching the whole art, has caused the deterioration of the martial arts.

Q: Do you think a certain amount of knowledge is lost when the art is taught from generation to generation?
A: Yes. The reason that techniques are lost is not because the teacher withholds the knowledge. Instead, it's because today's students don't work to understand what lies behind the physical movements. Sometimes you have a situation in which there are two students, and you spend a lot of time and effort on them. One turns out to be very good and the other turns out poor. The martial arts are not something you can copy. You must learn what lies behind the technique. The martial arts are taught today only like a good physical exercise. Unfortunately, they are lacking the true budo spirit. The training is not geared to a real life-or-death situation, and this single fact changes the whole approach.

"A student should be humble and honest with himself, because he should know his limitations and true possibilities. The martial arts are great as a physical exercise, as well as an excellent vehicle for mental health."

A student should be humble and honest with himself, because he should know his limitations and true possibilities. The martial arts are great as a physical exercise, as well as an excellent vehicle for mental health. Anyone should be able to become strong and more confident if he trains with the proper direction and goals in mind. Don't expect miracles though, because the martial arts won't bring any kind of mystical powers! It is important that a martial art instructor foster a sense of self-responsibility on the part of his students.

Q: Is it correct to change elements of the art and modify things that our teachers taught us?
A: I don't advocate change for change's sake, and this is what has happened recently in the world of martial arts. People with a limited amount of knowledge put together a little of this, a little of that, give it a new name and [suddenly] we have a new, complete martial art system that

will liberate all the practitioners in the world from the useless, traditional methods. I feel sorry for those students [who train with them] for not knowing any better. They follow these "instructors" and give them their money and their time. The traditional styles were put together with a sense of balance. Everything in a particular style was designed and glued together with meaning and reason. The techniques, the strategies and the principles found in the forms, et cetera, [all] work perfectly together like the pieces of a puzzle. If you have all the pieces and keep the final puzzle as it meant to be, you'll have a nice picture once you are finished. On the contrary, if you try to mix pieces from several different puzzles, you'll have a mess with no foundation and no reason to exist. People who do this often show big contradictions; they spend too much time repeating the words of other martial artist because they have nothing to offer and no central philosophy in what they are trying to teach. The old masters weren't so naive when they designed the different styles. Give them the credit they deserve because there is more in the traditional styles than what meets the eye. These martial artists who create new styles operate under the misconception that they are creating a perfect fighting method. To me, this concept is simply an illusion. The perfect style doesn't exit. Perfection is something that sounds very good, but it is unattainable. By simply eliminating classical techniques and replacing them with boxing does not make a new method better or superior. It makes it different. That's all. By changing the old styles and thinking that we have developed a superior method, we are creating a foundation for failure because that's another illusion. There is no perfect person, and there is no perfect style but the one that fits you and brings understanding and a peaceful spirit to your existence as a human being.

Q: Many people criticize the martial arts because they are loaded with rituals and protocols that are not necessary in the West. What is your opinion?
A: The martial arts are more than fighting. In Japan, they are part of budo. In China, they represent a way of life and a way of thinking that involves the principles of Taoism, and the same happens in every place where the arts were developed. Protocol and rituals have very little to do with the actual fighting, but they are vehicles to preserve education, politeness, etiquette, et cetera. All these are very important values for a student. The people who criticize this simply don't have the knowledge of what these aspects represent. The courtesy and proper protocol found in the traditional schools are the essence of the education. They are the true bones of

what's happening and keep everything within a serious environment for education. When you take away the protocol, the rituals like bowing and paying respect to your opponent, you are taking away from the history, from the legacy, from the bones and the essence of what a true martial art is all about. People should learn to differentiate between the rituals and the essence represented in these rituals. Maybe then they will realize why they are so important for the future generations.

Q: How important are the basics?
A: The technical foundations, which were dwelled upon for years, are unfortunately and often glossed over in a matter of a few months of part-time work. It is very important to train hard in the basics of the art. Never ignore these. Forms are composed of single movements or parts that make up the whole form. To become an expert, you should strive to learn how to use these parts. The basics, which are known as *kihon*, apply to the art of karate-do, as well as to the foundations of budo. It is very misleading [and wrong] if you move on and never give the basics another thought once you have learned them. To keep the foundation strong, you always have to go back to it, regardless of how many years of practice you have accumulated.

"People should learn to differentiate between the rituals and the essence represented in these rituals. Maybe then they will realize why they are so important for the future generations."

Q: Sensei, what kind of additional training is helpful for karate?
A: Traditionally, we had a series of supplementary training aids. They are classical implements that helped karate-ka to strengthen their bodies and prepare them for combat. The makiwara is one of them. Kobudo training also helps the wrists and hands.

Karate Masters

"Traditionally, we had a series of supplementary training aids. They are classical implements that helped karate-ka to strengthen their bodies and prepare them for combat."

Q: Is makiwara training beneficial for a practitioner?
A: If the student is guided by a knowledgeable teacher, it is definitely positive. You don't want to hit the makiwara without having a previous understanding and knowledge of what your goals are. You need to know the purpose of [training with the] makiwara, and the purpose is not to develop calloused hands. That's simply a consequence of the training. Your body, through correct training in the makiwara, will learn how to absorb the energy sent back to it after your fist hits an object. Thus, you will learn how to develop the right positioning when hitting an object with full force. It is a different [phenomena] to practice your punches and kicks in the air than it is to hit a solid object. The positioning of your legs, hip, back, shoulder, elbow, forearm and wrist must be properly aligned to exert all the possible power from your body and to absorb the shock of the impact. Basically, makiwara teaches you the right technique. If you do makiwara training simply to develop big knuckles and calluses, you won't get any benefit from it because that's not the purpose.

Q: Does the sportive approach change the teacher/student relationship?
A: Well, unfortunately, many people today think that karate is a sport, so they train for specific tournaments and competition, pretty much the same way that a basketball or football player trains for a game. Because the goal for every training session relates to sport competition, the person training them, correcting their movements and guiding them is a trainer

or coach. Never a sensei. The word sensei has very different connotations and meanings that extend way beyond winning a tournament. There are no coaches or trainers in budo.

The person who teaches you to discover yourself and your place in the world is not a coach. He is called teacher, master or sensei. He teaches you loyalty, courtesy, etiquette and all the important values that make a person a better human being. The person who trains a boxer is a trainer; the individual who trains and teach a karate-ka is a sensei. If the training is focused to win tournaments in a sport environment, other important qualities intrinsic in the true budo training, such as courtesy, loyalty, et cetera, are simply lost and forgotten. There can be an appreciation and respect for your coach but not in a budo way. Etiquette and proper attitude disappear. That's why we see coaches and competitors complaining constantly in a tournament if a referee's decision doesn't go their way. Proper etiquette is lost. Style is not as important as the spirit of the art.

Q: Is there anything you would like to add?
A: Yes, dedicate yourself to reach the higher levels of budo and put your heart and soul into it. The key to understanding the art of karate-do and most other budo arts is the underlying philosophy that runs so inseparably through all the forms of Japanese life. The principles of karate are based on the principles of life and the universe. It is the realization of an existing phenomenon—such as a punch or a kick—that gives meaning to that phenomenon, and it is the understanding of that meaning that allows one to master the phenomenon. It is for this purpose—understanding—that a person learns the art of karate-do. O

"The word sensei has very different connotations and meanings that extend way beyond winning a tournament. There are no coaches or trainers in budo. The person who teaches you to discover yourself and your place in the world is not a coach. He is called teacher, master or sensei."

Shigeru Sawabe

A Legacy of Excellence

SAWABE SHIGERU IS ONE OF THE MOST SENIOR SHITO-RYU PRACTITIONERS ALIVE TODAY. A DIRECT STUDENT OF BOTH KENWA MABUNI AND RYUSHO SAKAGAMI, SAWABE SHIHAN HAS KEPT THE ESSENCE OF THE VALUABLE TEACHINGS HE RECEIVED FROM THESE LEGENDARY MASTERS OF BUDO PURE. *"KARATE IS NOT A SPORT. IT SHOULD BE USED FOR SELF-DEFENSE AS A LAST RESORT ONLY. KARATE-DO IS A WAY OF LIFE ... A MEANS TO ACHIEVE SECURITY AND FEARLESSNESS."* AS WELL AS HIS CAREER AS LEADER OF JAPAN'S LARGEST CORPORATE SECURITY COMPANY, HE HAS LONG BEEN A LEADER IN JAPANESE KARATE-DO AND HAS HELD SEVERAL TOP POSITIONS WITH SEVERAL KARATE-DO'S GOVERNING BODIES. HE HAS ALSO AUTHORED SEVERAL HIGHLY REGARDED TEXTS ON KARATE AND IS THE LEADER OF THE JAPAN KARATE-DO SHUBU-KAI. SAWABE SHIHAN REMAINS ACTIVE AND EAGER TO SHARE THE GIFTS HE RECEIVED FROM HIS MASTERS AND EPITOMIZES THE TRUE DEFINITION OF THE "WARRIOR SPIRIT." IN HIS TEACHING, HE STRESSES THAT AS ONE GETS OLDER CONTINUOUS TRAINING BECOMES INCREASINGLY IMPORTANT. AND, ALTHOUGH HE IS CONSIDERED AMONG THE MOST KNOWLEDGEABLE OF LIVING KARATE MASTERS, SHIGERU SAWABE STRESSES THAT HE HAS NOT ARRIVED. INSTEAD, HE IS STILL A STUDENT WITH MUCH TO LEARN, AND HE INTENDS TO CONTINUE HIS QUEST FOR KNOWLEDGE AS LONG AS HE LIVES.

Q: When did you first meet Sakagami Ryusho?
A: I met Sakagami Sensei during wartime. I was in junior high school at the time. At that time in school we were required to do either judo or kendo. I chose kendo, and Sakagami Sensei was the kendo teacher. One day I saw Sakagami Sensei punching a tree. I asked him what he was doing, and he told me that he was practicing karate. Not long afterward I enlisted two of my friends, and we asked Sakagami Sensei to teach us. After the war in 1945, General MacArthur banned the practice of martial arts and Sakagami Sensei decided to stop teaching. After several months, my friends and I found where Sakagami Sensei lived. We went there and asked him to keep teaching us karate. We had to insist a little, but he finally agreed.

Karate Masters

"The training under Sakagami Sensei and Mabuni Sensei was very different compared to what we see today in any martial arts school. During the war, when I began, we had no gi and no dojo. We just trained outside."

Q: How were you introduced to Mabuni Kenwa?
A: Sakagami Sensei took me to Mabuni Sensei's dojo; that's how I met him. I continued studying karate-do with both Sakagami Sensei and Mabuni Sensei. After high school, I entered Osaka Kogyo University, where Mabuni Sensei was the instructor. I trained with the university club during the day and at night went to Mabuni Sensei's dojo to train more. During my third year at the University, Mabuni Sensei passed away. After that, I continued my training with Sakagami Sensei at his dojo. At that time, his dojo was located at his home.

Q: How was the training under these two great karate masters?
A: The training under Sakagami Sensei and Mabuni Sensei was very different compared to what we see today in any martial arts school. During the war, when I began, we had no gi and no dojo. We just trained outside. We trained barefoot even when it was quite cold with snow on the ground. The main thing then was the constant training. I would train for three hours at the university and then take the train to Mabuni Sensei's dojo for more training. The morale and mentality after the war dictated how all the practitioners felt and how dedicated they were to the training. It is difficult to explain, but there were mixed feeling inside each and every one of us. From the technical point of view, we weren't concerned about sport and our kata training was a method of training and researching for the most efficient self-defense techniques.

Q: How was the approach to kata training?
A: Well, to begin with, we didn't really care at all about the look of our kata. This is something that you see today. At that time, kata was not for show. By this, I mean that we never tried to make it look good. It was like a textbook in which you could take technical information. The essence and meaning behind the form were the most important things.

The outside or mold was simply perfected to match the proper delivery of the physical technique.

Q: Can you give us an example?
A: Sure. When we did *shuto-uke*, we did not hold our fingers perfectly straight. The idea behind shuto-uke is to use the outside edge of your hand to block or hit; therefore, if you straighten all of your fingers, you take force away from that specific area of the hand. We kept the fingers bent to focus more of the tension in that zone. The movement doesn't look as pretty as the "perfect" straight hand, but it is the correct way of doing it …when you are doing it for real use.

"The technical approach to the movements was more natural and the human body was taken more into consideration. The main idea in fighting was not to score a point based on speed and power. Instead, it was to attack the vital points in the opponent's body."

The technical approach to the movements was more natural and the human body was taken more into consideration. The main idea in fighting was not to score a point based on speed and power. Instead, it was to attack the vital points in the opponent's body. This is the reason why we develop each part of our body as a weapon. We used fingers to the eyes ands throat, side of the hand to the neck, instep to the groin, kicks to the legs and every other technique that allowed us to seriously hurt the opponent. That's how we learned karate. It was a method of self-defense and not a sport.

Q: Are you against sport in karate?
A: No, I am not as long as the true spirit of the budo stays during practice and training. Sport can be seen as a small part of the whole art called karate. That small part never is more important than the art.

Q: How do you remember Mabuni Kenwa?
A: He was a very special individual. His goal was to try to gather as much knowledge as possible, and that's the reason why he studied so many

Karate Masters

"I understand that modern practitioners do not need to study 60 or 70 kata, but Mabuni Sensei was in a very important position in the history of budo. He was the link between several styles in Okinawa and the acceptance of karate in Japan."

styles and accumulated so many kata. I understand that modern practitioners do not need to study 60 or 70 kata, but Mabuni Sensei was in a very important position in the history of budo. He was the link between several styles in Okinawa and the acceptance of karate in Japan. He was in a very important position, and he had to communicate and impart the knowledge in a proper way with the right information. He became a repository of traditional knowledge and kata and many other outstanding karate masters went to him for study and advice. For instance, Master Funakoshi studied with him and sent several of his main students [including M. Nakayama Sensei] to learn from Mabuni Kenwa. He was highly respected among all karate teachers and masters of his time.

Q: And Sakagami Ryusho?
A: He was a very special individual. His knowledge of budo was outstanding. Not only he was a master in karate but also in other arts like aikido, kendo kobudo and iaido. He trained with some of the best teachers ever and his understanding of how the different arts fit together in the perfect format for a budo warrior was amazing. He was capable of relating different techniques and explaining why they could work or why they couldn't. I haven't seen anyone like him, and his memory and legacy will stay with me forever.

Q: Did he teach kobudo, too?
A: Yes, and he was extremely knowledgeable about the history and application of each traditional weapon from Okinawa. He could relate history to technique in every weapon. He truly was an encyclopedia of knowledge.

Q: Why did he become the leader of the itosu-kai?
A: According to what I know, Mabuni Sensei had to leave the leadership

of the style [shito-ryu] to his son. This is the Japanese tradition in budo. Sakagami Sensei was older and senior to Mabuni's sons so Mabuni Sensei gave him the leadership of the Itosu-ha legacy that he had received from Grandmaster Itosu Anko. It was a way of allowing him to take the leadership he deserved, but Mabuni Kenwa couldn't give it to him for traditional reasons. Sakagami Sensei became the leader of the itosu-kai style of karate, but it is interesting to note that he was including the entire syllabus from naha-te and tomari-te in his teachings ... not only those techniques and kata from the Itosu lineage. The teachings of Kanryo Higaonna were present in the curriculum and syllabus of Sakagami Sensei. In fact, his teachings were pretty much the same as Mabuni Kenwa's. There were no substantial differences. And by all means, you can consider what Sakagami Ryusho Sensei was teaching as pure shito-ryu.

"Don't try to make sense of the complete kata at once because it was never meant to be that way. Pay attention to the little details in the structure of the form. There is more than meets the eye. Each kata requires time and effort to fully understand its meaning."

Q: Do you think that it is important for a shito-ryu or itosu-kai student to know all the complete kata syllabus of the style?
A: Not really. Each kata represents and teaches certain fighting principles. We have to look into kata using the following approach: Kata was not [originally] a set of fighting techniques. The fighting techniques were separated and they stood by themselves. Then, the old masters put them together in an organized format and created the kata. When you study the application of the movements, you must think this way and try to discover the meaning behind the technique. Sometimes you even have to reverse the kata to understand the bunkai!

Don't try to make sense of the complete kata at once because it was never meant to be that way. Pay attention to the little details in the structure of the form. There is more than meets the eye. Each kata requires time and effort to fully understand its meaning. Therefore, I think that the student in shito-ryu must learn those kata that provide him with the essence

Karate Masters

"To be a master of shito-ryu doesn't necessarily mean you need to know 60 different kata. Nobody can master this number of forms equally. Not even Mabuni Sensei had the same amount of knowledge about each single kata he knew."

of the different flavors found in the shito-ryu style (naha, shuri and tomari) and develop an appreciation for them. Then, focus on those kata that he feels a more natural inclination to and go deep into each one of them. Study the bunkai and oyo-bunkai, research the history of kata and find the true meaning behind the form. To be a master of shito-ryu doesn't necessarily mean you need to know 60 different kata. Nobody can master this number of forms equally. Not even Mabuni Sensei had the same amount of knowledge about each single kata he knew. Instructors and professional teachers need to have an extensive knowledge of the complete kata syllabus in order to pass them onto the new generation.

Q: Is it necessary to know different versions of the same kata to completely understand the form in all its interpretations?

A: Let's take *passai* kata. According to the opinions and interpretations of the different masters, there are many different versions of this kata. We have *matsumura no passai, ishimine no passai, passai dai, passai sho,* et cetera. All of these are simply versions of the same. To really get the proper benefit from the form, you don't need to know all of them. Some versions are closer to others, and others are very different to the point that they can be considered a different kata all together. This doesn't really mean anything because the practitioner should take maybe two or three different versions and try to understand their origin and differences. Also, it is important to start with an easier version before learning a more complex or advanced interpretation of the same form. Teachers need to learn more to be capable of passing these different interpretations to future generations.

Q: Are different kata used to develop specific qualities in the student's training?

A: Definitely. That's one of the advantages of the shito-ryu style. The teacher should use specific kata to develop the student in different technical and physical areas. For instance, you don't use passai dai to develop the student's strength and body conditioning. Other forms like sanchin and tensho should be used to that effect. Each kata has its specification, and it has to be used for that specific purpose. This is one of the reasons why it seems that Mabuni Sensei used the naha-te forms in the beginning of the student's training. Maybe he used that to develop the body so he could later introduce more subtle technical actions based on speed [shuri-te]. I think that basically it all depends on the student you are teaching. The training was done in almost one-on-one situations so the teacher used to give each student specifically what he needed. This doesn't happen today, and the instruction is more mass oriented. This reduces the possibility of the instructor giving the student those things that he really needs for himself.

"The training was done in almost one-on-one situations so the teacher used to give each student specifically what he needed. This doesn't happen today, and the instruction is more mass oriented."

Q: How does shito-ryu combine (under one format) the presentation of different styles (approaches) and fighting ideas from shuri, tomari and naha?

A: It is a difficult question to answer because it would take hours to explain all the details, but I'll try my best to keep it short. It is clear how the format of shotokan karate works, and it is also clear how the style of goju-ryu performs the kata. Shito-ryu doesn't use any of these extremes [if we can use this term]. It makes every form more natural ... more in an Okinawan way of performing the techniques. It is not as physical and strong as shotokan, but it is neither as hard as goju. This approach is something that people understand with time. When their bodies change and they get older, the hard approach can't be used any more because it is not natural for the body. Then you have to use a more natural way of doing the kata. Let me cite an example from shotokan. In this style, the kata has been changed and designed for young and strong people. So, when they get older, they can hardly do the kata as they used to. If you look at senior instructors of hard shotokan in the past, you'll see that now they do the forms very differently. They look more natural and closer to the way shito-ryu does the forms. They even use shito-ryu kata in their curriculum now because they have realized that the approach is more natural for the body and you can use it for a long period of time. Karate was never meant to be practiced only by young people. So, in my opin-

Karate Masters

"An intermediate movement can counter every basic technique, and an advanced movement can easily counter every intermediate movement. What people don't understand is that any advanced movement is very easily nullified by a basic technique."

ion, the idea of formatting karate for strong and physically talented students was not a very good move.

Q: Do you separate your teaching in basic and advanced techniques in kata?
A: Not really, because that is a mistake. I don't look at karate techniques and separate the movements into advanced and basic. There are no basic or advanced movements. Techniques are the same. Techniques are something that develop and improve with time and training. A fundamental technique becomes "advanced," as you like to describe, when it becomes a natural movement and a reflexive reaction. An intermediate movement can counter every basic technique, and an advanced movement can easily counter every intermediate movement. What people don't understand is that any advanced movement is very easily nullified by a basic technique. Please note that when I use the terms "advanced," "intermediate" and "basic" that I'm only referring to the technical difficulty of the physical action. Simply, don't forget that the more complex the technical action is, the less likely it will be successful.

Q: What is the difference between a sport coach and a karate teacher?
A: Many, but unfortunately and due to the fact modern karate is moving more and more into a sportive approach, teachers are becoming like football coaches. They use the sport approach to make students better and this is wrong. On the other hand, many karate champions become instructors immediately. Dan ranks are given to competitors because they have won a tournament. Then, you have a 5th dan instructor only because he has won an international championship. How do you think this instructor will coach his students? A competitor is focused on being better and stronger himself. Usually, they don't teach the student how to be great because they still have to think about themselves. And it is actually quite normal to think about your own importance when you are young and competing. A true sensei is a different thing all together. I have always enjoyed making my students better than me. Fortunately, young students have great teachers around the world they can go to for information, training and assistance.

Q: In modern competition, different scores are given to different techniques. Do you agree with that idea?
A: I like the idea of shobu-ippon because it represents what budo is all about. One punch, and you are dead. You can't get up and keep fighting. Even if you don't put your opponent down with one single technique that is what you should strive for. Even if you don't knock him down completely, he will be in very bad shape. In this condition, there is no guarantee of victory. When you know there is only one opportunity of doing it right—because otherwise you'll be doing it wrong—you pay

"The fighter needs to render himself empty as a mirror's polished surface reflects whatever stands before it. His mind should be empty of selfishness in an effort to react appropriately toward anything his opponent may give him."

more attention to everything. You know that a small mistake can be fatal. You know you can score three or four more points afterward ... like in soccer. It is only one clean shot. No second chances. Like the old samurai duels. You miss, and you are killed. This is budo, and I like this idea. Of course, it may be boring for spectators. For a budo-ka who understands what is happening, however, it is very interesting. This approach influences the mental state of the fighter because of the relevance of a single action. The fighter needs to render himself empty as a mirror's polished surface reflects whatever stands before it. His mind should be empty of selfishness in an effort to react appropriately toward anything his opponent may give him. He finds himself fighting in a controlled environment, but he maintains an attitude of facing death. This is the only way we can bring true budo spirit into modern competition without losing the traditional fighting spirit of the arts.

Q: Is it more difficult to perform proper kicking techniques or punching techniques?
A: Every technique has its difficulty, no matter what it may be. Personally, however, I see the necessary coordination, balance and use of all the proper lines of power in the body to be more difficult in the punching

Karate Masters

"Understanding the different types of kime when punching is extremely difficult. For instance, I see many practitioners only using their arms and hips when they punch. They don't know how to use their shoulders correctly in the movement. If they did, that would fully bring the back muscles into the punch."

techniques. I know many people think that kicking techniques are very difficult. However, if we understand all the body mechanics involved in a simple gyaku-tsuki, we'll realize that it is extremely hard to master the correct body positioning, hip rotation, back alignment, shoulder push, torque action, et cetera. Understanding the different types of kime when punching is extremely difficult. For instance, I see many practitioners only using their arms and hips when they punch. They don't know how to use their shoulders correctly in the movement. If they did, that would fully bring the back muscles into the punch. They, because of the lack of knowledge and understanding, use too many chest muscles to compensate for the technique. They also keep the muscular tension too long after the final part of the technique. Because of this, their breath stops, which is completely incorrect.

Also, the idea of snapping your body like a whip is something that has been developed in the last decades of research. It is important to fully understand how the body works and try to get the most out of it in every physical movement.

Q: What is the traditional model for teachers and students in Japanese karate and how do the Western students accept it?

A: The technical model is presented to the students, and they try to copy it as accurately as possible. They have faith and confidence in the sensei, which eliminates the need for lengthy verbal discussion about the technique. The student doesn't question anything. He accepts his role and the training environment. For a Western student, all this is really strange because it is a cultural thing. They accept more personal responsibility in their own progress in the art, which compels them to continually question the structure and content of each lesson. The questions need to be answered immediately, and students are not satisfied with the Japanese answer of *"because the sensei says so."* Considering all these differences, it is not difficult to understand why there are sometimes misinterpretations and misunderstandings. I believe that these important cultural aspects are the key to many problems in the art of karate today. For instance, many Japanese instructors living abroad need to find a reason for every technique they teach. They also feel they have to justify everything taught in class, as this is a desperate attempt to reassure the students that they are not wasting their time. Therefore, the value of the technique is expressed in relation to the potential such techniques have for scoring points and winning tournaments.

Q: What are the most important qualities of a good instructor?
A: The main point is that the instructor must know himself. He must understand his strong and weak points—both physically and mentally. From there he can look to the students and try to work with the capabilities and limitations they may have. This is very basic philosophy. Only when you understand yourself can you understand other people. Without this, it is impossible to teach other people properly. Also, a good instructor keeps training himself all the time. He doesn't stop his personal training or his learning process, and he places emphasis on the basics movements and techniques.

"A good instructor should be hard and dedicated to what he does. At the same time, he has to be understanding to the student's needs and be there to help him when he needs it. This applies not only inside the dojo but outside as well."

A good instructor should be hard and dedicated to what he does. At the same time, he has to be understanding to the student's needs and be there to help him when he needs it. This applies not only inside the dojo but outside as well. A good sensei in the traditional budo concept is much more than a simple teacher of a fighting art.

Q: What should an instructor be looking for in a grading session?
A: From the technical point of view, it depends on what dan level the student is testing for. Based on this, the requirements are different. But there

Karate Masters

"Any technique, regardless of how perfect it may be from a physical point of view, is irrelevant without the correct spirit. I'm not talking about anger or rage. I am talking about good spirit, which is something creative and positive."

are basics concepts and principles the students must physically display according to the rank they are testing for; such as body control, hip action, kime, zanchin, stances and overall coordination, et cetera. These are some of the elements that every karate practitioner should have, depending, of course, on their skill level. Regardless if they pass or fail, students should present themselves with etiquette and decorum. If the attitude is wrong, I personally don't care much for the physical ability.

Q: What is karate to you and how would you describe its benefits?
A: Karate represents many different things. To me, it is a beautiful art that can be used as a physical activity to keep in shape and also a method of perfecting character. It is an art form, but not only because someone designed a set of physical moves that make it look artistic. It is art because karate teaches us to use the body in a perfect way. The movements are designed to be used in the best possible way. Every single muscle and body part work together to generate the body's maximum potential in power and speed. Through the attempt to perfect these techniques, you can use your body like a tool for self-improvement. Once you have the necessary skill, that is when the true spirit of budo must take over. Any technique, regardless of how perfect it may be from a physical point of view, is irrelevant without the correct spirit. I'm not talking about anger or rage. I am talking about good spirit, which is something creative and positive. With it, we can surpass our physical and mental limitations and improve ourselves.

Q: Why do you think students stop training after three or four years?
A: There is a threshold in which most of the students quit training, and this is between 1st kyu and sho-dan. After this period of time [three or four years], the student is not motivated any more because the initial illusion has gone away. Now the students realize that to progress there is only one way to go ... constant repetition of what they have learned and

this becomes a boring chore. Another reason is that their technical foundation hasn't been set properly, and they start to see their own limitations and get disappointed. If they don't have a precise understanding of the art and basics from the very beginning, it is impossible for them to keep motivated to progress. They simply have no desire to stick to it. In the Japanese culture, the student is not supposed to enjoy the training. Training is a challenge and something difficult the student has to face every day. It is not a hobby or a pleasure as it is in the Western world.

"Dedicate yourself to your instructor. When you become a teacher, teach anyone who is willing to learn. Karate teaches you how to gain and keep control of any situation in life. When you face a difficult task, push yourself into it until you can do it."

Q: Finally, what advice would you give to all karate-do practitioners, regardless of style?
A: My advice is to keep practicing all the time. Even if you feel tired, bored and with no motivation whatsoever … keep doing it. You'll understand one day. Because the more you practice, the more you understand when the right time comes. Never neglect the basics and take the kata training seriously. Never forsake one kata for another and treat them all the same because they bring different benefits to you. Dedicate yourself to your instructor. When you become a teacher, teach anyone who is willing to learn. Karate teaches you how to gain and keep control of any situation in life. When you face a difficult task, push yourself into it until you can do it. Don't give up under pressure. Keep a good attitude and strong discipline. O

Tatsuo Suzuki

The Pure Essence

TATSUO SUZUKI HAS REMAINED—THROUGHOUT THE YEARS—TRUE TO THE TEACHING AND PHILOSOPHY HE LEARNED FROM HIRONORI OHTSUKA, HIS INSTRUCTOR AND FOUNDER OF WADO-RYU KARATE. ONE OF THE FEW CHOSEN TO DIRECTLY TRAIN UNDER THE LEGENDARY MASTER, SUZUKI SENSEI'S TECHNICAL LEVEL IS AMONG THOSE WHO HAVE A RESERVED PLACE IN THE HISTORY OF MARTIAL ARTS. ALTHOUGH HE AGREES THAT "SPECTACULAR TECHNIQUES ATTRACT STUDENTS," HE SAYS THESE [TYPES OF TECHNIQUES] ARE NOT PART OF TRUE KARATE, "THE EVOLUTION OF WARRIOR TECHNIQUES TO SATE HIGH ENOUGH TO BE CONSIDERED AN ART IN THEIR OWN RIGHT REQUIRES A DEVELOPMENT OF SEVERAL GENERATIONS AND THESE ARE NOT FOR FUN OR ENTERTAINMENT."

WITH AN ALWAYS FRIENDLY AND HUMBLE ATTITUDE, THIS KARATE MASTER'S GOAL IS TO PRESERVE THE TRUE SPIRIT OF BUDO IN MODERN SOCIETY. AMONG THE GREAT KARATE MASTERS OF OUR TIME, TATSUO SUZUKI IS QUITE UNIQUE, BOTH IN HIS PROFOUND KNOWLEDGE OF MARTIAL ARTS THEORY AND IN HIS INNOVATIVE SPIRIT. HIS VIRTUES, MARTIAL QUALITIES, MASTERY AND CONSCIENTIOUSNESS ALL MAKE HIM ONE OF THE MOST REMARKABLE INSTRUCTORS OF JAPANESE KARATE-DO IN THE WORLD.

Q: Is it true that you began your karate training under Kimura Sensei?
A: Yes, it is true. I began training in 1942 when I was 14 years old. Kimura Sensei was an extremely talented instructor and one of the best Ohtsuka Sensei instructors. Before that, I did practice karate. The brother of one of my friends was training at Tokyo University. When he came back for school holidays, he taught us. At that time [before the war], all the training was fighting-oriented and featured real contact. About two years later I moved to Yokohama, where I was born.

Q: Did you practice kata?
A: Not much. The training was based on hard sessions of kihon (basic movements in a system) and lots of sparring and fighting. There was a difference between the private clubs and the university dojo. The training at the university was very hard, and the instructors didn't care if the students quit because there were another 100 students waiting to enter the next

Karate Masters

"The instructors taught us to punch and kick to defeat the opponent so our mentality was simply to attack. Of course, when we got seriously hit, we had to figure out how to block! But instructors didn't spend time showing the defensives aspects of combat."

month. But the privates clubs were different. They couldn't afford to lose students so the training was more humane. This is the reason why the university had great fighters with a strong spirit and fearless determination. Many people got injured and ended up with bruises and cuts. Others suffered broken teeth and noses. Sometimes people were really hurt. They were trained that way. The emphasis was on attacking more than in learning how to defend.

Q: What do you mean by that?
A: The instructors taught us to punch and kick to defeat the opponent so our mentality was simply to attack. Of course, when we got seriously hit, we had to figure out how to block! But instructors didn't spend time showing the defensives aspects of combat.

Q: What kind of man was Ohtsuka Sensei?
A: He was a real Japanese samurai. He had the right spirit and attitude. I have never met a man with such a great personality. He was one of the greatest karate men ... both physically and mentally. I have never seen such a complete martial artist.

Q: How were things after World War II?
A: They changed very much because we [Japanese] weren't allowed to practice anymore. The American government prohibited all kinds of martial training, including judo and kendo. Most practitioners stopped their training at that very same moment, but there were some clubs where you could train because they managed to keep them open under the name of "Japanese boxing." Actually, this was pure Japanese karate and had nothing to do with boxing.

Q: How was the training at the university?
A: It was very hard. I was at Nihon University, and we had a pretty decent group of students. Unfortunately, the training was so hard that the atten-

dance dwindled from 200 to 20. The rest simply decided it was too hard. When I was in my first year at the university, I was already *san-dan*. The highest senior university student was *ni-dan*. So, I outranked all of them. Don't forget at that time *go-dan* was the highest rank given.

Q: How many go-dan were there in wado-ryu at that time?
A: Not many. Only the senior students.

Q: Is it true that you went straight from san-dan to go-dan?
A: Pretty much. I never worried about rank, so even if I was san-dan, I never cared about the next rank. Testing for 4th Dan was not on my mind at all. All the junior students began to push me to test because if I didn't test they would have never been promoted. So, after many years of 3rd Dan, I decided to test for 4th Dan. After the test, Ohtsuka Sensei gave me the 5th Dan. I said that it was "too much." And I didn't want to accept it. I asked Ohtsuka Sensei for him to give me the 4th Dan because the go-dan was the highest rank. He answered, *"No. You take this. All the examiners agree your are 5th Dan, so you must accept it."* So I did.

Q: Did you fight against practitioners from other dojo or schools?
A: Yes, I did. It was normal and accepted to arrange meetings to train together. These training sessions ended up in real fights. At that time, you could easily recognize the practitioner's style because of his style of fighting. For example, the goju people in neko-ashi-dachi, the shotokan practitioners using a long distance approach, et cetera. Our [wado-ryu] style was something in between, but we used a lot of tai-sabaki and body evasion techniques.

Q: I have heard that you had a tokui-waza and that it was a low side kick. Is this true?
A: Yes! I used *sokuto-geri* to the knee and leg a lot. It is a great technique to stop your opponent in his tracks, and I did get very good at it. I developed perfect timing and sensed when to throw it to stop the attack. This is a great technique for real fighting and self-defense because it causes a lot of damage. At the same time, it stops the attack immediately. The problem today is that nobody uses it because you need power and force to be effective. If you control the technique, it won't be effective at all.

Q: So, at that time you used kicks to the legs ...
A: Of course! Why not? We used kicks to the legs, headbutts, attacks to

Karate Masters

"I trained very simply, but I did thousands of repetitions of the same movement. I also did a lot of makiwara, which I consider to be a very good training tool. In this day and age, most practitioner's fists are very weak."

the groin, et cetera. It was—without a doubt—a different way of practicing karate.

Q: When was the best time period (years) of your training?
A: Maybe around 1953 or 1955. Immediately after the war the training was not that strong because of the moral state of the people. Later on, however, we caught up and there were excellent training days.

Q: Did you get seriously hit during these training sessions?
A: I have never been knocked down, but I have been hit and hit hard! I had a bad experience with one of Motoyoshi Sensei's students. He was a kendo student, a very tough karate-ka and very big. I was much faster than him so I used my speed, but he waited and waited until he had his chance. Then he stamped kicked to my knee. I felt a great deal of pain when he hit me. I kept fighting, but I needed to stay in bed for one week to recover. During this, I also got a couple of black eyes.

Q: What kind of personal training did you do at that time?
A: I trained very simply, but I did thousands of repetitions of the same movement. I also did a lot of makiwara, which I consider to be a very good training tool. In this day and age, most practitioner's fists are very weak. Thus, they are not real weapons. I also used *tetsu-geta* for my kicks. I did everything, because I used to spend 10 hours everyday in the dojo. In 10 hours, you have time to do almost everything everyday!

Q: How was the training under Ohtsuka Sensei?
A: When I graduated from the university, I wanted to be a professional karate teacher so I basically decided to follow Ohtsuka Sensei anywhere. We had our Honbu dojo in Tokyo. This dojo was built by Mr. Tanaka for Ohtsuka Sensei. I spent all my time training and teaching for Ohtsuka Sensei. The spirit was very strong and good. And the training was very hard.

Q: Was jiu-jitsu part of Ohtsuka Sensei's teachings?
A: It was, and he mixed it in. There were no special classes for this. He used to teach these jiu-jitsu elements and *tanto dori* and *idori*. I never saw him to teach it as a separate entity.

Q: How do you remember him?
A: He was a very active individual and always enjoyed what he was doing. His techniques were very fast, especially his *ura-ken* [backfist]. I believe that he had formulated the wado-ryu style a few years before I started training under him.

"Older people should not train for physical power. They have to train differently. Every action should be a softer way to bring the power from the internal organs."

Q: There are many misinterpretations about the different kinds of training practitioners should do based on their age. Why is this?
A: Simply because a 50-year-old karate-ka sees a 25-year-old individual and thinks he has to train the same. Then, when he gets older, he already has this incorrect idea of what he has to do and tries to follow it. What they don't understand is that if a 40-year-old practitioner tries to train the same as a young man, he will actually get weaker. And this is a fact. Older people should not train for physical power. They have to train differently. Every action should be a softer way to bring the power from the internal organs. When they have to react to a real situation, they will be able to because of the right training.

I have seen many great karate-ka quit karate after a certain age because they thought that they couldn't do the art the same way they did when they were younger. They can't kick high and they can't jump as they used to … so they quit. In karate-do, you don't have to kick or jump high to do good karate. The art has absolutely nothing to do with that. Everybody has physical limitations. What many people don't understand is that the old masters knew about this. So, when they designed the struc-

Karate Masters

"We have become intellectually knowledgeable of the activity we practice. In the past, we didn't know about lines of power, centrifugal force or any of these scientific principles used in karate. Today, maybe the training is not as hard as it used to be, but it is more scientific."

ture of the art, they did it in such a way that these changes were accommodated when the right time came in the practitioner's life. Instructors must understand this point and ensure that older students do the things in the right way and train within their own limitations. Karate is not hard to the body if it is properly done, Unfortunately, many of the instructors around the world don't have the proper understanding to help the older students. In true karate-do, if a person is using the same kind of power when he is 60 than when he was 30, then something is wrong.

Q: Do you think that the karate training today is better than what you received when you were young?
A: This is a difficult question to answer. What I can say, however, is that the basic foundation of the art should not be changed at all. By this, I mean the kihon, kata and kumite structure. These three basic elements of karate should be kept together and the same. The truth is nobody ever gave me a good reason to change any of these elements to make it better. People change kata but not to make it better. They do it because it looks better ... to them or because it is good for competition. But this has nothing to do with karate. On the other hand, today we have more scientific knowledge of why and how to perform the techniques. We have become intellectually knowledgeable of the activity we practice. In the past, we didn't know about lines of power, centrifugal force or any of these scientific principles used in karate. Today, maybe the training is not as hard as it used to be, but it is more scientific. I'm not sure if this is good or bad, to be honest. The truth is people may reach the same level with less effort because of the understanding of how things work.

Q: How important is the rank in Japan?
A: Rank was never a relevant thing in Japan. In fact, rank is something that became popular in the Western world. Teachers in Japan don't go around bragging about their rank. It is something that only brings a bad

reputation and proves how immature they are.

Q: How important is it for a practitioner to train for real impact in the techniques?
A: Extremely important. How do you know if a car is useful unless you turn the key, start the engine and push the gas? Unfortunately, many instructors think of karate technique as something that has to be mastered by punching and kicking in the air. And this is not correct. Students must learn the basic body mechanics and form by punching and kicking in the air. This is simply the first step. It is at this stage in which the instructor should correct the technical mistakes. Students need to learn the proper use of the body, muscles and joints to generate power. Once the student has this skill down, impact training should be included. The body reacts completely different when you punch or kick a heavy bag or focus mitt compared to when you perform the technique in the air. The feedback from the object being hit goes back into the body. Therefore, the student needs to get use to absorbing that energy. At the same time, he has to learn how to exert energy into the blow. There are many different tools that can be used for this training, including the makiwara, the heavy bag, the focus pads, et cetera.

"Rank was never a relevant thing in Japan. Teachers in Japan don't go around bragging about their rank. It is something that only brings a bad reputation and proves how immature they are."

Q: You keep yourself in such great shape with expert technical skill. How do you manage to do it?
A: Ohtsuka Sensei told us to continue training everyday and never stop. He practiced daily until his death. I try to imitate him and train everyday of my life. The only secret is to never stop training. Although a lot of my time is spent in teaching, I train everyday and everywhere. It doesn't matter where I am. I allocate time for my personal training. I try the old way, polishing my basics and trying to make my kata stronger every time. I just try to reach my personal best each day I put the gi on. As far as strength,

Karate Masters

"The only secret is to never stop training. Although a lot of my time is spent in teaching, I train everyday and everywhere. It doesn't matter where I am. I allocate time for my personal training."

I am not really concerned with creating big muscles, but I do some strength training to keep my muscles in good condition. It is not good to have too much muscle if you can't move quickly.

Q: So, you emphasize the importance of basics in your personal routine?
A: Definitely. I work on the basics first and then I move on to kata and some fundamental exercises to maintain the necessary body coordination required to perform the techniques correctly. Stance training is also very important because everything else is based on how you move and how strong and coordinated your stances are.

Q: Speaking of stances, what are the most common errors students commit when working on their *dachi*?
A: Most practitioners tense and fix their positions very well, but they make the mistake of maintaining the tension between stances too long. When you punch, you immediately relax your muscles after the moment of impact (kime). When moving from one stance to another, students should do the same ... tense and relax.

Q: Do you think there is still a gap between Japanese instructors and the Western students?
A: Yes. It is cultural gap because the senior karate instructors were trained under the strict principles of budo. There are things than can't be explained or understood because we [Japanese and Westerners] look at it from a completely different point of view. I know it is hard to understand, but there seems to be a gap, regardless of how much everybody tries to understand everybody else. For instance, the concept of *senpai-kohai* is mostly misunderstood in the Western world and difficult to incorporate properly in a dojo when you teach outside Japan. For the Japanese, these kinds of things are natural. Outside of Japan, students don't understand it.

It is simply not part of their culture and other rules are developed naturally based on the specific culture and belief of that given country.

Q: Is it possible to duplicate the state-of-mind of the old samurai in modern budo matches and competitions?
A: It is very difficult because old samurai fought with swords and the loser died. These kinds of events require demanding physical training and a mental training that is capable of dealing with life-or-death situations. In real fighting, if you make a mistake, you are dead, so you must make no mistakes of any kind. Of course, it is normal for a human being to be afraid of death, so the idea of accepting death is difficult to absorb. If competition today was like it was when I was young, then I'm sure that a lot of mental training should be done before getting into such type of confrontation. We weren't killing each other, but people used to get seriously hurt. Zen is a good way to learn how to deal with these situations.

"There are things than can't be explained or understood because we [Japanese and Westerners] look at it from a completely different point of view. I know it is hard to understand, but there seems to be a gap, regardless of how much everybody tries to understand everybody else."

Q: Are you interested in Western boxing?
A: Very much. I love to watch and study boxing films. You can see and learn a great deal from these excellent fighters. In boxing, because they only use the hands to fight, they have developed excellent techniques based on scientific principles. Much better than karate, I think. If you use your feet too, that is a different game. With hands only, I feel boxing is very strong. Ohtsuka Sensei told us that karate is not perfect and that if we see something good from other sports or another martial art we should add it to build up our karate technique. He did this himself when he formulated wado-ryu.

Q: Do you think Olympic recognition would be good for karate?
A: I'm sure that more people would get involved in karate and the governments would help the federations with money, but I also know something else. If that ever happens [Olympic recognition], I'm very sure that

Karate Masters

"If competition today was like it was when I was young, then I'm sure that a lot of mental training should be done before getting into such type of confrontation. We weren't killing each other, but people used to get seriously hurt."

karate would lose its martial content forever. Today, karate in most schools is only a sport, and this is wrong. I must agree that there can be a sport side to it, but the instructor should balance this and teach the student the two sides of the coin. If karate gets into the Olympics, it will be extremely difficult to maintain the mental and spiritual side of the art. That's why I said that it would lose its content forever.

Q: Are you interested in Zen?
A: Yes, I am, and I have always been interested in the old legendary martial artists from Japan. All of them studied Zen at some point of their lives. I wanted to follow their example so I began study it, too. Mr. Tanaka, who was the patron of the club where I was training, introduced me to Genpo Yamamoto, a very well-known priest, and Soyen Nakagawa, his top disciple. I used to visit the Temple of Ryutaku-ji and take some of my karate students with me. I believe that the kind of thinking that Zen provides to the martial artist is very important. It is important to study and practice it everyday ... the same that you do with your physical techniques. You must be able to continue the things that you have started. Don't drop things in the middle.

Q: How different is teaching and practicing Zen from practicing karate-do?
A: Zen is difficult to teach in a few lessons. The student can't get an idea of what it is. It takes time and patience ... pretty much like good karate. For that matter, it takes time to make the students understand things in both karate and Zen. The difference is that in Zen the student must do it by himself. Only he can find the real meaning.

Q: Wado-ryu has different branches today. How do you feel about that?
A: Not very happy. I have always tried my best to unify people, but it seems that this is an impossible dream. So I decided to do what is good for

me. I can't bring people together when all what they want is to fight and argue all the time. That's why I created my own association. I'm sad to see that they change kata and some important principles of the style. Those individuals received early training from me, which means they are my juniors. I teach the wado technique that I learnt from Ohtsuka Sensei. And this is pure wado-ryu. After many years of training 10 hours per day, it is not my mind that remembers the technique. Instead, it is my body that knows how to do the technique right. This is where other people are different; they try to remember with their minds, and memory—with time—goes away. For me, it is the body. Today, what you see being practiced in other wado-ryu groups is different from what Ohtsuka Sensei was doing. A lot has been completely changed, and I don't want to be like that. I am not interested in making money or getting more recognition around the world. I made the association for one simple reason ... to preserve the teachings of Ohtsuka Sensei and the continuation of pure wado techniques. That's all.

"Today, karate in most schools is only a sport, and this is wrong. I must agree that there can be a sport side to it, but the instructor should balance this and teach the student the two sides of the coin."

Q: What would you recommend to someone who is interested in starting karate?
A: I would say find a good instructor. Someone who teaches budo and not only sport. Someone who knows how to help the student grow and mature. If they don't find a good instructor, their karate will never be good. Invest all the necessary time to find the right teacher.

Q: What are your plans for the future?
A: I would like to go back to Japan and stay there. In Japan, I could live well because I have a lot of supporters there. I would like to have a small private dojo and teach very hard. I would also like to develop a few students who I can pass all my knowledge to, and they would carry on the legacy of Ohtsuka Sensei. O

Katsutaka Tanaka

The True Way of Budo

SENSEI TANAKA IS ONE OF THE MOST WELL-KNOWN MARTIAL ARTS LEADERS IN AMERICA AND A PIONEER OF JAPANESE KARATE IN THE WEST. BUT MORE THAN THAT, HE IS A REMARKABLE MARTIAL ARTIST AND A TRUE ICON IN THE WORLD OF KARATE-DO. KATSUTAKA TANAKA'S SKILLS IN THE TRADITIONAL WEAPONRY ART OF *KOBUDO* HAVE IMPRESSED THOUSANDS OF PEOPLE THROUGHOUT THE YEARS. SENSEI TANAKA WAS BORN AND RAISED IN JAPAN AND LEARNED HIS ART THE HARD WAY—A WAY THAT CAN ONLY BE FOUND IN THE ORIENT. ALTHOUGH DEEPLY INVOLVED IN THE TECHNICAL COMMITTEE OF THE WORLD KARATE FEDERATION, TANAKA'S VIEWS ARE A RETURN TO THE TRADITIONAL VALUES OF THE MARTIAL ARTS, "THE SPORT ASPECT OF KARATE IS VERY IMPORTANT NOWADAYS, BUT WE CAN STILL MAINTAIN THE TRADITIONAL ROOTS AND MORAL VALUES OF BUDO. BOTH WORLDS CAN LIVE TOGETHER—THEY ARE NOT THE OPPOSITE OF EACH OTHER. IT'S UP TO THE TEACHERS TO PRESERVE THE ETHICAL PRINCIPLES OF KARATE-DO FOR FUTURE GENERATIONS, AND AT THE SAME TIME KEEP IT AN INTERESTING SPORTING ACTIVITY." RESIDING IN ALASKA SINCE HIS FIRST VISIT TO AMERICA, SENSEI TANAKA HAS TAUGHT MARTIAL ARTS TO THOUSAND OF STUDENTS FROM ALL OVER THE WORLD. HE STILL TEACHES HIS DAILY CLASSES AND STICKS TO THE TWO MOST IMPORTANT PRINCIPLES OF KARATE—HARD WORK AND INNER SPIRIT. HE IS TRULY A MASTER OF THE OLD WAYS.

Q: When did you start training martial arts?
A: My first experience was at the age of 14. My brother came home one day and found me kicking at some decorative beads hanging from the ceiling. "Hey!" my brother yelped. "Do you want to learn karate?" I shrugged my shoulders and said: "I don't know." "Come on, then," he said. "Let's find out." He took me to a karate school in the city where my brother's friend was an instructor. When we arrived, we found that there was by a guest from one of the university karate teams in central Japan—and he was really tough! One by one, he fought all of the school's black belts. Not one of them could go the distance against him in a two-minute match. He was too awesome. Knees, elbows, head butts—everything. He was crazy.

Karate Masters

"A karate team at a Japanese university is much like a football team at an American university. Personal pride and school spirit are invested in the team's performance."

Q: What was your impression?
A: I was terrified. That was not something I wanted to study. I went home and tried to put the incident out of my mind. But the memory haunted me. I was forced to consider my reaction more profoundly. "I know I'm scared," I thought to myself. "And I don't want to go back. But if I don't, I might do the same thing with everything in life. I don't want to go, therefore I must."

Q: Did you immediately enroll in the dojo?
A: Yes, soon after I began my karate lessons. And, of course, the karate supplemented the judo and kendo classes which were a required part of junior high school physical education in Japan. Yet being a student following a college prep curriculum, I did not have much time to devote to serious study of the art. Then in 1965 I joined the new karate team at Nagoya-Gakuin University, where I was studying for a Bachelor's degree in Economics. The karate team practiced three-to-four hours a day, six days a week. I submerged myself in the training. The art I practiced at the university was *seidokai,* a sort of cross between shotokan karate and Japanese kempo, but with a lot of boxing-like footwork. However, I soon grew dissatisfied with the karate team, and especially with the team seniors. A karate team at a Japanese university is much like a football team at an American university. Personal pride and school spirit are invested in the team's performance. But Nagoya-Gakuin's team was still inexperienced and not very successful.

Q: What do you mean by that?
A: When the team showed up at major tournaments, the other university teams would laugh at us. The team seniors were often chastised and mistreated. I really took the insults personally. I wanted my seniors to stand-up to the abuse, physically. They did not. They lacked the mental component of the art—the self-confidence and determination. I felt that I had to do something. I wanted to silence the laughter and restore respect for the name "Nagoya-Gakuin." So one member of the team and I approached our seniors with a proposition: "Please. Treat us rougher! Make us do the things we must to become winners." The seniors listened but they did not act. They seemed almost afraid of our fervor.

Q: What happened then? Didn't they react to your words?
A: Not really—and in free-sparring practice, on occasion, I would defeat one of the seniors. Several months passed and I progressed to the point where I consistently defeated my seniors. As a freshman I was inexperienced compared to the polished technique of the seniors—but spirit-wise I was superior. Unfortunately, as my skills became more improved, my seniors grew more removed. Once again, I called the seniors aside and said, "Look. Even though my friend and I can beat you in free-fighting, we still respect you. You are our seniors. So go ahead and give us orders. Tell us what we must do to become winners." It was there when I really began to wonder if my seniors even knew how to train champions.

"Several months passed and I progressed to the point where I consistently defeated my seniors. As a freshman I was inexperienced compared to the polished technique of the seniors—but spirit-wise I was superior. Unfortunately, as my skills became more improved, my seniors grew more removed."

Q: How did that affect the way the team performed in competition?
A: Soon afterwards, the seniors entered Nagoya-Gakuin in the team competition at the Central Japan Karate Championships. Team competition in Japan is conducted much like the team competitions in America. One squad of fighters faces another one-on-one, utilizing the point system of scoring. The team that scored the most points at the conclusion of the

Karate Masters

"The nature of the fighting in Japan was radically different from that in the West. The competition was more blood and guts. There was no safety equipment. Broken bones, knockouts, and an assortment of other injuries were commonplace."

last match was declared the winner. However, the nature of the fighting in Japan was radically different from that in the West. The competition was more blood and guts. There was no safety equipment. Broken bones, knockouts, and an assortment of other injuries were commonplace. The Japanese style of fighting was based on stability. They charged straight ahead, never backed up, and never quit. Backfists were rarely scored as points, and the hit-and-run tactics of the mobile fighters were never seen.

Q: Do you have some special memories of your competition days?
A: Yes, I remember that in the first round of the team competition, my school had to confront our closest rival, the team from Nagoya Commercial College. The rival school's team was anchored by one of the most feared fighters in all of Japan, a man called "Monster." He stood five-foot-ten inches tall, was built like Joe Frazier, and liked to knock people out. Nagoya Commercial College sent out Monster—and we sent out our own giant, a friend of mine who stood six foot three. Monster laughed when he saw him. Yet once underway, it was the giant who launched the opening attack. Whap! A front kick found Monster's belly. Monster grabbed the leg and cradled it against his side, like a football. Then he looked the giant square in the eyes, screamed, and charged forward and deposited the giant on the floor in the next ring. Monster turned around and slowly walked back to the starting position. The match was over. Monster's teammates howled with laughter.

Q: What happened then?
A: Our team fought back in the later matches, and after the last fight the two teams were tied. The captains of each team met in the ring with the referee to decide who would fight to break the tie. When the captains began to return to

the sidelines, Monster assumed his position in center ring. I turned to our giant and said, "Who's going to fight that beast for us?" Over the loudspeaker came a sudden announcement: "Representing the Nagoya-Gakuin karate team is Katsutaka Tanaka!" I was surprised and I protested, but the Giant just slapped me on the back. "Well," he said, "you wanted to do anything to be a winner." I shook my head and gulped deeply. "This is going to be your last match ever kid," yelled one of Monster's teammates. I gulped again and thought to myself: "This is the man to beat. If I can stop him, I can stop anybody. I am not going to back up." I defeated Monster that day and went on to finish second in the tournament.

Q: Was it then that you were elected captain of the university team?
A: Yes, and from then on everything changed. I made the practice sessions tougher—much tougher. I trained the team not to back up and not to quit. If they got hit once, they were to hit back twice. Punishment training was emphasized. No one was to get knocked-out in a tournament. The team needed leadership and discipline, and I was determined to set an example. Most everyone thought I was a little crazy because of the kamikaze attitude that I had about fighting—but they did

"I made the practice sessions tougher—much tougher. I trained the team not to back up and not to quit. If they got hit once, they were to hit back twice. Punishment training was emphasized. No one was to get knocked-out in a tournament. The team needed leadership and discipline, and I was determined to set an example."

respect my intensity and my results—and that was exactly what I was after. I figured I had three more years to spend at the university, and was going to get as much out of it as I possibly could. The first thing I did was develop a one-year plan, sort of a crash course to get us on par with the rest of the universities. I started a schedule of very hard training and kept pushing them until they fell. Even then, we poured water on them and kicked them until they got up again. They realized they had to push themselves beyond being tired or hurt because I wouldn't accept anything less. We hit them, kicked

Karate Masters

"I started a schedule of very hard training and kept pushing them until they fell. Even then, we poured water on them and kicked them until they got up again. They realized they had to push themselves beyond being tired or hurt because I wouldn't accept anything less."

them, and we made them get used to getting hurt so they wouldn't care anymore. It really worked. We became the roughest university team in central Japan within that first year—not the most technically sound but the roughest. You can't imagine what an intimidating influence that can have on an opponent. They just didn't know what to expect from us because we got a reputation for being a bunch of crazy fighters. This, in turn, pumped-up the whole team and gave them the confidence that they could win anything. I wanted my team to be the best in Japan, and in 1968 I took the team to the Central Japan Karate Championships and came away with the first place trophy. My dream had come true.

Q: When did you came to the United States?
A: After graduation, I went to the Alaska Methodist University, which had an exchange program with Nagoya-Gakuin University. I started teaching karate during the day as part of the university's physical education programe, and at nighttime I taught a women's self-defense class. When I arrived at AMU, I started teaching the way I was taught in Japan. I had 40 students when we started and two months later I didn't have any. No one came back because I hit them and I kicked them—and if their stance was no good, I tripped them. I was finally told by the head of the P.E. department that I couldn't do that. And I told him, "Don't tell me what to do. This is the way it should be done." He explained that he was getting a little bit scared, and thought we were going to get sued! So I decided not to hit students anymore. I'm getting very Americanized (laughs). But I still believe in the traditional ways—martial arts should be very strict.

Q: So you had to modify the traditional Japanese teaching methods to Western culture?

A: When I first came to Alaska, I was still *gung-ho* and quite convinced that my training methods would be effective and well-received. But I quickly realized that I was no longer in Japan and that I couldn't treat American people like Japanese people. I tried to take it easy and I really thought I had successfully tailored a program that would be acceptable to everyone. I was wrong. I had one student who refused to listen to my comments on the narrowness of his stance. I came up from behind him and swept him to the floor with relative ease. He stood-up glaring at me and asked why I tripped him. I told him his stance was too narrow and to try again. Again his stance was too narrow and again I swept him to the floor—this time very hard and very fast. Admittedly, I made him look like a fool. The next day he came to class acting really tough, saying that he wanted me to know that he had a gun and that I'd better watch out. I knew that if I showed fear I'd have a difficult time controlling him. When he finally showed me the gun I grabbed it and emptied the bullets. It was then that I realized that I didn't want to have to contend with this type of behavior for the rest of my life, and that many people take the discipline in the classroom as a personal affront. I've since found a number of ways to accomplish the same end by alternative means. It's still rough and it's still intense but I don't find it necessary to pummel a student to get his attention. I've been told my classes are not unlike Marine Corps Boot Camp. That's not so bad.

"When I first came to Alaska I was still gung-ho and quite convinced that my training methods would be effective and well-received. But I quickly realized that I was no longer in Japan and that I couldn't treat American people like Japanese people."

Q: After settling in the United States, did you go back to Japan to update your training?

A: Yes, I did. In 1972 I returned to Japan briefly. I found that seidokai stylists were then turning to kickboxing, a move that I could not support. I began to search Japan for a new style to serve as my foundation art. I

Karate Masters

"I looked at shotokan, kyokushinkai and goju-ryu, but finally settled on shito-ryu. I don't believe that one system is good enough—none of them. No single one is fully adequate. Each system has good points. So what I teach combines everything."

looked at shotokan, kyokushinkai and goju-ryu, but finally settled on shito-ryu. I don't believe that one system is good enough—none of them. No single one is fully adequate. Each system has good points. So what I teach combines everything. My fighting technique comes from my days with the university karate team.

Q: How can a karate practitioner develop a fighting instinct to survive a real threat situation?
A: It's a rather simple concept, but it's very difficult to teach. What it boils down to is a person's ability to refuse to be beaten. Injury and pain must be accepted as minor obstacles. The ultimate concern is to prevail and to convince yourself that nothing else matters. To the layman, this might sound a bit extreme, but fighting must be viewed in its own separate context. I agree with those who say that fighting should only be a last resort to any altercation. But there are going to be times when there is no other alternative. When that time comes, there can only be one thing in your mind—get in, do as much damage as possible, and get out. Resign yourself to the fact that you're going to get hurt. Accept it. But be confident in the fact that your opponent is going to get hurt a lot more than you.

Q: What about the idea of pushing yourself beyond your physical limits?
A: Again, the concept is simple but the execution is difficult. The human body has the ability to go beyond conventional limits of strength. When you feel like you can't go on anymore, that's when you really learn, that is when you really make progress. When you're really tired and you are able to push yourself past the point of exhaustion, you suddenly forget about being tired. You are past that point and you no longer have to think about what you are doing. You have passed all points and your mind is

free of your body so you're ready to do anything.

Q: Do you follow the strict shito-ryu method?
A: I earned my black belt in the shito-ryu, and yes, I follow that style as far as foundation and kata training goes. But 90 percent of what I teach is actually a highly stylized combination of many styles—at least in principles and concepts of technical functionality. I think that a majority of instructors will tell you how to do a technique without telling you why it is going to be useful. I shun soft, flowing techniques and concentrate on hard kicks and punches—particularly punches. The main thing that I want my students to learn is to punch well, because in terms of self-defense, how many people on the street jump up and kick you in the head? They just grab and punch. For that type of situation, you've got to have good, dependable hands—where you're confident that if you hit your attacker he won't be getting up for a while. If you have

"The main thing that I want my students to learn is to punch well, because in terms of self-defense, how many people on the street jump up and kick you in the head? They just grab and punch. For that type of situation, you've got to have good, dependable hands."

good hands you feel more secure and will be calmer. You'll see the situation better and maybe try to talk your way out of a fight altogether. I tell my students to avoid trouble as much as they can. My master in Japan said that the highest skill in karate is not winning 100 fights out of 100, but avoiding 100 out of 100 fights. But in order to avoid these 100 fights you must be very smart—you must have good self-control, be calm, and clearly evaluate how the situation is developing. But if they are pushed to the point of fighting, I encourage them to go all the way. Either you fight all out, or you don't fight at all. There is no halfway in self-defense.

Karate Masters

"They say that studying martial arts is like walking on a stony road. It's very painful—nothing but pain. But that's how you learn the answers of life. The real truths come from fighting with yourself. No matter how good anything seems on the surface, you must be convinced—you have to convince yourself. That is the answer."

Q: So for self-defense, you advocate having powerful and definitive techniques?

A: Definitely. This is the main reason why I concentrate on what you can be described as "hard" techniques. I stress hard punches and kicks to vital points on the body. If you're fighting someone who is big and muscular, so what? Kick the groin and pull him down. The groin, throat, nose, eyes and neck are basically the only areas that I want my students to attack. Don't even bother with joint locks and throws. Throwing a guy is not going to put him away, it will just get him more enraged. So before you throw him, knock him out—and fast. I want my students to know exactly what's going to work for them and why. This is a bit of a departure from the traditional Oriental approach, where if you have a question about something you are told to practice until you find the answer. I don't agree with this and that's probably why I had so much trouble in school—I always wanted to know "why." When my instructor told me to do a technique I would ask why it was a good technique. In many cases, I don't think they really knew why. They would just say, "That's the way it's always been done, so do it." I think that my questioning attitude brought me to where I am today. I understand now, though, what my instructors were trying to say—most answers in life come through self-realization. They say that studying martial arts is like walking on a stony road. It's very painful—nothing but pain. But that's how you learn the answers of life. The real truths come from fighting yourself. No matter how good anything seems on the surface, you must be convinced—you have to convince yourself. That is the answer.

Q: How important do you think the study of kata is in the art of karate-do?

A: It is very important. The more I study kata, the more I can see how important they are for fighting. To fight better than your opponent, you must make him move as you want—with proper spirit, and well-balanced techniques. Your technique has power when your body moves as a single unit. Kata helps you learn that unity. In Japan, maybe we put too much weight on fighting and not enough on kata. I mean, when you think about it, so many masters have practiced this art. Maybe for one master to develop a kata, it took him a lifetime. He thought about a lot of things. You know, if my opponent does this, what can I do? So the katas are the result of all his training and experience. And the more time you spend exploring a kata, the deeper will be your understanding of the art of karate and its uses. You have to go deeper and deeper into the study of the kata. You just can't stop on the surface and simply try to master the physical and external appearance of the kata.

Q: What is your teaching philosophy for the budo arts?

A: I truly believe the old ways are the best and still work. Perfection in the martial arts is to make the mind and body work together. That's the final goal. I try to teach my students how to perfect themselves. That's the true way—the way of budo. O

"You have to go deeper and deeper into the study of the kata. You just can't stop on the surface and simply try to master the physical and external appearance of the kata. Perfection in the martial arts is to make the mind and body work together."

Mikio Yahara
The Unconquerable Spirit

YAHARA SENSEI WAS BORN ON APRIL 4, 1947, IN THE EHIME PREFECTURE. AFTER GRADUATING FROM KOKUSHIKAN UNIVERSITY, HE BECAME KENSHUSEI, OR JUNIOR INSTRUCTOR, IN THE JAPAN KARATE ASSOCIATION. HE RAMPAGED THROUGH THE WORLD, MONOPOLIZING THE HIGH RANKINGS IN MANY TOURNAMENTS, ESTABLISHING LEGENDARY FAME. KNOWN FOR HIS LEOPARD-LIKE CARRIAGE, BEAUTIFUL JUMPING TECHNIQUES AND ADAPTATIONS, HIS UNIQUE KARATE STYLE FASCINATED KARATE-KA ALL OVER THE WORLD.

IN APRIL 2000, TO FURTHER DEVELOP HIS IDEA OF KARATE, YAHARA SENSEI ESTABLISHED THE *KARATENOMICHI WORLD FEDERATION,* AND THE CONCEPT BEHIND THE FEDERATION WAS SIMPLE: THE ESSENCE OF KARATE IS TECHNICAL, AND THAT IS EXACTLY WHERE KARATE STARTS. FOR EXAMPLE, THE NATURE OF HIS KARATE ENTAILS SEVERAL KEY ELEMENTS, INCLUDING THE NECESSITY TO STRIVE PERSISTENTLY TOWARD GOALS DESPITE THE GENERAL CURRENT TREND TOWARDS SPORTIVE ASPECTS IN THE KARATE WORLD; TO ATTAIN *IPPON* TECHNIQUE OR EFFICIENCY IN THE EXECUTION OF THE KILLING BLOW CONCEPT, AND TO STAKE ONE'S LIFE ON THE OFFENSIVE AND DEFENSIVE ACTIONS INSIDE A SPLIT SECOND. YAHARA SENSEI'S KARATE TECHNIQUES, HAVING BEEN FORMED DURING COUNTLESS FIGHTING SCENES, MAKE USE OF THE MAXIMUM POSSIBILITIES OF HUMAN MUSCLES AND THE MAXIMUM POSSIBLE MOVEMENT OF THE JOINTS. THE POINT IS TO FOCUS ALL THE POTENTIAL ENERGY OF THE BODY INTO THE FISTS OR FEET DURING THE BRIEFEST OF MOMENTS. THE THEORY BEHIND THESE TECHNIQUES IS—WITHOUT A DOUBT—AN EYE OPENER, EVEN TO KARATE-KA WHO HAVE PERFORMED MANY YEARS OF ARDUOUS PRACTICE.

Q: The name of your organization is the *Karatenomichi World Federation.* Is there any difference between karatenomichi and shotokan? And, do you teach shotokan karate or is it more like another style of karate?
A: Shotokan was the original style. The simple thing I teach is that karate is changing, and it is possible that it could disappear. I know karate as a martial art, but now it seems [more] like dancing. I would like to return to the original karate ... to its sources. Budo karate, as far as I am concerned, is a situation in which I may finish my opponent definitively by one killing

Karate Masters

"I am against the type of competition that promotes the development of game karate. Many people don't understand my karate. You have to be spiritually strong because karate must be spiritually strong, too."

blow. My work basically consists in forming ways and methods to increase my technical level to the perfection I require and that is one blow should be enough to cause an opponent's defeat.

Q: How did you develop the Karatenomichi World Federation as an organization?
A: First of all, it's a true budo karate that has very effective techniques, and the purpose of the organization is to teach people the kumite methods that I referred to earlier. I want to teach my students so well that they are capable of winning any competition, and then I want them to travel worldwide. I also want people to know and learn my techniques and understand my aim for perfection. Sports karate is very popular now and many people consider karate a game. These people usually forget about karate immediately after competition. If necessary, I would like my students to be able to use karate in real life, but I don't want them to treat it like it was strictly a game.

Q: Sensei, does competition help competitors to understand the essence of budo?
A: I am against the type of competition that promotes the development of game karate. I frequently have debates and conversations with representatives of other organizations to defend my opinion about karate, and it is possible that my actions remind them of true karate.

Q: What is your perception of the art?
A: Many people don't understand my karate. You have to be spiritually strong because karate must be spiritually strong, too. Then the correct technique will grow from it. I have seen some people who think they are strong, but the truth is they are bigheaded. If you ask me—even after many years of training—I will tell you that I still don't know karate. I look

for perfection in what I do, but I still have a long road ahead. Technique comes to some students quickly and to others slowly. But if they keep training hard and follow the principle of *nichi-nichi-no-keko* (train harder over and over again), they will be alright.

Q: You were highly ranked in many tournaments and you were also the world and JKA champion many times. What victory do you remember most?
A: Certainly, I, as well as many other people, remember those tournaments. The most important moments that remain in my memory are those times in which I realized that my opponent wasn't able to control the situation and his skill wasn't as perfect as mine. Everyone applauded when I used the techniques that amazed my opponent and made him nonplused. Perhaps, these moments are the ones that I remember most of all.

Q: Is physical or spiritual victory more important for you? And did you ever feel moral satisfaction in spite of defeat?
A: Is it possible to be happy after suffering a defeat? When a strong person loses, he doesn't feel any satisfaction, and he will never find both spiritual and psychological victory. However, victory and spiritual satisfaction could come later, because your defeat stimulates new feats. You try to improve your skill, and as a result, you win. In this case, you will understand that the victory is the result of your last defeat.

"The most important thing that I want to pass on to you all is that you should never forget about the source of karate, its basic functions and purposes. If you ignore this and do not diligently execute all techniques, you will absolutely walk the other way, which is very far from the karate that I try to bring to your country and to your life."

Q: The chairman of the Karatenomichi World Federation is internationally renowned fashion designer Yohji Yamamoto. Could you please tell us why this person came into the world of karate?
A: Actually, it is not as difficult to answer your question as you would expect. I think that there are two reasons. The first reason is psychological. The world of Mr. Yohji Yahamoto is a magnificent world with a bril-

Karate Masters

"Recently, many people have turned to Zen, and there are many books about this; however, it is a fake. Why? Of course, Zen could be indicated in a fight. But what is the sense of Zen? If two opponents had a knife, it would be too easy if they just killed each other."

liant atmosphere and amazing surroundings. Of course, this atmosphere dims the enthusiasm. Photographers, cameras, beautiful people and clothes have a very strong influence on his emotional condition because he is part of this world. Karate allows him to restrain himself and allows him to follow the spiritual way, which is defined by conscience. Karate is the deterrent that gives him a chance to remain himself. The second reason is physical. Mr. Yamamoto's world creates a sedentary way of life, and it does not have a good effect on his health. Weak muscles are not good for man. Due to his karate practice, he now is in good physical condition. I think that Mr. Yamamoto has the budo consciousness that only a true samurai could have. Mr. Yamamoto has practiced karate with me for about 10 years, and he is very zealous while training. He came into shotokan due to our friendship, and we have been friends more than 10 years.

Q: There are many books about Zen Buddhism and budo philosophy. Is there any connection between karate and Zen?
A: Recently, many people have turned to Zen, and there are many books about this; however, it is a fake. Why? Of course, Zen could be indicated in a fight. But what is the sense of Zen? If two opponents had a knife, it would be too easy if they just killed each other. In this case, it would be an ordinary murder. Both of the opponents would die, and they would be absolutely tranquil, because there is no difference for each opponent. But there is a significant problem. Each adversary keeps wondering what will occur in case of a mistake? Maybe someone will be wounded. The body becomes enslaved and the mind just thinks about fear. This fear disturbs the use of your actual power. Kumite teaches us to stay tranquil. If you follow the Zen way, you will have the emptiness in your mind while doing kumite. Fear and thought disappear from your mind, and you don't feel the fear. In this moment, you are able to demonstrate your true power

... the power that is available only to you. No emotions, no thoughts about past and future. This is Zen. That is why people who write books about Zen Buddhism in the martial arts without experiencing serious fighting or mortal combat are liars.

Q: What is the philosophy of karate?
A: Karate has no philosophy. Some people think that the tradition of karate came from Buddhism and karate has a connection with the absolute, space and universe, but I don't believe in that. My philosophy is to knock my opponent out with one technique. One finishing blow!

"Karate has no philosophy. Some people think that the tradition of karate came from Buddhism and karate has a connection with the absolute, space and universe, but I don't believe in that. My philosophy is to knock my opponent out with one technique. One finishing blow!"

Q: Do you have any time for rest?
A: Karate is the rest in my life. You know I am very busy, because I have my own business, as well as karate. This arrangement keeps my mind busy but often creates tension because I always have to think about some deals. Of course, this can have a negative influence on my sleep and mind. While training, my body feels tremendous stress, but this enables me to step closer to the art of karate. My body relaxes after training, and I can sleep. By falling asleep after a grueling training session, I am collecting and re-charging my power for a new day ... to make it as useful as possible.

Q: Besides karate, what do you like?
A: I like music very much. I like Tchaikovsky. I am very tired after training, and music helps me to relax. I think that music is even necessary for me. I listen to music when I am resting and when I am driving.

Q: I understand that you like to drive fast and once experienced a terrible accident.
A: Yes, I like speed very much. I even do some road events. Some time ago I was in an unbelievable road event. I was driving a Porsche, which is my favorite car, and my speedometer indicated that I was going 250 kilometers per hour. The speed limit of my car was 280 kilometers per hour, and I tried to reach that speed. The car in front of me wasn't going that fast, so I went around him. While I was in the passing lane, I noticed another car

Karate Masters

"Mishima became angry and started to shout at him, 'Let's do it—faster!' After that, he [Morita] struck, but he missed and split part of Mishima's skull. Mishima then screamed even more loudly, 'You are fool! What are you waiting for? Let's do it quickly!'"

coming toward me at about 100 kilometers per hour. If there had been a head-on collision, it would have been a terrible accident. Thankfully, and probably due my reactions as a skilled karateka, I avoided the oncoming car by swerving toward the curb. I made this decision instantaneously; otherwise, we would have slammed into each other with a combined speed of 350 kilometers per hour! I remember how my car turned over, and I remember all my movements and actions at this time. At the time, it all seemed like slow motion. The only thing I thought to protect was my head. I did everything to receive as little damage as possible. The car was so destroyed that it could not be restored. Fortunately, I was OK.

Q: Sensei, do you like to read in your free time?
A: Yes, I like to read very much. Usually I read books about the samurai and how they bravely passed away as a result of hara-kiri (ritual suicide). It is very important for me, and I will tell you about this without any embellishment. Three of my friends have died in such a way and the last one occurred in December 2003. The most courageous way to die from hara-kiri is the crisscross. [Using a sword], you go from left to right and then bottom to top. This gives you the hieroglyph "ju," and that means 10. Maybe you know the famous Japanese writer Yukio Mishima; perhaps you even read his books. He was my student. We trained together for one and half a years. He was much older than me. When he was 45, I was 24. One week before his passing we were training together. After training, we were in the traditional Japanese bath or *furo*. His behavior was normal, he laughed and nobody—even I—suspected that he was going to leave this life. Something like this is a very important decision, and I am sure that one week prior to his death he certainly knew that he would do it. I very much respect him for it, and I believe that he was a really great person.

Yahara

It's even documented how it happened. It began when he entered the commander's office at the Japan Defense Agency. And let me state right now. No one, including those who suspected something might be wrong, had time to stop him. He and his friend, Masakatsu Morita, went into the room and locked the door. He was with a friend because the code of the samurai requires that a friend, colleague or student—someone he trusts—chop the head off after the suicide. Having opened his stomach with his blade, he felt an inhuman pain. In the meantime, Morita held a sword in his hands, and his hands shivered because of excitement or inexperience. Mishima became angry and started to shout at him, "Let's do it—faster!" After that, he [Morita] struck, but he missed and split part of Mishima's skull. Mishima then screamed even more loudly, "You are fool! What are you waiting for? Let's do it quickly!" The second impact of the sword of Morita fell onto Mishima's shoulder. Only after the third attempt had he completed the task [beheaded him]. Subsequently, the police rushed into the office. Please trust me. These events are true and fixed in the police report. I do not want to scare you; I just want to say that this person, I believe, had a strong spirit.

"The famous Japanese writer Yukio Mishima was my student. We trained together for one and half a years. He was much older than me. When he was 45, I was 24."

Q: Why did Mr. Yukio Mishima commit suicide?
A: The purpose was rather great. By then he was already a well-known writer, and he knew that people would speak widely and frequently about his death. Shortly before his death, Mishima made a political declaration from a balcony of the same building. By his death, he wanted to draw the public's attention to new Japanese orders and laws. He was very much against them, and he wanted people to protest these. Certainly, he achieved this purpose.

Karate Masters

"Traditional karate training places great emphasis upon the mind, and makiwara training helps this, because in many ways, it is the basis of the art."

Q: Do you practice any other kind of budo except karate?
A: Yes, I practice iaido. I like the spirit of this martial art. One single sword blow results in the death of the opponent.

Q: What is love for you?
A: I do not know how to answer, and this is actually a very difficult question. If I were to say something, I'd say that love is the impossibility of personal happiness in loneliness. What I mean is that it would be necessary to give everything [you have] completely up and make sure that your sweetheart has everything and is happy [to really experience love]. And, of course, you'd have to be happy with this result. In addition to that, you must be ready for everything, even death. I'm not saying that you should look for such things, but you should be ready for anything that life may send your way.

Q: You are a strong advocate for makiwara training. Why?
A: The makiwara is not only a tool to be used for conditioning, but when used correctly, it makes the body strong, especially the hips and hara areas. Makiwara training brings control to the technique. Traditional karate training places great emphasis upon the mind, and makiwara training helps this, because in many ways, it is the basis of the art.

Q: Do you recommend cross-training in different arts?
A: In the beginning, it is good for a student to concentrate on a few things that he can develop strongly. I don't like to give students too many things to concentrate on. Not aikido one day, the next karate, judo and then something else! That is not good. Unfortunately, some students think this is the correct way because they want too much too soon, and there is nothing the instructor can do about it. Their minds are diffused over too many ideas. That's why it is very important to train the mind of the stu-

dent in the right direction. If the student has "no mind" in training, he will get into these kinds of situations and will make incorrect decisions. Hard, physical training helps to develop the right mind for karate. And technique isn't the only important thing; you must also make good, true karate.

Q: What is missing in some forms of sport competition today?
A: The way we always competed was very budo-oriented. We always looked for the "kill," but I understand your question. Since the advent and growth of freestyle karate, the main goal in many dojo around the world is simply competition. Unfortunately, many associations that regulate the competition rules allow participants to do strange things. For instance, punching with good and strong positioning and scoring with a simple touch is one of those. Also, contestants lack zanchin. They concentrate more on what the referee will say than on their opponent. They should look at the opponent and not the referee. Forget the referee! Many students around the world never learn this serious approach to kumite karate, and the art becomes a simple sport. This approach brings a lack of confidence to the students simply due to the fact that they haven't been trained properly. They must be trained to kill with one blow, but they also have to learn how to control their power and techniques.

Q: Would you like to wish something to the karate practitioners?
A: Everybody should ask himself the following question: "What is the most important thing for me in karate?" I think that we all should practice karate with the same spirit, mood and ideas. Likely, people who practice karate with very similar ideas have identical inquiries, needs and purposes. The name of our organization—*Karatenomichi*—means "Way of karate, way to karate, way due to karate." Perhaps this also is the way in which we walk the karate path together, and we should meet many people on this way. Somewhere this way could become wider and somewhere it could become narrower. The most important thing that I want to pass on to you all is that you should never forget about the source of karate, its basic functions and purposes. If you ignore this and do not diligently execute all techniques, you will absolutely walk the other way, which is very far from the karate that I try to bring to your country and to your life. Control your ego properly because the true enemy is inside yourself, and this is the toughest opponent to beat. O

Gogen Yamaguchi

Simply "The Cat"

A KARATE LEGEND WHOSE FAME TRANSCENDED THE ART, GOGEN YAMAGUCHI WAS BORN ON JANUARY 20, 1909, IN THE CITY OF KAGOSHIMA IN SOUTHERN KYUSHU, THE THIRD SON OF TOKUTARO YAMAGUCHI. REGARDED AS ONE OF THE FOUR MAJOR KARATE MASTERS OF ALL TIME, HIS CHARISMATIC AND POWERFUL PERSONALITY, COMBINED WITH HIS CAT-LIKE MOVEMENTS, GAVE HIM BOTH HIS NICKNAME AND A RECOGNITION THAT FEW MEN OF BUDO EVER ACHIEVE. DEVOTED TO PERPETUATING THE SPIRITUAL TRADITIONS OF SHINTO AND YOGA, IN CONJUNCTION WITH THE ART OF KARATE, YAMAGUCHI SENSEI ESTABLISHED A REMARKABLE REPUTATION, NOT ONLY FOR HIS EXCELLENT TECHNICAL KARATE-DO SKILLS BUT ALSO FOR HIS UNSURPASSED ABILITY TO APPLY THE PHILOSOPHICAL ASPECTS OF BUDO TO DAILY LIFE. DURING HIS MANY YEARS OF TEACHING AND INSTRUCTING, STUDENTS ALL OVER THE WORLD COULD FEEL HIS PROFOUND LOVE AND RESPECT FOR HIS TEACHERS—A LEGACY THAT HE DILIGENTLY UPHELD UNTIL THE LAST DAY OF HIS LIFE ON MARCH 20, 1989. SELDOM HAS A SINGLE MAN HAD SUCH A PROFOUND EFFECT ON THE DEVELOPMENT AND PROPAGATION OF KARATE-DO. IN RECOGNITION OF HIS DEDICATION TO THE JAPANESE MARTIAL ARTS, HE WAS HONORED IN 1969 BY EMPEROR HIROHITO OF JAPAN WITH RANJU-HOSHO, THE BLUE RIBBON MEDAL.

Q: Master Yamaguchi, it is said that your nickname "The Cat" comes from a ferocious fight you had with a tiger, is that true?
A: Let me ask you something; what does karate have to do with fighting a tiger?

Q: I believe, nothing.
A: So whoever said that is either a fool himself or is trying to fool others. Karate-do has nothing to do with fighting animals, breaking boards, walking on fire or similar things. You are not a better karate-ka for breaking 10

Karate Masters

"Karate-do has nothing to do with fighting animals, breaking boards, walking on fire or similar things. You are not a better karate-ka for breaking 10 boards or fighting a bull or a tiger. You are a better karate-ka for practicing good karate."

boards or fighting a bull or a tiger. You are a better karate-ka for practicing good karate. Do you understand my point?

Q: Completely, Sensei.
A: The nickname of "The Cat" came when someone said that my physical movements doing karate were similar to those used by a cat. I have always used short and fast hand actions and my favorite posture is *neko-ashi dachi*, or "cat-stance." That was the reason.

Q: When did you first start martial arts?
A: I was 13 when I started to study *goju-ryu karate kenpo* with a man named Takeo Maruta, who was a carpenter from Okinawa. He taught me everything he knew and helped me to truly understand the real art of karate. My physical condition really changed after starting karate training under him. Before that, I had trained in other arts like *iaido* and *kendo.* I studied Law at Kansei University in 1928 and Ritsumeikan University in Kyoto from 1929 to 1932 and received my law degree. To this day, I am still qualified as an attorney. While studying at the university, I initiated a karate club for training and to develop the free sparring that I consider very important. I did that based on the fact the ancient training consisted mainly of *kihon* and *kata.* By this time, all karate schools in Okinawa and Japan practiced kata and pre-arranged application exercises, and they never attempted to practice any free-form sparring. I decided that it was a positive thing and started to introduce it in my classes. At that time, the art of karate-do was not considered a part of budo by the Butoku-kai. I was one of the karate masters who really worked hard for karate to be accepted as a true Japanese martial art form. This happened thanks to Mr. Seizaburo Fukishima, who at that time was in the Judo Department of the Butoku-kai and also was the leader of the Giho-kai.

Q: When did you meet Miyagi Chojun?
A: In 1931, when I was 22 years of age. Meeting Choyun Miyagi was the best thing that could have happened to me. Under his guidance I realized that I wanted to practice this art for the rest of my life. He not only influenced my physical training but also the philosophical and spiritual aspects of my life as well. His personality had a profound influence on me. I remember he told me I had already mastered the hard part of goju, but that I needed to concentrate on the soft side of the style. Master Miyagi gave me the name of Gogen, which means "rough," due to the way I was doing karate then. Years later, he appointed me as his successor and the leader of the goju-ryu school in Japan.

Q: Is it true that you went into isolation for long periods of time in order to train and mediate?
A: Yes, it is. I often spent long periods of time staying at Mount Kurama where I subjected myself to ascetic exercises and hard physical training, especially training *sanchin* kata, meditating and enduring intense fasting.

"Master Miyagi gave me the name of Gogen, which means "rough," due to the way I was doing karate then. Years later, he appointed me as his successor and the leader of the goju-ryu school in Japan."

Q: How was your experience during the Japanese-Russian war?
A: Not very good. Between 1938 to 1945 I was sent to Manchuria on government and military assignments. On several occasions, my skills in karate and my mental training kept me alive. I was taken prisoner of war and sent to a prison camp in Mongolia. For over two years I was there under very bad conditions.

Q: Did you keep training?
A: Yes, I did. I believe that was what gave me the strength, both physical and mental, to survive.

Karate Masters

"My advice for practitioners is to focus on individual aspects of the art so you can prioritize your goals. Undertake the practice of karate-do as a lifetime journey so you can improve little things here and there without being overwhelmed by the idea of being an expert at everything. Don't fool yourself, you'll never be an expert at everything karate has to offer."

Q: What is your opinion on how the art of karate is evolving these days and its future direction?

A: The art of karate is gaining international recognition now—but this has nothing to do with how I was taught in the past by my teachers. Things change and we all have to understand this. Unfortunately, I see practitioners emphasizing only the sport aspect of karate. They focus only on trophies and prizes and not on the true spirit and essence of what the art is all about. They are becoming like baseball players. When you put your mind only in winning you are making a big mistake. Karate-do is mainly about learning to overcome defeat. When you lose is when you are facing your fears and your limitations. It is then when the true values and spiritual foundations of karate-do come to your life. You have to use them in order to move on. That's the value of karate-do and not simply winning trophies.

My wishes for the future are few and very specific. Some day, the leaders of karate-do, the ones who learned the art directly from the first masters, we won't be here anymore, and it is important that the new generation knows how to preserve the art and philosophy of this beautiful art. I would like to see practitioners all around the world study yoga and some kind of religious philosophy such as Shinto to balance their lives. In sports there are losers and winners—but in true karate-do everybody is a winner because everybody has a chance to become a better individual. Through sport you simply can't understand budo, because budo is about life and death, it is about to kill or be killed. My goal is to teach students to understand karate-do in the spiritual way.

Q: Do you think change to a sport emphasis is happening only in the West or also in Japan?

A: Sadly, it is happening in Japan, too. The lack of spirituality in the practice of karate-do is not something that you only see in the Western world, whom are not the ones to blame since their cultural background is totally different than Japan. Too many people think the power of karate-do is only physical, but it is not. Karate relies on inner strength and power, an invisible power that is not recognizable by the human eye. That's why the spiritual aspects are so important.

Q: Why did you found the International Karate-do Goju-kai Association?
A: I simply founded IKGA in order to regulate and maintain uniformity among my students all over the world. It was never meant to be a controlling nucleus or a dictatorial organization. It is true that I am the Chairman of the Board, so to speak, and things are done my way. In every boat there is only one captain, and I know what I want for the art of goju-ryu within the Goju-kai.

Q: How have you seen your karate change with the passing of the years?
A: When I was younger my training was very hard and demanding. I have tried almost everything possible. But with the passing of the years I have realized that karate-do is a very simple art if you have the right attitude. Don't misunderstand me, I am not saying it is easy, I am saying it is simple. After years of training your karate becomes more natural, more supple and more straightforward. You become one with the art. You don't practice karate; you *are* karate. You find the right ways of practicing and training the techniques and it eventually saves you time and unnecessary injuries. When you practice right, you save a lot of pain and suffering to your body. It is true, though, that hard training will bring you to a higher level of consciousness—but it is also true that your body will pay for it. My advice for practitioners is to focus on individual aspects of the art so you can prioritize your goals. Undertake the practice of karate-do as a lifetime journey so you can improve little things here and there without being overwhelmed by the idea of being an expert at everything. Don't fool yourself, you'll never be an expert at everything karate has to offer. And some

"Karate-do is mainly about learning to overcome defeat. When you lose is when you are facing your fears and your limitations. It is then when the true values and spiritual foundations of karate-do come to your life. You have to use them in order to move on. That's the value of karate-do and not simply winning trophies."

Karate Masters

"If my student's character is good, then I'll do my best to teach him everything and make him as good as he is able. A good teacher is like a parent who wants his child to do better than him. I'm not really interested in physical ability since this is something that usually creates problems in the student's mind."

karate styles that I see can't be practiced when a person gets older. Proper karate is "natural" for the human body. It is a difficult point to understand but it is true.

Q: How important is it for students to copy their teachers?
A: It depends on who the teacher is and what the student is trying to accomplish. To begin with, some teachers perform the techniques in a very specific way, and by this I mean that they have already adopted the main principles of the physical technique to their own characteristics, to their own bodies. If a student tries to simply copy his teacher's movements without analyzing and studying the principles behind the technique, then he is going to have some problems later on. Problems begin when a student with insufficient technical knowledge and understanding tries to make the techniques fit their body and starts to change and modify things. The understanding of one's own body is crucial to the correct execution of the techniques, but today we have lost understanding of how our bodies work because of our daily chores and responsibilities. We have too many devices to do physical work for us.

Q: What qualities do you like to see in your students?
A: To me, the most important quality a student can have is good character. Without good character, everything else is irrelevant. He must respect others and be a good person, otherwise I'll never teach him the essence of the art. If my student's character is good, then I'll do my best to teach him everything and make him as good as he is able. A good teacher is like a parent who wants his child to do better than him. That's my philosophy and that is the most important thing a student should have. I'm not really interested in physical ability since this is something that usually creates problems in the student's mind. When they see they are capable of doing things better than other students, they get a big head and humbleness

goes by the window. I want a student with good character and humble attitude.

Q: How effective is karate as a self-defense method?
A: The art of karate *is* a self-defense method. What you are trying to ask me is how good karate is compared to other arts. All I can say is that karate-do is a martial art and as such it is as effective as any other martial arts style—but the important point here is the level and skill of the practitioner. If a karate-ka loses a fight, we can't say that karate is not good but rather only that the practitioner has not achieved real karate skills.

"All I can say is that karate-do is a martial art and as such it is as effective as any other martial arts style—but the important point here is the level and skill of the practitioner. If a karate-ka loses a fight, we can't say that karate is not good but rather only that the practitioner has not achieved real karate skills."

Q: And what is "real" karate skill?
A: Being able to use karate not only for health and sport but to protect yourself. This is a very advanced aspect of the art since it requires understanding techniques that are not used in sport competition. These are techniques that can seriously hurt another person such as groin kicks, finger jabs to the eyes, blows to the throat, kicks to the knees, et cetera. This kind of karate has to be trained for specifically, and kata bunkai is the main tool for this. This is a kind of karate that you don't usually see at most of the dojos around the world. The style of goju-ryu is very useful for this since it involves close and tight hands movements for attack and defense, uses postures covering the groin, and employs many empty-hand attacks combined with low-line kicking. Goju-ryu can be described as a close-quarter style of karate. If you know where to look and how to look, you'll find very interesting elements for effective self-defense in the goju-ryu method.

Q: Do you teach women karate?
A: Yes, I have female students and I have to say they are very conscious of the little details, especially in kata training. They don't have the hard-

Karate Masters

"I obtained the rank of Swami in yoga and I tried to adapt some things to make the breathing in karate much better and healthier. To me, goju-ryu karate and yoga are complementary to each other. By practicing karate, you improve your yoga breathing and by practicing yoga you help your karate technique. They complement each other perfectly."

headed mentality a man has, therefore their approach focuses more on the details that make the kata beautiful and graceful. My own daughter Gogyoku (Wakako) trains diligently under my guidance and she has achieved a high level of skill.

Q: So kata training must focus on the details?
A: Yes, but not only that. Kata training can be divided in two simple aspects—the actual performance of the form and the application and use of the techniques found in the form. If you are good at performing the kata but you don't have a deep understanding of how to use the techniques of the form, then your training is meaningless. It becomes simply like a ballet. That's good if you are practicing ballet, but if you are training in budo then you need to know more about kata that simply the movements. I practice karate-do as a discipline, the budo way. In the early days, we practiced a lot of basics and kata. Kata was broken down into segments that we trained repetitively. Nowadays the emphasis is on the overall phys-

ical performance of the form, not in the self-defense principles hidden in the kata and their combative value as fighting tools. If the student wants to develop a good understanding of kata, then he needs to develop good basics of bunkai and kumite, because every single part is interrelated with the others. The basic requirement for good karate is good kata.

Q: What is your opinion about the different styles of the art of karate?
A: In Japan we have many different styles of karate. This is good and bad. It is good because it makes the art richer by keeping different traditions. On the other hand, it creates differences and make practitioners think their system is better than the one practiced by other karate-ka. To combat this, we organized the *Japan Karate-do Federation*. We are trying to organize the art of karate-do for future generations.

Q: Goju is said to exemplify both soft and hard karate aspects. How can it do both?
A: Both ends are complementary. Please don't look at them as opposites because they are not. Both principles are exemplified by the katas *sanchin* and *tensho*. Sanchin shows the hard side of goju-ryu karate and tensho teaches the soft principles of defense and attack. These two are the basic kata that teach the student the fundamental principles used in any other form in the style. The training of both forms balances the body and is very healthy for the practitioner. Don't forget goju-ryu is a close-quarter art which is calm and relaxed. From this calm and relaxation comes great speed.

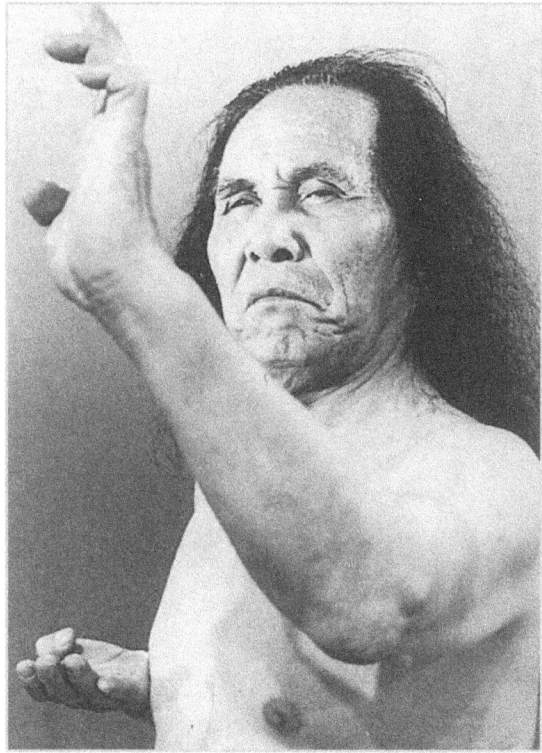

"I practice karate-do as a discipline, the budo way. In the early days, we practiced a lot of basics and kata. Kata was broken down into segments that we trained repetitively. Nowadays the emphasis is on the overall physical performance of the form, not in the self-defense principles hidden in the kata and their combative value as fighting tools."

Karate Masters

"The main objective of karate is to bring enlightenment, which includes humility and self-respect. It is not right to go out and look for trouble or to get into fights to get experience. Not only does this go against the code of karate-do but it's also against Shinto teachings. It is important for young men to have a purpose in life which they can direct themselves toward."

Q: How do the breathing methods you teach apply to the practice of these two katas?

A: We have two different breathing methods. One is *ibuki* which concentrates on keeping tension in the body. The other form is called *yin* and is softer. You have to learn to combine these two breathing methods to get the most out of it. Properly combined, these two breathing methods will develop what is called "*kyoku*" power, which is a kind of power that comes from the internal organs. It is not based on muscle but on internal energy. This type of power can only be achieved by using proper breathing methods.

Q: Yoga strongly focuses on breathing. Did this influence you to adapt it to karate?

A: I never adapted yoga breathing methods to karate. There are similarities and, of course, masters of karate and masters of yoga came to the same conclusions as far as the right breathing methods are concerned. Both practices complement each other perfectly. I obtained the rank of Swami in yoga and I tried to adapt some things to make the breathing in karate much better and healthier. But, for instance, the *ibuki* method of breathing is called *kumbaka* in yoga terms. To me, goju-ryu karate and yoga are complementary to each other. By practicing karate, you improve your yoga breathing and by practicing yoga you help your karate technique. They complement each other perfectly.

Q: Shinto has been a big influence in your style of karate and your life. What can you tell us about it?
A: First of all, I must say that Shinto has its roots in the cultural heritage of Japan and therefore is common to all budo students. It is used for the spiritual aspect of the training. Karate-do requires a spiritual aspect to balance the physical techniques, and that's when Shinto comes into play. Only through practice, meditation and spirituality can you achieve the invisible power that I mentioned previously. Shintoism is practiced for yourself—I do it for myself, you do it for yourself. It is a very individual and private thing. With a better understanding of Shinto, your karate practice will improve.

Q: How do you combine these three elements of karate, Shinto and yoga?
A: The main idea of karate is to hit someone hard. This is only physical. Using Shinto you can defeat an opponent without fighting. That's the highest level of Shintoism and karate. I like to think of it like a pyramid—one dimension is the physical side of karate, the next dimension is the Shintoism aspect, and the third is the yoga training. Maybe this is difficult to understand but this is the way it is.

Q: Is any style better than the rest?
A: You always hear people saying that this or that style is the best. There is no "best" style, it is simply a matter of personal preference. I've yet to see an art that I don't rate. But I have seen many individuals I don't rate—but that's is due to their personal weaknesses and does not reflect on their art or style. The main objective of karate is to bring enlightenment, which includes humility and self-respect. It is not right to go out and look for trouble or to get into fights to get experience. Not only does this go against the code of karate-do but it's also against Shinto teachings. It is important for young men to have a purpose in life which they can direct themselves toward. This purpose will give them direction and will be a tool to experience things and know themselves better. I would recommend that instructors teach not only the physical art of karate but also the spiritual aspect of life, too. Although I have been very busy all my life, I have never neglected my spiritual side. A true man, a true karate practitioner will always balance his existence in this world. O

Notes

"A true martial arts practitioner—like an artist of any other kind—be this a musician, a painter, a writer or an actor, is expressing and leaving part of himself in every piece of his craft. The need for self-inspection and self-realization of 'who' he is becomes the reason for a journey in search of that perfect technique, that great melody, that inspiring poetry, that amazing painting or that Academy Award performance. It is this motivation to reach that 'impossible dream,' that allows a simple individual to become an exceptional 'artist' and 'master' of his craft."

—Jose M. Fraguas

www.ingramcontent.com/pod-product-compliance
Lightning Source LLC
Chambersburg PA
CBHW081343080526
44588CB00016B/2365